Striking Terror

America's New War

Striking Terror

America's New War

by

PHILIP C. WILCOX JR.

TONY JUDT

ISAIAH BERLIN

STANLEY HOFFMANN

ORHAN PAMUK

PANKAJ MISHRA

CHRISTOPHER DE BELLAIGUE

TIM JUDAH

TIMOTHY GARTON ASH

RICHARD L. GARWIN

MATTHEW MESELSON

DANIEL BENJAMIN AND STEVEN SIMON

KANAN MAKIYA AND HASSAN MNEIMNEH

THOMAS POWERS

edited by

ROBERT B. SILVERS AND BARBARA EPSTEIN

NEW YORK REVIEW BOOKS

nyrb

New York

THIS IS A NEW YORK REVIEW BOOK

PUBLISHED BY THE NEW YORK REVIEW OF BOOKS

STRIKING TERROR:

AMERICA'S NEW WAR

This edition published in 2002
in the United States of America by
The New York Review of Books
1755 Broadway
New York, NY 10019

www.nybooks.com

3 5 7 9 10 8 6 4 2

Library of Congress Cataloging-in-Publication Data

Striking terror : America's new war / Philip C. Wilcox, Jr. ... [et al.] ; edited by Robert B.
Silvers and Barbara Epstein.
    p. cm.
    ISBN 1-59017-012-1 (pbk.)
    1. Terrorism. 2. Terrorism — United States. I. Wilcox, Philip C. II. Silvers, Robert B.
III. Epstein, Barbara.
    HV6431 .S765 2002
    363.3'2 — dc21

                                                                                        2001008628

ISBN 1-59017-012-1

Printed in the United States of America on acid-free paper.

March 2002

Contents

Introduction

In the weeks following the attacks of September 11, we heard from a great many writers, some of them offering to go to Afghanistan, others sending reflections on the war or suggesting how the *Review* should respond. Of the articles we asked for, we publish here some that we think will last beyond the rush of events, whether they describe what our correspondents observed in Afghanistan, Turkey, Europe, and Washington, or explain, as the physicist Richard Garwin has done, the "many threats of terror," or put forward critical perspectives on foreign policy and the conduct of the war during its different phases. In some cases our contributors have added epilogues that take account of subsequent developments and try to look ahead, hazardous as any attempt to anticipate historical consequences is bound to be.

We thank our fellow editor Michael Shae for all his work in making this collection possible.

ROBERT B. SILVERS
BARBARA EPSTEIN

COMMENTS

PHILIP C. WILCOX JR.

The Terror

(The following was written in the first few days after September 11 and was the first commentary on the attacks published in The New York Review.*)*

THE BUSH ADMINISTRATION has declared "war" against terrorism, suddenly shocked into realizing that it is now the foremost danger to America's national security. The administration has not yet defined this war, although a head of steam is building for military action. Armed force, however, while politically popular, is usually an ineffective and often counterproductive weapon against terror. Before acting, the US would be wise to construct a more sophisticated strategy. This should include strengthening traditional methods of counterterrorism, while reserving the use of force as a limited option. But a new national security strategy must also include a broader foreign policy that moves away from unilateralism and toward closer engagement with other governments, and that deals not just with the symptoms but with the roots of terrorism, broadly defined. The catastrophe of September 11 could give powerful momentum to such changes.

Islamist terrorists, who are thought to be responsible for the September 11 attacks, were first identified by analysts as the main terrorist threat to the US after a similar, although less sophisticated, gang carried out the first attack on the World Trade Center in 1993. These terrorists, so far as we know, are not sponsored by states; they have been recognized as posing a more complex and lethal challenge than state sponsors of terrorism, such as Libya, which are now mostly inactive, or anti-American secular terrorist groups, which are practically all moribund.

The deep hatred and suicidal fanaticism of the Islamist terrorists, their lack of a rational political calculus, and their belief in divine sanction make the penalties and deterrents traditionally used against terrorists far less effective. It is difficult for intelligence agencies to penetrate their cells, which are loosely structured and often act on an ad hoc basis, and therefore are extremely hard to identify and keep under surveillance. Porous borders, fake documents, and sympathizers who offer cover in a great many countries give such terrorists global mobility. Worst of all, as analysts have predicted and the horror of September 11 confirmed, Islamist terrorists seek mass casualties, and are heedless of public opinion and conventional morality. Searching for a pattern in this maze, US analysts believe Osama bin Laden is the mastermind of a global network of fanatic Islamists and the prime suspect behind the September 11 attacks.

Some of President Bush's civilian advisers want a tough new policy of military retaliation and preemption of terrorism, in place of tedious and uncertain criminal prosecution, the preferred policy of the Clinton administration. Bush himself seems to believe that a dramatic military effort could be a popular catharsis for public outrage and demands for action.

But on the rare occasions that the US has tried to carry out military attacks on terrorist targets, the attacks have failed or backfired. The US bombing of Tripoli in 1986, after a Libyan terrorist attack on Americans in Germany, killed dozens of Libyan civilians. Qaddhafi struck back in 1988 by bombing Pan American Flight 103, killing 270 people. Also, US cruise missile attacks on targets in Sudan and Afghanistan after the bombing of American embassies in East Africa in 1998 had no discernible effect on terrorism and provoked widespread international criticism.

In contrast to Bush's civilian hawks, many American military officers are skeptical about using military force against terrorists. They point out that a target like bin Laden, who is thought to be hiding in the mountains of Afghanistan, probably could not be hit from the air and that his physical "infrastructure" is negligible. Moreover, abducting or killing him with US ground forces, especially in such a remote and hostile environment, presents grave intelligence as well as tactical and logistical challenges. A better approach would be a concerted international effort, with carefully calculated pressures and incentives— and cooperation from Pakistan, which is essential—to persuade bin Laden's Taliban hosts to hand him over for trial. He is already under a previous US indictment. Bombing the Taliban to make them give up bin Laden might kill innocents and would probably fail.

The use of military force is questionable for other reasons. Islamist terrorists throughout the world seek death through martyrdom. Far from deterring these self-proclaimed holy warriors, US military attacks would likely inspire them to carry out even more dangerous acts of terrorism; the effect could well be to increase recruitment and raise the stature of the terrorists in the underworld of militant Islam. Without minimizing the threat they pose, we should regard these people as criminals and murderers, and not dignify them as warriors. We must also understand that getting rid of bin Laden will eliminate neither the ideology of Islamist terrorism nor its often inchoate and diffuse operations.

At the same time, using military force against terrorists in sovereign foreign states is likely to raise difficult legal issues. Unilateral attacks may violate international laws, including treaties against terrorism that the US has worked hard to strengthen; and they may alienate governments, especially in the Islamic world, whose cooperation we need. Although NATO governments have pledged solidarity with the US after the September 11 attacks, some have already expressed wariness about an American military intervention or attack. In any case, if the US government cannot show a clear evidentiary trail of foreign direction of the September 11 attacks, using military force will not be a credible strategy, especially since many of the terrorists and suspected terrorists, who came from several countries, have lived in the US, and at least some of the training and planning for the attack took place here.

If a military solution is not advisable, what can be done to minimize the risk of further disasters? Improving aviation security should clearly be the first step. Because aircraft hijacking had virtually stopped during the past decade, US analysts no longer concentrated on this threat, much less on the nightmare of using hijacked aircraft as suicide bombs against mass civilian targets. After the bombing of Pan American 103, US officials knew that the additional measures that were then taken to strengthen aviation security were hardly foolproof. But they were looking at other mass threats, like the use of chemical and biological weapons, and were reluctant to provide more funds; the airlines prevailed in arguing that more effective security would be too costly for them and too unpopular.

Intelligence and analysis should also be improved; but there are limits to our ability to collect intelligence abroad, especially in hard-to-penetrate terrorist networks. In the US, where some of the training and planning for the recent attacks might have been discovered and preempted, the FBI is constrained by constitutional limits on eavesdropping and on other intrusive measures. A debate is already under way about whether these protections have now become a luxury that Americans cannot afford. Many will be loath to sacrifice these freedoms. Citizens and politicians must accept the grim reality that while we can do more to prevent further catastrophes, terrorism in open societies can never be eliminated entirely. We must also be prepared for the possibility that, even as we improve intelligence and aviation security, terrorists will adopt new tactics, perhaps using weapons such as chemicals and biotoxins and striking at other vulnerable targets.

The most important deficiency in US counterterrorism policy has been the failure to address the root causes of terrorism. Indeed, there is a tendency to treat terrorism as pure evil in a vacuum, to say that changes in foreign policy intended to reduce it will only "reward" terrorists. Moreover, many argue that terrorists care little about particular American policies and hate the US simply because it is powerful, rich, modern, and democratic and because its dynamic secular culture threatens their identity.

But the US should, for its own self-protection, expand efforts to reduce the pathology of hatred before it mutates into even greater danger. Conditions that breed violence and terrorism can at least be moderated through efforts to resolve conflicts and through assistance for economic development, education, and population control. Limiting the proliferation of lethal materials also deserves higher priority as a measure against terrorism as well as for arms control.

The US must also realize that, notwithstanding our great power, indeed because of it, we cannot dictate respect and cooperation. Other nations will not fully help us in combating terrorism, whatever pressures we apply, unless we are sensitive to their legitimate interests and are willing to reciprocate. Certainly the US should reappraise its policies concerning the Israeli–Palestinian conflict and Iraq, which have bred deep anger against America in the Arab and Islamic world, where much terrorism originates and whose cooperation is now more critical than ever. We can do all this without abandoning our basic commitments, including to the security of Israel.

We should also search for ways to strengthen the common bonds between Western values and Islam in order to combat the notion of a "clash of civilizations" and to weaken the Islamist extremist fringe that hates the West and supports terrorist actions. Such new departures in US foreign policy would require devoting far greater resources to supporting a more engaged, cooperative, and influential American role abroad. Redefining national security and counterterrorism in this broader sense is the most promising way to fight the war against terrorism. It is vital that we do this soon, now that the stakes have been raised so high.

—September 19, 2001

EPILOGUE

America's sudden progress in routing the Taliban in Afghanistan through bombing and support for opposition forces has put the squeeze on Osama bin Laden and his apparatus there, although as I write in December bin Laden is still at large. The difficult task of creating a multiethnic government that is needed to stabilize Afghanistan and prevent it from being used in the future as a terrorist sanctuary is under way.

Success in rehabilitating Afghanistan will require, above all, that its neighbors can be persuaded to abandon their previous policies of using Afghan warlords as instruments for their own ends, and will also require US support for a national government created by Afghans themselves. While the UN takes the lead in government-building, and perhaps peacekeeping in the interim, it will be critically important for US diplomacy to discourage interference from neighboring states. Success will require, especially, that Pakistan can be persuaded to support a multiethnic Afghan government and stop the training of Islamic militants on Afghan territory to fight India in Kashmir. The US should also accelerate efforts to carry out the humanitarian relief and the sustained program for reconstruction and development in Afghanistan to which it is committed.

Some Bush administration officials, encouraged by success against the Taliban and, perhaps, bin Laden, are talking about wider use of force against terrorist groups and, perhaps, other countries that harbor them. Although some of the difficulties that I and others

anticipated the US would encounter in Afghanistan did not material-
ize, it should be clear that the circumstances of the American engagement there have been unique and that the US benefited from factors
unlikely to be repeated elsewhere. They included the absence of an
effective Afghan government; worldwide sympathy for America
because of the enormity of the September 11 attacks; disgust with bin
Laden and the Taliban; and the presence of willing military partners
for the US on the ground.

There is no real prospect for US air or ground attacks on the other
Arab or Muslim states—or example, Syria or Lebanon—that harbor
groups named by the US as terrorists. These groups have not attacked
American targets for years, and Washington knows that military
attacks on these countries would enflame the entire Middle East and
create an international uproar. Also unlikely are both a US attack on
Saddam Hussein and US sponsorship of an exile invasion. Some sub-
cabinet officials and others are now advocating such strategies more
strenuously on the theory that Saddam might arm terrorists with
weapons of mass destruction. President Bush has left this possibility
open, in theory, to keep Saddam guessing. But the plans mooted in
Washington for expanding the war by an attack on Saddam Hussein
that would not involve American ground forces or risk shattering the
antiterror coalition Washington has constructed are not realistic. For
these reasons, the use of military force is unlikely to become the cen-
terpiece of a new US counterterrorism strategy after the Afghanistan
conflict subsides. Rhetoric aside, America's "war on terrorism" will
have to continue to rely on other governments to help us in arresting,
prosecuting, or extraditing to the US terrorist suspects.

President Bush's executive order allowing for trial of terrorists
before secret military tribunals could actually be an obstacle to bringing foreign terrorists to justice in America. Between 1993 and 1999,
foreign governments, working with US officials, extradited or simply
handed over thirteen such suspects to the US, all of whom were tried

and convicted in federal or state courts. Already, Spain, which recently arrested a group of al-Qaeda suspects, has said it has reservations about extraditing terrorist suspects to US military courts, and other governments might also be reluctant to do so. The rationale for military courts is that we are at war, that terrorists do not deserve protections given to American defendants, and that extraordinary measures are needed. The administration also cites the need to protect secret intelligence evidence, even though this problem has not prevented the prosecution and conviction of terrorist suspects in regular courts in the past.

One test of a free society is how it defends the rule of law in times of crisis. Bush's proposal for military courts is a radical change, as are his authorization of FBI eavesdropping on conversations between terrorist suspects and their lawyers, and prolonged detention of many Muslim-Americans. There have, moreover, been reports that the FBI may restore the highly intrusive surveillance powers against Americans that it used, and abused, in the past. The first duty of the US government is to protect its citizens; but the administration has not made the case that these inroads on civil liberty are necessary to protect our security.

If we assume that the US is successful in dealing with Afghanistan and bin Laden, the threat of anti-US terrorism by extremists in the Arab and Muslim world will persist. Bin Laden and his network of terrorists are only an extreme symptom of anti-American hatred that festers on the fringes of troubled societies throughout the Arab and Muslim worlds. History tells us also that anti-US terror is not unique to the Islamic world. Secretary of State Colin Powell has spoken of the need to address the root causes of terrorism in order to discourage further bin Ladens. But there are no signs yet of more ambitious plans to deal with the many problems and conflicts in the developing world that breed alienation and violence. Not the least of these is the failure of authoritarian regimes in the Arab world to provide economic growth and political participation. America's potential influence in promoting political liberalization and broad-based economic growth in the Middle East has limits; but these problems deserve far greater priority in our foreign policy and far more resources than they have received in the past.

The bloody spasm of terrorist attacks against Israel by Palestinian Islamists in early December and Israel's retaliation against Arafat are a serious challenge to the President's antiterrorist strategy. The perception in the Arab and Muslim world of American favoritism toward Israel is the single most important cause of anti-American anger in that region, and demagogues and terrorists like bin Laden feed on it. Secretary of State Powell's eloquent speech of November 19 and retired General Anthony Zinni's mission to the region were designed to show new American resolve to restore peace talks through the Mitchell cease-fire plan. But the upsurge of terrorism in December and Israel's harsh response have made the situation worse.

Arafat knows he must try harder to stop violence and terrorism if he is to regain credibility in Washington and in Israel as a negotiating partner and if he is to overcome Sharon's efforts to portray him as the Palestinian bin Laden. But unless the Palestinians have reason to hope they can achieve a viable state through negotiations, even a Draconian effort by Arafat to subdue his own militants and his Islamist adversaries will not succeed, and public support for his leadership will continue to decline. Thus far, Sharon has offered Arafat and the Palestinians no reason to hope they will benefit in return for a cease-fire. Only the US can offer this through a bolder American vision of peace that goes beyond the Mitchell Plan and does more than offer to help the parties to resume negotiations. Such a new initiative would challenge both Arafat and Sharon. By offering an alternative to violence, it would also revive hope among the traumatized majorities on both sides who, according to polls, still want peace and are willing to compromise. Such a vision should address the issues of security, borders, settlements, Jerusalem, and refugees in a way that meets the basic needs of both peoples.

Without more aggressive and imaginative American leadership and diplomacy, Israelis and Palestinians are likely to continue to brutalize each other, at great cost to Israel's security, to the Palestinians' need for freedom from occupation, and to America's need for Arab and Muslim support in the war against terrorism.

—December 17, 2001

TONY JUDT

America and the War

"AMERICA IS SOLIDLY organized egoism, it is evil made systematic and regular." Osama bin Laden? No, Pierre Buchez, a French socialist writing in the 1840s. Anti-Americanism goes back a long way. It was not born of American global domination—when Edmond de Goncourt wanted to express his horror at Baron Haussmann's new Paris he observed that "it makes me think of some American Babylon of the future." That was in 1860, when the US was still at best a regional power. Much has changed since then, though America is still seen in many quarters as the embodiment of rootlessness, disruption, cosmopolitanism: modernity, in short. But if the US is to make sense of its place in the world, if the present war is to have any beneficial long-term outcome, Americans need to make a sustained effort to understand what it is that so many millions of foreigners claim to dislike and fear about their country.

In the present mood, this subject elicits little serious discussion. Some on the left, whether in the US or Europe, have slipped comfortably back into familiar routines: peace vigils, teach-ins, and finger-pointing. The real problem, it sometimes seems, is not terrorists but the American government. "They" (George Bush, the Establishment) will use the crisis as an excuse to trample on our civil liberties—for Terry Eagleton, writing in the *London Review of Books*, the US is already "a one-party state." And as for the horror of September 11, some just can't help feeling that, as the historian Mary Beard put it, "however tactfully you dress it up, the United States had it coming." Professor Thomas Laqueur of Berkeley writes that "on the scale of evil the New York bombings are sadly not so extraordinary and our government has been responsible for many that are probably worse." Frederic Jameson of Duke University argues that "the Americans created bin Laden during the Cold War. . . . This is therefore a textbook example of dialectical reversal." We devised the world's problems—imperialism, exploitation, globalization—so we shouldn't be surprised at the backlash.[1]

There is an ugly hubris in these lofty self-condemnations—as though all the world's crimes and sins were just another American invention. In this view, if the US were not running amok in the world, projecting power and cruise missiles into Panama, the Sudan, Iraq, and Afghanistan, we would not now be suffering such terrible retribution. But American intervention in Kosovo, at least, saved the local (mostly Muslim) population from a catastrophe of genocidal proportions. In its foreign dealings, America typically does both harm and good.

But this nuance is lost on many domestic critics from the left; and as a result they are often at a loss to explain what has happened. As *The Nation* put it in a recent editorial, "Why the attacks took place is still unclear." This view of the world mirrors that of its opponents on the isolationist right. The attacks on the Pentagon and the World Trade Center would never have happened, the logic runs, if we had minded our own business. What is wrong with (us) Americans? We're overpaid, overarmed . . . and over there.

Among conventional politicians of the bipartisan middle, consensus takes a different form. Here the attacks on New York and

---

1. For the views of Eagleton, Beard, Laqueur, and Jameson, see the *London Review of Books*, October 4, 2001.

Washington merely illustrate America's distinctive virtues. "They" hate us not for what we do but for what we represent: pluralism, freedom, democracy, civilization. Even those who once argued for a more nuanced American engagement with the world—against the unilateralism of the Bush administration before September 11—now confine themselves to variations on a worn theme: realism.

The old realism insisted that the US put its "interests" first and last. The new realism demands that our foreign friends stand up and be counted—and willingly accepts for the time being that our enemies' enemies be included in the census. And so we assemble a heterogeneous and fissile posse of Russians, Pakistanis, Syrians, Saudis, Tajiks, Uzbeks, and the rest—most of whom have at some point in the recent past been the object of American ire and condemnation for their mistreatment of civilians or their active support of murderous terrorists.

But if the war goes according to plan and we dismantle the Taliban and capture bin Laden, what becomes of this international coalition? We are unlikely to solicit its views on what to do with bin Laden, if we have him. And while the Northern Alliance will be helpful in a ground war against remaining Taliban forces, and Uzbekistan, like Turkey, can provide logistical help, our military need for outside assistance is limited—we have not even called on the French. As the fight against terrorism goes on, what shall we make of the terrorizing proclivities of our friends? Shall we undertake nation-building in Afghanistan? With the Uzbeks and Tajiks of the Northern Alliance? With the exiled king? Or with the "moderate" Taliban representatives, as Pakistan (many of whose citizens are Pashtuns, like the Taliban themselves) would much prefer? Shall we further commit ourselves to stabilizing and securing Pakistan? And eventually Syria and Iraq? Or shall we walk away and concentrate on "homeland protection"? And what will the world say of us, in any event?

Anyone who has lived or traveled away from the US knows something of the shape of contemporary anti-American sentiment. In the first place, it is driven by humiliation, the feeling of worthlessness and hopelessness shared by hundreds of millions in the Islamic world and elsewhere. In a world of easy communications, the wretched of the earth see and feel their abjectness reflected in their encounters with the guardians of prosperity. In itself, however, this is not about America. What ties this widespread sentiment of wounded pride to a certain image of America in particular is American "arrogance."

This is the first of a number of themes masterfully exploited by Osama bin Laden in his televised interviews and speeches.[2] For the US, in its foreign dealings, is often arrogant: it asserts a preemptive right to be where it chooses, to do as it sees fit, with scant attention to the consequences for others. Richard Armitage, the deputy secretary of state, was asked on television, on October 11, about bin Laden's reiterated obsession with the presence of US troops near Muslim holy places. Should we not pay attention to Muslim sensibilities in this matter? Armitage ignored the question—we're there, he asserted, to protect Persian Gulf oil sites against the threat from Iraq, and we are staying. If you even raise this issue, he warned the (American) interviewer, you are playing in bin Laden's ballgame. His reply will doubtless be run and rerun on al-Jazeera television—it will make fine recruiting material for the next generation of terrorists.

All great powers are arrogant—it just so happens that America is the only one around. But America, as bin Laden and countless Arab (and European) editorials never tire of repeating, is also inconsistent—or, as they would say, hypocritical. Rhetorically committed to a moral universalism quite unlike the patronizing elitism of older imperial powers ("We hold these truths to be self-evident..."), the US cannot help but come across as saying one thing and doing another;

---

2. See in particular a long interview given by bin Laden to al-Jazeera television in December 1998 and made available in English on line by the BBC Monitoring Service. Quotes from bin Laden are from this source unless otherwise indicated.

and it is perhaps unfortunate to be the only great power at a time when anyone in the world can scrutinize its every word. America switches overseas allegiances with disconcerting ease: now India, now Pakistan; now Iraq, now Iran. We embrace countries and then abandon them. Picking (and then dropping) one's friends overseas for short-term advantage is the surest way to make enemies.

Even in the Muslim world, not everyone is a priori offended by American example and leadership. But they are wounded and scarred by Washington's shifting treatment of them, with its wild swings from engagement to indifference. It is in this respect that hard-nosed "realism" is its own worst enemy. Today we are at war with "rogue states" and terrorists, and now is not the moment, we are told, to pay overmuch attention to the fine print. But what is a "rogue state"? One that allows terrorists to raise cash and buy guns on its soil? What is a terrorist? Is an armed Kurd a freedom fighter in Iraq but a terrorist in Turkey? Was Iraq a rogue state when the US backed it against Iran? Were al-Qaeda volunteers terrorists when they joined the US-financed war in Afghanistan?

These are not fixed terms with agreed meanings that last for long (witness the careers of Menachem Begin and Gerry Adams, among many others). To assert otherwise, as American leaders now do, to claim that terrorism is a moral given and you are either for it or against it, is imprudent. It is particularly imprudent for a country like the US to adapt its moral categories to immediate requirements, however urgent. We need Russian cooperation, to be sure. But Putin needs us, too, for many reasons. It should not be beyond our ingenuity to secure his support without consigning the Chechens to oblivion, or—worse—relabeling them terrorists just to please him. The less we say now, the fewer hostages we shall offer to hostile fortune.

You have only to read or hear Osama bin Laden at some length to understand how fluidly he plays off these matters. His own motives, if we take them at face value, are to push the "infidel" out of the Arabian peninsula, to punish the "Crusaders and the Jews," and to wreak revenge on Americans for their domination of Islamic space.³ He is not a spokesman for the downtrodden, much less those who seek just solutions to real dilemmas—he is cuttingly dismissive of the UN: "Muslims should not appeal to these atheist, temporal regimes." But he is adept in his appeal.

He makes much, for example, of the "feebleness and cowardice of the American soldier." Americans are "unmanly"—and so, therefore, are those (notably the ruling Saudi family) who align with them or accept their protection. This allusion to US reluctance to accept casualties and Washington's insistence on fighting wars from 15,000 feet up attracts a wide and sympathetic constituency, and not only among Arabs; for it tidily combines the themes of arrogance, hypocrisy, and pusillanimity while reminding his audience of terrorists' own willingness to die for their cause. I don't think Washington, or many American citizens, have taken the full measure of the propaganda price that America has paid for its manner of waging risk-free war.

And then there is Israel. It is disingenuous to suggest that the crisis in the Middle East is unconnected to bin Laden. In my reading of European and Near Eastern sentiment today, the Israel–Palestine conflict and America's association with Israel are the greatest single source of contemporary anti-US sentiment, crossing political, ideological, and national boundaries. Osama bin Laden may not care one way or the other for the Palestinians, and he is certainly not interested in an agreed solution to their predicament; but when he says (as he did in December 1998) that "we must consider Israel the real perpetrator of any attack on any state in the Islamic world," he strikes a deep chord.

Arabs and other Muslims from Rabat to Jakarta have watched Israel build settlements in occupied territory in defiance of UN

---

3. In his December 1998 interview bin Laden invokes "crusades" and "Crusaders" seven times. In his lexicon they are interchangeable with Christians.

resolutions and international law. They've been shown footage of the Israeli army destroying houses and land; they've heard Israeli leaders acknowledge state-sponsored assassination; they've noted the election of Ariel Sharon in spite of his shameful record in Lebanon; and they've seen the American president assure Israel of unwavering US support. When bin Laden claims that he is striking back for the Palestinians, too, he renders the Palestinian cause no service—but he doesn't lose friends, either.

Is there anything the US can do about anti-Americanism? Actually, quite a lot. If Osama bin Laden is taken alive (and we had better hope that he is), he should be tried by an international tribunal. There is not yet an International Criminal Court (thanks in some measure to Washington's refusal to countenance indictments against Americans...), but an ad hoc court for the purpose is one option. A trial in the US, however fair and open, would be imprudent. It would be widely perceived abroad as "victor's justice." Nuremberg was victors' justice too, and set important precedents as well as punishing major criminals. But we forget too readily that in the aftermath of Nuremberg many Germans privately dismissed the verdicts (and therefore the charges against the Nazis) as imposed on them by force.[4] It would be a catastrophic error were something comparable to flow from an American court's verdict on the terrorists of September 11.

The US must also take its political case to the constituency that matters. In recent weeks Tony Blair has been giving interviews to Arab-language TV stations in an effort to convince his audience not just that we have no quarrel with Islam (pace bin Laden's repeated claims), but that Osama bin Laden does not speak for anyone. What has the US done? Well, we complained to the emir of Qatar that al-Jazeera, the Qatar-based television station that has carried many of

---

4. In polls taken in 1950, 30 percent of West Germans thought the postwar trials had been "unfair."

bin Laden's statements and which has a huge popular audience in the Arab world, was providing terrorism with a platform and should be curtailed. The unelected emir duly reminded the representatives of one of the world's oldest democracies that a free press is essential to democratic life.[5]

Finally, the US needs thoroughly to reassess its relationship to the rest of the world. Those who hate us for our "values" (which in any case are Western, not American) are vastly outnumbered by those who resent us for our foreign policy. Our efforts to eradicate terrorism will go for nothing if we keep uncritical company for tactical ends with rulers who practice at home the very crimes we claim to abhor. The same goes for the actions of our friends. The policy Israel has been pursuing is "worse than a crime, it is a blunder,"[6] and the US does neither itself nor Israel any favors by providing implicit cover for its policies toward the Palestinians. If Washington cannot prevent Israel from behaving in destructive and self-destructive ways, then it must at the very least distance itself from it. Sharon has doubtless helped this process along by his revealingly brutal outbursts since the atrocities of September 11.

The US should surely abandon the embarrassing practice of treating international agencies and agreements as foreign-policy "options" which it can cherrypick or neglect at its own convenience. The ingratiating alacrity with which Washington paid its back dues to the UN when it needed international help did not pass unnoticed overseas. Is this the beginning of a fresh approach, or just another hiccup in the history of America's inattention to international affairs? It depends on how the Bush administration understands the importance of the choice facing it. In view of its starting point last January, this is not a

---

5. Reported on the BBC Web site, October 12, 2001.

6. "*C'est pire qu'un crime, c'est une faute.*" Attributed to Antoine Boulay de la Meurthe on hearing of Napoleon's execution of the Duc d'Enghien in 1804.

suitable government for such a purpose; but it is the only government we have.

Whether President Bush and his advisers can find it in themselves to look long and hard at America's past mistakes—at a time when, understandably enough, Americans are being exhorted to feel proudly patriotic—is not yet clear. Edward Said recently admonished Arabs for failing to denounce suicide missions and hiding instead behind the excuse of their own suffering; how many of us, he asked, have taken responsibility for the poverty, ignorance, illiteracy, and repression in our own societies, and the political manipulation of Islam, while complaining about Zionism and imperialism?[7] It is a timely question, and no doubt an uncomfortable one too. But we in the US should be asking uncomfortable questions of our own. The American political concentration span is famously short; and despite the atrocities and the anxieties, less may have changed here than people say—there will be a deep collective urge to get back to normal once the crisis has passed. That would be a grave mistake.

—*October 18, 2001*

EPILOGUE

It is now more than a month since the "war on terror" began. At the time of writing the Northern Alliance has captured Mazar-e-Sharif and Kabul: the Bush administration can claim a significant victory and real progress in its effort to destroy the Taliban. On the US home front there have been no more anthrax-laden letters for a while and the edgy public mood has calmed. No one is quite sure what "normal" should now be, but there is a widespread public desire to return to

---

7. Edward Said, "Backlash and Backtrack," *al-Ahram*, weekly on-line edition, September 27–October 3, 2001. I'm grateful to Jim Sleeper for bringing this to my attention.

it, even—perhaps especially—in New York City. The President continues to enjoy record levels of public support.

How justified is the American public's continuing confidence in its government? Washington's handling of the anthrax scare, and of domestic security as a whole, has not been very reassuring. This is not so surprising. In Republican administrations especially, the departments of health and transportation, the postal service, and even the office of attorney general are typically filled with second-string political friends and time-servers, men and women elevated beyond their competence to posts in which their party has little interest. Bush's appointees never expected to find themselves in the front line of a major national crisis and their performances have been inept. Like the FBI and the CIA, they appear overwhelmed and underprepared.

The secretaries of state and defense of the Bush administration have performed much better, as might have been expected from their background and experience. They have even begun to mount a propaganda offensive in which an Arabic-speaking professional US diplomat at last went on the al-Jazeera television station and presented the US case. The military has been less convincing. On the evidence to date, and notwithstanding the retreat of the Taliban forces to their strongholds in the south, the United States has been fighting not so much the war it needs to fight as the one for which its forces are best prepared. That, of course, is what peacetime armies always do at the start of wars—the learning curve is protracted and usually bloody. In this war, given America's overwhelming strength, we shall probably win all the battles in any case. Whether we shall win our war remains an open question.

Up to now, Washington's main concern has not been winning the war so much as securing the "coalition." Our priorities since September 11 have been clear: Washington, and especially the Pentagon, has taken extra special care to make friends, purchase allies, neutralize opponents, assuage local sensibilities, appease Pakistani fears of a

Northern Alliance victory, ensure the safety of its soldiers and airmen, fine-tune its bombing campaign, and in general behave like a good international citizen. These are all worthy objectives in peacetime, and one can only hope that the US will continue to be so solicitous of international sentiment once the war is over.

In the meantime, however, the war on the Taliban has taken longer than anticipated—just a week before the fall of Kabul the Pentagon was expressing its surprise that the Afghans had held out so long. As a consequence, and despite the best efforts of Secretary of State Colin Powell, the fault lines within the international coalition have begun to show. The Pakistanis, who are far from happy at the presence in Kabul of the Northern Alliance, have publicly spoken of submitting the bill for their support. The Russians have warned Washington not to forget India, and no one should forget Kashmir. The administration has not acted effectively to address the conflict in Israel's occupied territories, and is paying the price for this caution in the Middle East.

Even in Europe, support for what is now increasingly referred to as "America's War" has dropped very rapidly. Newspapers and television news reports in Britain, France, Germany, and elsewhere have routinely reminded their readers and viewers of how much havoc has been wrought in Afghanistan. Americans seem quite unaware of this shift. When it is brought to their attention they react with incomprehension and dismay—understandably, since US mass media rarely report on overseas reaction. The Bush administration has successfully kept information about the war to a minimum, and Osama bin Laden's interviews and pronouncements are still kept out of the US media.

All of this, it seems to me, points to a paradox in America's current international position. Before September 11 the US was widely seen as arrogant and unhelpful in international affairs, and on the verge of retreat into a smug unilateralism, washing its hands of foreign crises and shared concerns. In the aftermath of the attacks on New York and Washington the country was awash in genuine international sympathy.

The Bush administration set out to mobilize these good feelings behind its war against terrorists, and it mostly succeeded. But the "coalition" was an inch deep, in large measure a figment of American imagination, energy, and money. Worse, most of its members were not being asked to do anything much beyond lining up behind American military action. In short, the world was expected to place its faith in what amounted to American unilateralism, albeit in a very different key.

Understandably, that faith has proven shaky. There is some resentment at being made to share responsibility for American actions while having no say in them. Indeed, the US might have been better off had it paid less attention to the need for Saudi, Syrian, Iranian, Pakistani, and other allies and considered instead a lightning campaign to remove the Taliban and capture bin Laden. Washington would certainly have taken flak, but that would have been the price of being a great power, and anyway success would have silenced most critics. As it is, we have spent a month dropping very heavy ordnance on a country whose people were not the ostensible object of our wrath, and have put our allies to the trouble of justifying this to their domestic constituencies. Blair, Schröder, Chirac, and Berlusconi are now fighting on two fronts—side by side with the Americans against terror, and at home against critics of their unquestioning alignment with the United States. And this even before the political difficulties begin in Kabul, and with Osama bin Laden still at large.

So what happens next? We are about to engage in nation-building in Afghanistan, with the help of some rather unappetizing local forces whose ambitions we shall now have to rein in, and neighboring countries whose interests we do not share. It will be crucial for the US to provide heavy and sustained humanitarian aid to a country where many are threatened with starvation. But that is only the beginning. For a brief moment following September 11 there really was something resembling an international consensus on the nature of terrorism and the need to extirpate it. But already local prejudices and agendas have resurfaced. In Yugoslavia, for example, President Kostunica has exploited the international campaign against "terrorism" as a cover for inflammatory rhetoric about Albanian "terrorists" and their misguided American backers.[8]

In Macedonia the Slav-dominated government has capitalized on antiterrorist rhetoric to retreat from its undertaking to work with the Albanian minority. Muslims there and elsewhere have good grounds for fearing the implications for them of America's new focus, despite President Bush's best efforts to convince them otherwise. What is more, American attention—vital for their well-being—is once again far away. America's reengagement with the world in one region is thus offset by its departure from the scene somewhere else. This is a pity, because even after September 11 there will be more to foreign policy than the hunt for international criminals.

Short of another atrocity, the US is going to find it hard to mobilize the rest of the world for a sustained struggle against shadowy enemies. The bombing campaign, whatever its tactical benefits in the anti-Taliban cause, has directed attention away from the main issue of criminal prosecution of terrorist networks and reminded America's critics everywhere of all their longstanding complaints about American power. If the US decides to identify, for example, Baghdad or Damascus as a fomenter of terrorism and acts accordingly, then it will be on its own. Even the British will slip away, as Tony Blair has already made clear.

As I write, President Bush has just delivered a series of speeches demanding that our coalition partners and others give more than mere verbal support to our battle with terrorism. That is fair enough (and the Western Europeans have indeed done so). But when the call first went out from Washington after September 11 for countries to stand up and be counted, it sounded the trumpet for mobilization in a

---

8. *Politika*, September 21, 2001, cited in the International Crisis Group, "Bin Laden and the Balkans: the Politics of Anti-Terrorism," *Balkans Report*, November 9, 2001.

common fight. Now it sounds a bit like the FBI's pathetic admission that it has no idea what to do about the anthrax attacks and would "welcome" public input. And it is even less convincing: seen from abroad, the war in Afghanistan is Sheriff Bush's affair, and everyone else is in the posse, following orders.

Our priority now should therefore be to complete our business in Afghanistan as quickly as possible, do our best to ensure that something stable is put in place of the Taliban, and then pay serious attention not just to the threat of terrorism but to the state of America's relations with the rest of the world. The longer the war drags on, the more the US will be perceived as unable to accomplish its goals and the greater will be the difficulty of even our closest allies in holding the line in the face of public opposition at home.

—November 15, 2001

ISAIAH BERLIN

Notes on Prejudice

Isaiah Berlin liked to allude to a passage in Bertrand Russell's History of Western Philosophy *where Russell says that, if we are to understand a philosopher's views, we must "apprehend their imaginative background,"*[1] *or the philosopher's "inner citadel," as Berlin calls it.*[2] *The character of one of the main rooms in Berlin's own citadel is vividly expressed in some hurried notes Berlin wrote for a friend (who does not wish to be identified) in 1981. His friend was due to give a lecture, and wrote to Berlin to ask for suggestions about how he might treat his theme. Berlin had to go abroad early on the day after he received the request, and wrote the notes quickly, in his own hand, without time for revision or expansion. The result is somewhat breathless and telegraphic, no doubt, but it conveys with great immediacy Berlin's opposition to intolerance and prejudice, especially fanatical monism, stereotypes, and aggressive nationalism. Its relevance to the events of September 11, 2001, hardly needs stressing.*

Berlin's manuscript is reproduced here in a direct transcript, with only a few adjustments to make it easier to read. I have omitted material relevant only to the specific occasion.

—Henry Hardy

---

1. *History of Western Philosophy* (Simon and Schuster, 1945), Chapter 23, para. 2.

2. For example, in *Liberty* (Oxford University Press, 2002), pp. 246, 288.

1.

FEW THINGS HAVE done more harm than the belief on the part of individuals or groups (or tribes or states or nations or churches) that he or she or they are in sole possession of the truth: especially about how to live, what to be & do—& that those who differ from them are not merely mistaken, but wicked or mad: & need restraining or suppressing. It is a terrible and dangerous arrogance to believe that you alone are right: have a magical eye which sees the truth: & that others cannot be right if they disagree.

This makes one certain that there is one goal & one only for one's nation or church or the whole of humanity, & that it is worth any amount of suffering (particularly on the part of other people) if only the goal is attained—"through an ocean of blood to the Kingdom of Love" (or something like this) said Robespierre:[3] & Hitler, Lenin, Stalin, & I daresay leaders in the religious wars of Christian v. Moslem or Catholics v. Protestants sincerely believed this: the belief that there is one & only one true answer to the central questions which have agonized mankind & that one has it oneself—or one's leader has it—was responsible for the oceans of blood: but no Kingdom of Love sprang from it—or could: there are many ways of living, believing, behaving: mere *knowledge* provided by history, anthropology, literature, art, law makes clear that the differences of cultures & characters are as deep as the similarities (which make men human) & that we are none the poorer for this rich variety: knowledge of it opens the windows of the mind (and soul) and makes people wiser, nicer, & more

---

3. Berlin may be referring to the passage where Robespierre writes that "*en scellant notre ouvrage de notre sang, nous puissions voir au moins briller l'aurore de la félicité universelle*" ("by sealing our work with our blood, we may see at least the bright dawn of universal happiness"). *Rapport sur les principes de morale politique qui doivent guider la Convention nationale dans l'administration intérieure de la République* [Paris, 1794], p. 4.

civilized: absence of it breeds irrational prejudice, hatreds, ghastly extermination of heretics and those who are different: if the two great wars plus Hitler's genocides haven't taught us that, we are incurable.

The most valuable—or one of the most valuable—elements in the British tradition is precisely the relative freedom from political, racial, religious fanaticism & monomania. Compromising with people with whom you don't sympathize or altogether understand is indispensable to any decent society: nothing is more destructive than a happy sense of one's own—or one's nation's—infallibility, which lets you destroy others with a quiet conscience because you are doing God's (e.g. the Spanish Inquisition or the Ayatollas) or the superior race's (e.g. Hitler) or History's (e.g. Lenin–Stalin) work.

The only cure is understanding how other societies—in space or time—live: and that it is possible to lead lives different from one's own, & yet to be fully human, worthy of love, respect or at least curiosity. Jesus, Socrates, John Hus of Bohemia, the great chemist Lavoisier, socialists and liberals (as well as conservatives) in Russia, Jews in Germany, all perished at the hands of "infallible" ideologues: intuitive certainty is no substitute for carefully tested empirical knowledge based on observation and experiment and free discussion between men: the first people totalitarians destroy or silence are men of ideas & free minds.

2.

Another source of avoidable conflict is stereotypes. Tribes hate neighbouring tribes by whom they feel threatened, & then rationalize their fears by representing them as wicked or inferior, or absurd or despicable in some way. Yet these stereotypes alter sometimes quite rapidly. Take the nineteenth century alone: in, say, 1840 the French are thought of as swashbuckling, gallant, immoral, militarized, men with curly moustachios, dangerous to women, likely to invade England in revenge for Waterloo; & the Germans are beer drinking, rather ludicrous provincials, musical, full of misty metaphysics, harmless but somewhat absurd. By 1871 the Germans are Uhlans storming through France, incited by the terrible Bismarck—terrifying Prussian militarists filled with national pride etc. France is a poor, crushed, civilized land, in need of protection from all good men, lest its art & literature are crushed underheel by the terrible invaders.

The Russians in the nineteenth century are crushed serfs, darkly brooding semi-religious Slav mystics who write deep novels, a huge horde of cossacks loyal to the Tsar, who sing beautifully. In our times all this has dramatically altered: crushed population, yes, but technology, tanks, godless materialism, crusade against capitalism, etc. The English are ruthless imperialists lording it over fuzzy wuzzies, looking down their long noses at the rest of the world—& then impoverished, liberal, decent welfare state beneficiaries in need of allies. And so on. All these stereotypes are substitutes for real knowledge—which is never of anything so simple or permanent as a particular generalized image of foreigners—and are stimuli to national self satisfaction & disdain of other nations. It is a prop to nationalism.

3.

Nationalism—which everybody in the nineteenth century thought was ebbing—is the strongest & most dangerous force at large to-day. It is usually the product of a wound inflicted by one nation on the pride or territory of another: if Louis XIV had not attacked & devastated the Germans, & humiliated them for years—the Sun King whose state gave laws to everybody, in politics, warfare, art, philosophy, science—then the Germans would not, perhaps, have become quite so aggressive by, say, the early nineteenth century when they became fiercely nationalistic against Napoleon. If the Russians, similarly, had not been treated as a barbarous mass by the West in the nineteenth century, or the Chinese had not been humiliated by opium wars or general exploitation, neither would have fallen so easily to a doctrine which promised they would inherit the earth after they had, with the help of historic forces which none may stop, crushed all the capitalist unbelievers. If the Indians had not been patronized, etc., etc.

Conquest, enslavement of peoples, imperialism etc are not fed just by greed or desire for glory, but have to justify themselves to themselves by some central idea: French as the only true culture; the white man's burden; communism: & the stereotypes of others as inferior or wicked. Only knowledge, carefully acquired & not by short cuts, can dispel this: even that won't dispel human aggressiveness or dislike for the dissimilar (in skin, culture, religion) by itself: still, education in history, anthropology, law (especially if they are "comparative" & not just of one's own country as they usually are) helps.

STANLEY HOFFMANN

On the War

1.

AS SOON AS the shock of the terror attacks on New York and Washington was felt, commentators began saying that September 11, 2001, marked the beginning of a new era in world affairs. It is a misleading interpretation of a horrible event. What was new was the demonstration that a small number of well-organized conspirators could cause thousands of victims in the territory of the "only super-power" and thus show that the US was not any safer from attack than far less mighty nations. But the change of scale and the location of the targets do not represent a transformation of international relations. The terrorists brutally drew our attention to a phenomenon that had long been partly hidden from sight by the cold war and by decolonization, two historical developments that were quite traditional: an epic contest between two great powers, and the troubled birth of a large number of (more or less shaky) new states.

While these struggles went on, something drastically new was emerging: a global society in which states were no longer the only or even the essential players. Insofar as they keep the appearance and trappings of sovereignty, the states are still, on the surface, the shapers of their foreign policies. But unlike in the dominant model of world affairs taught to future academics, statesmen, and businessmen, the goals of states are now only partly "geopolitical," consisting of territory, resources, security from rivals, prestige, etc. States have increasingly had to take into account the demands and wishes of their people—jobs, welfare, ethnic or religious sympathies and hatreds, protection from internal or external wars, etc. Governments that neglect such preferences and pressures do so at considerable peril. Nothing is purely domestic or purely international anymore.

Even more important has been the recent emergence of a global civil society, made up of people and groups that operate across borders and whose decisions and acts sharply reduce the freedom of maneuver of governments: not only multinational corporations, secular and religious nongovernmental organizations, and investors able to move their money at lightning speed from one stock market to another (and thus to shake up domestic currencies), but also drug cartels, mafias, and terrorists. The distinction between state and civil society is of course artificial. Many of the components of civil society want governments to adopt measures aimed at satisfying their demands, whether for education, protecting the environment, or treatment of AIDS or other illnesses; there are very few "private" actors who do not need and obtain financial or political support from governments. But global civil society has suffered both from neglect by students of world affairs and from being even more unmanageable than a world of states with only a fragmentary collective governance. The shock of monetary crises in the 1990s was fortunately not strong enough to destroy the world economy. The shock of September 11 has been so great because it resulted from an attack; it was not, moreover, an attack by anonymous speculators on national currencies but by a small group of minimally armed terrorists on the national security and sense of confidence of the world's greatest power. Suddenly, rogue states lost their status as the greatest potential threat. A world of millions of private actors means a world of virtually unlimited vulnerability.

This is, paradoxically, especially frightening for the United States, the country that has done most to destroy borders and walls, to shape a world market, to promote freedom of communications, information, and movement. Americans have known, since the Vietnam War, that awesome firepower does not guarantee victory against a determined small nation. Concentrated will and the ability to accept casualties can compensate for inequality in economic and military might. The fact that American power was partly unusable (nuclear weapons, for example), and partly ineffective when used, was disturbing enough when the foe was a relatively small state. It is even more disturbing to think that a few thousand terrorists may have the same effect: Gulliver no longer tied by Lilliputians, but assaulted by clever gnats. The weapons of economic and military warfare (including those for mass destruction) are now available not merely to states, but to the peoples of the world.

2.

How do we deal with this change? The Bush administration has shown a great deal of schizophrenia. On the one hand, the President himself has declared war on terrorists and regimes that support them, thus evoking images of large-scale campaigns fueled by the huge American arsenal. And he has proclaimed that whoever does not support us will be considered to be against us. On the other hand, this grand display of threats has been tempered by the increasingly numerous references by Cabinet members to the duration, complexity, and uncertainty of this war; to the financial and other nonmilitary aspects of it; and to the fact that we expect certain states to support us for some tasks, and other states for different ones. This schizophrenia reflects both division within the administration and the difficulties of the task.

The first question that comes to anyone's mind has still not been answered. Whom are we fighting? If it is bin Laden and his associates, formidable as they may be, we risk finding that dismantling their network is likely to be a slow and frustrating task in a world without walls, and that even successes in this particular struggle will not put an end to many other murderous forms of terrorism. To proclaim a war on terrorism in general, even if one means only terrorist cells and forces not directly sponsored by states, is ambitious indeed, for we need to distinguish among types of terrorists. Some have limited missions and do not see the US as their principal enemy. In Sri Lanka or Northern Ireland, in Corsica or Chechnya, in Palestine or in the Basque province, most terrorists see themselves, convincingly or not, as "freedom fighters." It is hard to imagine US forces acting directly against them. It is the groups that have declared war on America, or on the entire Judeo-Christian world, that the US must respond to.

Many insist that the US make war against states that serve as hosts and helpers of terrorists. Here again distinctions are essential. Are all the states in which terrorists operate their willing accomplices? In this case, the category includes states incapable of exerting control because they are too weak (Lebanon) or because they are insufficiently vigilant (the US and many of its democratic allies). Should the "war" be directed only against the states that sheltered or aided bin Laden? This risks sending us into an Afghan quagmire of disastrous proportions, causing a huge new exodus of miserably poor people, and creating revulsion and perhaps revolt among the Pakistanis, or at least some factions among them. Should the US make war against those whom it has declared to be terrorist, or terrorist-sponsoring, states, even if their links to bin Laden are hypothetical or dubious? This list includes states that have now promised to help the US (Syria, Sudan) as well as longstanding enemies (Iraq) or semi-enemies (Iran); trying to "punish" these could all too easily boomerang and reduce international support for the US. A determined project of ridding the world of all rogues and terrorists is a dream that would be seen abroad as a demonstration of rabid imperialism. The US has to be more modest in its goals.

The second question concerns the means by which war is carried on. The administration's recent emphasis on diversity of tactics has been wise. Terrorism should be fought as a crime against the innocent, just as organized crime is at home. More effective than military operations are likely to be the methods of police and counterintelligence, including the patient collection of information, the silent penetration of cells, the cutting-off of financial support, the dismantling of the communications used by the networks. Military attacks risk causing both political damage, by weakening regimes that would let us operate from their soil or friendly governments whose domestic support is shaky (Pakistan, Egypt, Saudi Arabia), and what is euphemistically called collateral damage, i.e., killing innocent victims, among whom the terrorists have been living. Indeed, the very scope of our military forces makes surprise attacks difficult. Small teams of US Special Forces are reported to be inside Afghanistan; but it seems likely that by the time our planes and combat forces arrive, training camps and former hiding places for terrorists will be empty. This is particularly the case in Afghanistan, as many past attackers have found out: there, more is definitely less.

As Reverend J. Bryan Hehir has argued, attacks that do not take every precaution against killing the innocent or destroying the infrastructure of the society in which the civilian population lives would be both immoral and counterproductive.[1] This brings us to the third question. How can we fight terrorism without undermining our position in a world where the support of other governments and peoples is essential? One reason for prudence in punishing governments that help terrorism is that we can hardly avoid punishing their societies as

---

1. "What Can and Should Be Done?" *America*, October 8, 2001.

well (and in doing so we may sharply increase popular hostility to ourselves). At worst we'll be faced, after the collapse of those currently in power, with the formidable task of finding new leaders who will not appear as our puppets. Our choice of local allies during the cold war days was often sufficiently catastrophic that we should now be dubious about the kind of nation-building, or rebuilding, we could undertake in regions we don't understand. After all, the Taliban derived from programs supported by the CIA and the American-supported Pakistanis not so long ago. Should the Taliban's rule collapse, it is far from clear that an eighty-six-year-old exiled former king and a Northern Alliance that has little support in much of Afghanistan (and that Pakistan dislikes) could provide very effective rule. There are more than enough tribes, factions, and animosities in Afghanistan to make an extremely cautious policy desirable.

To demand that the often besieged governments of other countries be with us, or else, makes sense only if they are in a position to be with us without committing suicide or reinforcing their internal enemies. Such a demand may be far less than successful in getting hostile or critical governments to side with us out of fear of American power. It may push friendly but frightened governments to seek a fence to sit on out of fear of their domestic foes.

3.

Another question concerns American unilateralism. Commentators may have announced its demise too soon. In a situation infinitely more complex than the one we faced when one unpopular leader, Saddam Hussein, invaded and annexed a small Arab state, we must ask how the coalition that Secretary of State Powell has been skillfully building is being seen by his colleagues in the government. Do they see it as a partnership in which our allies will not only provide various forms of support, but also take part in the major decisions? As often before in NATO, the danger is that we will look at our allies as junior partners of our firm, asked to supplement our forces and to pay for the common good.

There are two reasons to worry about this. One is that we have a large enough number of critics in the world, as well as old friends who do not want to be seen as protégés of the US, to need and seek a seal of international legitimacy (especially at a time when Russia, as in 1990, is cooperative and China discreetly nonhostile). That legitimacy could be provided by the Security Council of the United Nations, and the administration has acted wisely in suspending its suspicion of the UN and in persuading the council to pass on September 28 a resolution obliging UN members to cooperate in combating terrorism. If ours is the cause of humanity, if terrorism against civilians is something that threatens everyone, if security from terror attacks is a universal public good, we should behave not as a country that seeks revenge for what it has endured, and has the power to twist arms throughout the world, but as a country that seeks a broad mandate by accepting the norms and constraints of international law. The Security Council resolution is a step in that direction, although it contains no definition of terrorism and provides for no specific action by the UN itself.

A considerably more direct involvement of the UN in the campaign against terrorism would have legal and practical advantages. Legally, the International Criminal Court (resisted so reflexively by American "sovereign-tists") should be allowed to extend its jurisdiction to crimes against humanity committed by terrorists. A UN agency or office against terrorism could facilitate—especially among states that are not particularly friendly with one another yet have their own reasons to combat terrorism—exchanges of intelligence and arrangements for cooperation. There may also be a need for a temporary UN trusteeship over a post-Taliban Afghanistan, to preserve peace, to rebuild an administration, and to reconcile factions.

Another reason to resist the itch of unilateralism and of what I have elsewhere called bossism[2]—the use of international and regional institutions to impose our views—is that in order to succeed, the struggle against terrorists and the states that support them needs to begin with an adequate understanding of our adversaries' grievances, if only to allow us to shape a perceptive policy and to avoid acting in a self-destructive way. Reading newspapers and listening to public officials and commentators since September 11 has been a disconcerting experience. While the press and television in friendly countries have, mostly without animosity, discussed why the US is the target of so much hostility (and not only in the Islamic world), in the US the question has largely been dismissed. Or the answer has been self-serving, simplistic, and summary—it's the virtues of democracy, or of capitalism, or of an open society, that make others envious and angry.

It would be far better to realize that this hostility toward the US has many layers. Some of the terrorists and their supporters are religious fanatics who see in the US, the West, and Israel a formidable machine for cultural subversion, political domination, and economic subjection. The kind of Islamic revanche bin Laden projects in his statements is both so cosmic and based on so peculiar an interpretation of the Koran that there is very little one can do to rebut it. But there is a great deal one can do to limit its appeal. This kind of an ethics of conviction feeds—like so many other forms of totalitarianism—on experiences of despair and humiliation, and these can be understood and to some degree addressed.

But there are more limited bills of indictment against the US, focused on specific American policies. Sometimes, the targets are the corrupt or brutal regimes that have been propped up by American economic and military assistance. Sometimes there is solidarity with

---

2. See "The US and International Organizations," in *Eagle Rules?*, edited by Robert J. Lieber (Prentice-Hall, 2001), pp. 342–352.

the Palestinians' demand for an end of occupation and, at last, genuine self-determination. Sometimes there is concern for Iraq's children, who are claimed to be victims of US sanctions. Sometimes it is a sense of having been used and discarded—acute among many Pakistanis after the end of the war against the Soviet Union in Afghanistan. Throughout the developing world, resentment of American wealth is accompanied by protest against the misery of refugees, or continuing mass poverty.

It is dangerous to confuse those different categories and lump them as anti-American. We have tended, in the last ten years, toward a form of self-congratulation that can be grating for others: we are the "indispensable nation," the carriers of a globalization that will bring peace, democracy, prosperity, etc., the champions of an economic system that will eventually lift all boats, the catalysts of world order. We have not been sufficiently sensitive to other peoples' fears for their cultures, and to others' sense of shock at the inequities that come with capitalism and globalization.

No policy the US adopted would affect the implacable hatred of bin Laden. But we need to know why others sometimes feel threatened by us. We have been celebrating the solidity of our status as the dominant nation after the collapse of Soviet power and of the Soviet threat. There are, when it comes to overall power, no rivals in sight, and benign American hegemony, we often say, provides a modicum of order without threatening anyone. And yet a powerful country can both attract and repel.[3] By conventional measures of power we may be unbeatable, but those who feel threatened by us or annoyed by our self-righteous, ostentatious, and opulent predominance can do us great harm. We need not only to protect ourselves better at home (instead of waiting for a decisive victory abroad), but also to understand why

---

3. See Philip C. Wilcox Jr., "The Terror," pp. 3–14, and Joseph S. Nye, "Defending our Homeland," *The New York Times*, September 25, 2001, p. A29.

even nonterrorists sometimes feel smothered by America's cultural, economic, political, and military omnipresence.

Who will wage "America's new war"? The (mainly civilian) professionals of violence, or those who realize the limits of our power? A prudent policy would concentrate on the bin Laden networks of underground plotters and the financial manipulations that support them. It would use minimal military force only when the chances of success were good, aiming at isolating and neutralizing the Taliban regime rather than at immediately overthrowing it (and risking thereby a worsening of the sufferings of the Afghans)—unless it disintegrates through desertions and divisions. It would draw as much as possible on the expressed willingness of UN members to cooperate in actions against terrorism. But it would not let the present need for allies against it obliterate our efforts to combat human rights violations by regimes, for example on Afghanistan's northern borders, whose repressiveness risks driving more of their victims into terrorism.

Such a policy would give diplomatic priority not only to coalition building but to resuscitating the Israeli–Palestinian peace process. It would also show that, after the atrocities of September 11, we can listen both to the imperative of justice and to the views of others. It would avoid turning the lurid predictions of a "clash of civilizations" from a gloomy fantasy into a high risk. It could take advantage of the opportunity offered by the tragedy of September 11 to try to strengthen control over the most dangerous and elusive part of global civil society. But this should be done not only by states (in a porous world) or through interstate cooperation (always dependent on momentary circumstances) but by international and regional agencies.

Some US leaders have expressed verbal support for such a policy. Let us hope they have the commitment, patience, and skill to make good on their words and will not plunge into military action that will kill innocent people. Let us also demand of them the intelligence and compassion to understand that beyond lining up allies against terror, the national interest means seeking partners in a quest for the many and differing solutions to the pursuit of life, liberty, and happiness in a bewildering world. We should now realize that we cannot safely enjoy these values at home if others, abroad, cannot hope for a share of them.

—*October 3, 2001*

EPILOGUE

It is, of course, too early to predict the scope of victory in "America's new war." But it is not too early to point to some of the paradoxes and dilemmas that have marked its beginning, and to wonder about its immediate and long-term effects.

America's war in Afghanistan was dictated by the need to react to the horrors of September 11 and by the felt obligation not to appease an implacable and murderous enemy. Hence George W. Bush's choice of targets. One was bin Laden's al-Qaeda, the other was the Taliban regime that had given him a base. This second objective was meant to show that harboring and supporting terrorism does not pay and that the punishment for doing so would be extremely severe. The problem with the first goal—capturing or killing bin Laden and dismantling his network—isn't only the difficulty of finding him and the scope and resilience of his organization; it is also that there is no good reason to believe that the elimination of bin Laden and the demise of al-Qaeda in Afghanistan would remove the threat that terrorism creates for the ordinary people it attacks all over the world. To obtain a drastic reduction in terrorist acts would require a coherent effort to address at least the specific and often justified grievances that both drive humiliated and despairing people into terrorism, and provide sympathy and support for them.[4] Such a program would obviously have to take place over a long period, and its goals would never be completely achieved. The "crushing humiliation that has infected the third-world countries," the "feeling of impotence deriving from degradation," as the Turkish novelist Orhan Pamuk put it,[5] run so deep, and the remedies are so elusive, that one cannot have much hope of ultimate and definitive success.

This may be among the main reasons why the war shifted, during the first phase, from settling accounts with bin Laden to settling accounts with the Taliban. It thus soon moved from the uncharted terrain of war between a superpower and a private warrior-prophet to the familiar one of a war between states. Battering the Taliban seemed easier than getting rid of al-Qaeda. The desire for quick retribution led to a policy that aims at more than inflicting heavy losses on the military might of the Taliban. To discourage states from sponsoring terrorists, American officials concluded that the Taliban had to be removed from power. At first our adversary proved far tougher and far more resistant to bombing than we had thought, and our pounding resulted in civilian casualties, and hence more anti-Americanism in a world where many of those who do not endorse terrorist mass murder are also repelled by the spectacle of a huge power beating on a small one, already devastated by thirty years of war and famine. When American strategy shifted from the bombing of the Taliban's rather feeble infrastructure to an attack on its front-line forces, and used its sensors, its drones, and the information provided by its Special Forces to find appropriate targets and to coordinate its efforts with those of the Northern Alliance, the Taliban crumbled first in the north and soon in most of Afghanistan's provinces. The sense of liberation manifested in the cities the Taliban had ruled and

---

4. See Stanley Hoffmann, "Why Don't They Like Us?" *The American Prospect*, Vol. 12, No. 20 (November 19, 2001), pp. 18–21.

5. See Orhan Pamuk, "The Anger of the Damned," pp. 59–66.

oppressed mitigated the intensity of opposition to the US in the Muslim world.

Leaving the Taliban battered but in place would have looked timid to much of the American public, as well as to some of our allies and to some of the countries we wanted to understand that they had to choose between being with us or against us. It would also have resulted in preserving a safe haven for bin Laden's organization. However, getting rid of the Taliban raised two formidable problems: How much force would be required to do so, and what would replace it? Paradoxically, as Taliban resistance became concentrated in a few places, there was a greater and greater need for American forces in Afghanistan and in neighboring countries, especially in order to help the Taliban's enemies wrest control from it in places where its popularity was greater than in the North. A complete collapse of the Taliban might still leave the possibility of guerrilla warfare in these regions—and perhaps in others as well, if the postwar scene turns bloody and chaotic, in which case American military involvement might have to persist or even increase.

One important factor in the Taliban's defeat has been the increasing tension between its Afghan members, many of whom clearly preferred to extermination a defeat that left the future open, and the foreign members—largely Arab, Pakistani, and Chechen—who were not welcome in a country in which even opposed factions and ethnic groups of Afghans had old links and understandings. (This was brutally confirmed by the revolt of foreign members of the Taliban captured at Mazar-e-Sharif, and their massacre by their Northern Alliance captors.) But since the speed of the war has been much greater than the progress of negotiations toward a new regime, the US found itself in a quandary. Between the Taliban tyranny and the old feuding warlords who reemerged, there were few visible local leaders (except a very old ex-king), and the jockeying for power among factions became fierce. Even the current transitional government cobbled together under American and UN pressure might not last, especially if the Pashtuns decide they are underrepresented.

It will not be easy to find a tutorial force capable of preventing any new government from following the murderous precedents of the pre-Taliban years. The US has shown little enthusiasm either for taking on that task or for any kind of political trusteeship and peacekeeping by the UN (as distinguished from relief and reconstruction work). The UN, without the kind of standing force Sir Brian Urquhart has called for,[6] has insufficient means even for relief, and the Afghan warlords prefer to be left to themselves, without any external control or constraint.

The biggest issue that the US will face in the short term as a result of its war in Afghanistan is raised by repeated statements of the President promising (or threatening) to pursue the war against states that support terrorists throughout the world. Paradoxically, pressures for such escalation could grow, in either of two different developments. First, in Afghanistan itself, a protracted guerrilla war could be compounded by a renewed factional and ethnic war, so that US escalation beyond Afghanistan would serve as a diversion. Second, if there is lasting success in Afghanistan, the argument that there is "no substitute for victory" could be interpreted to mean that victory against the Taliban needs to be extended and completed before our enemies in Iraq and other rogue states recover from the shock of that victory.

The administration seems still divided between those who see a need to strike while it is succeeding militarily and would prefer to crush regimes that support terrorism, and those who would rather address the grievances that feed or provide support for terrorism. (There is here, obviously, the complex underlying issue of what would best ensure Israel's security. An all-out war on terrorism favors the hard-liners in Israel; an attempt to deal with Muslim and Arab

---

6. See "For a UN Volunteer Force," *The New York Review*, June 10, 1993.

grievances favors the Palestinians.) A policy of military attacks on Iraq and other terrorist states (even though some, like Syria and Libya, are openly or silently supporting us against bin Laden) would vindicate the complaints of our critics and enemies about American brutality and hubris, especially if such a policy aims at overthrowing existing regimes. We would lose many of our allies not only in the Muslim world, and practice what the French call *la politique de Gribouille*, after the hapless character who sought refuge from the rain by diving into a river.

When we think about the long term, we must distinguish between what is likely and what is desirable. What is likely is a mixture of good and not so good developments. On the one hand, despite the Bush administration's decision to scuttle the ABM treaty, the current rapprochement with Russia and the reduction of tensions with China may last; and the US government may shelve more decisively its unilateralist and anti-UN inclinations, if only because international cooperation will be indispensable in the fight against terrorism as well as in the attempt to prevent the world economy from declining further. On the other hand, the events in Afghanistan, combined with the effects of September 11, will push terrorist networks toward dispersion and clandestinity. The asymmetry of power between them and modern states could turn out to be the terrorists' greatest asset, and could make rooting them out extremely difficult.

In turn, antiterrorism at home is likely to slow down the "retreat of the state," in a world where the chief enemy is the terrorist who takes advantage of all the transnational facilities—open borders, open information and communications, etc.—that globalization has fostered, where supranational organizations are rare and international ones weak. We may instead find a "return of the state" in often unattractive guises: restrictions on internal liberties and on immigration and travel; increased powers for the police and the military; and a state obsessed with order and security rather than justice. How far this trend will go and how long it will last in the US are major questions for Americans concerned with protecting their values. One of the casualties of this trend, abroad, could be further European integration, especially in the domain that had remained the Achilles heel of the EU: common diplomacy and defense. Since September 11, the European nation-states, not the EU, have been the actors, and Britain has returned to its old role of best ally of the US.

What would be desirable? No one should doubt that the fight against global terrorism must continue. But it should take as its model and method—in the US as well as abroad—a patient and shadowy policy involving police cooperation with friendly countries, improved intelligence, support for democratic forces, and, if need be, support for US Special Forces actions in hostile countries and regions. It also has to be accompanied by a long-term strategy aimed at addressing the reasonable complaints of the third world.

We would help to achieve the goal of protection against terrorism by linking it to the cause of human rights. After all, those rights can be attacked both by individuals and by states; freedom from terror is, or ought to be, a basic human right and there ought to be a right of collective intervention that ranges from diplomatic pressure and sanctions to military action against extreme violations by terrorists. Such collective intervention could address cases of acute terrorism (state-sponsored, or by individuals) and instances of state crimes against humanity or genocide, such as those in Bosnia, Kosovo, East Timor, to name only a few. Captured terrorists and murderous statesmen, future bin Ladens and future Milosevics, should be judged by the same international criminal court.

As part of this new kind of international law, one could think of a convention defining the conditions under which a collective intervention against terrorism could legitimately occur. Such intervention could punish or even try to topple a regime that sponsors and encourages terrorism against foreign people or against its own. An explicit authorization by the UN, showing broad support for such an action, would be necessary. The "return of the state" resulting from security concerns that I deplored above would thus be counterbalanced by a reinforced defense of human rights.

More generally, if I had to summarize what is desirable, I would say: an end of the old and tiresome battle between "realists" concerned only with the defense of a national interest defined by military and economic strength, suspicious of humanitarian moves, and distrustful of international agencies that don't serve our interests, and "idealists" disturbed by the emphasis on and the effects of national power. Today idealism is often the best form of realism. We have, during and after the cold war, collected allies whom we needed at the moment, but whose internal and external policies in the long run created more grief than benefits for us. Saudi Arabia, Pakistan, and Egypt have supported Islamic fundamentalism in Afghanistan. Religious schools that teach hatred of the US have been funded by the Saudis. Mubarak's regime has supported an anti-American press. Our support for Pakistan has encouraged Islamabad to help terrorism against India in Kashmir.

The most basic requirements of realism and the best protection against fundamentalisms can take the form of support for causes that have been too easily dismissed. These include not only the protection of human rights abroad but also aid for economic development given even to governments that are not democratic but are willing to push for economic and social reforms at home so as to narrow the gap between the rich and the poor, the powerful and the dispossessed. (The establishment of a genuine democracy in a country that has never experienced it takes time.) It is brutalization and misery that drive their victims into millennial and violent religious fantasies.

A "Realist," however proud of American predominance and power, should understand that it is in the American national interest that the US stop being the universal scapegoat—deemed responsible, for instance, for the failings of Arab, Islamic, or third-world societies. Some of this scapegoating is inevitable, the price of the success of the American economy and the diffusion of American culture. But some of the hostility can be avoided. In some cases, in the disputes over Palestine or Kashmir, for example, it is American timidity that allows our critics to blame us for bloody stalemates that result in part from their own actions. In other cases, the US will be safer and have more support and authority than it enjoys today if it follows a policy combining greater humility, greater attentiveness to the plight of others, more concern for doing what is just than for doing what is expedient, more determination to reduce our dependence on dubious allies (such as our dependence on Saudi oil), and more willingness to let other actors do more. We live in a world in which no single country, however rich and strong, can rule over the rest, or even assure its own security.

—*December 15, 2001*

ORHAN PAMUK

The Anger of the Damned

I USED TO think that disasters strengthened people's sense of community. Right after the great Istanbul fires of my childhood and the earthquake of two years ago, my first instinct was to share my feelings, to discuss the disaster with others. But this time, seated facing the television in a small Istanbul coffeehouse near the quay frequented by carters, tuberculosis patients, and porters as the twin towers in New York blazed and collapsed, I felt desperately alone.

Immediately after the second aircraft hit the tower, Turkish television channels commenced live broadcasting. A small crowd in the coffeehouse watched the unbelievable images on the screen in detached amazement, astonished but apparently without being deeply affected. At one point I felt like standing up and declaring, "I spent three years of my life in Manhattan. I lived among those buildings. I walked those streets without money in my pocket. I kept appointments with people in those towers." But, as in a dream in which one feels increasingly alone, I remained silent.

I went out into the streets because I could not bear to see what was happening, and even more because I wanted to share what I had seen with other people. A short while later I saw a woman on the quay weeping as she stood in the crowd waiting for a ferryboat. From her expression and the faces of those around her, I saw immediately that she was not weeping because she had a relative in Manhattan but because she thought the end of the world was approaching. In my childhood, when it was feared that the Cuban crisis would give rise to a third world war, I had seen similarly distraught women weeping, as middle-class Istanbul families stocked up with packets of lentils and macaroni. I went back to the coffeehouse, and resumed watching the scenes on television with the same irresistible obsession as the rest of the world.

Later, as I walked the streets again, I met one of my neighbors. "Sir, have you seen, they have bombed America," he said, and added fiercely, "They did the right thing."

This angry old man is not religious at all. He struggles to make a living by doing minor repair jobs and gardening, and gets drunk in the evening and argues with his wife. He had not yet seen the appalling scenes on television, but had only heard that some people had done something dreadful to America. I listened to many other people express anger similar to his initial reaction (which he was subsequently to regret). At the first moment in Turkey, many spoke of the brutality of terror, and how despicable and horrifying the attack was. Still, they followed up their denunciation of the slaughter of innocent people with a "but," making restrained or resentful criticism of America's political and economic power. To debate America's role in the world in the shadow of terrorism that is based on hatred of the "West" and brutally kills innocent people is both extremely difficult and perhaps morally questionable. But in the heat of righteous anger at vicious acts of terror, and in nationalistic rage, some will find it easy to speak words that might lead to the slaughter of other innocent people. In view of this, one wants to say something.

Everyone should be aware that the longer the recent bombing lasts, and the more innocent people die in Afghanistan or any other part of the world in order to satisfy America's own people, the more it will exacerbate the artificial tension that some quarters are trying to generate between "East" and "West" or "Islam" and "Christian civilization"; and this will only serve to bolster the terrorism that military action sets out to punish. It is now morally impossible to discuss the issue of America's world domination in connection with the unbelievable ruthlessness of terrorists responsible for killing thousands of innocent people. At the same time, we should try to understand why millions of people in poor countries that have been pushed to one side, and deprived of the right to decide their own histories, feel such anger at America.

We are not always obliged, however, to look with sympathy at such anger. Moreover, in many third-world and Islamic countries, anti-American feeling is not so much righteous anger as an instrument employed to conceal their own lack of democracy and to reinforce the power of local dictators. The forging of close relations with America by insular societies like Saudi Arabia that behave as if they were determined to prove to the world that Islam and democracy are mutually irreconcilable is no encouragement to those working to establish secular democracies in the Islamic countries. Similarly, a superficial hostility to America, as in the case of Turkey, allows the country's administrators to squander, through corruption and incompetence, the money they receive from international financial institutions and to conceal the gap between rich and poor that in Turkey has reached intolerable dimensions.

There are those in the US today who unconditionally support military attacks for the purpose of demonstrating America's military strength and teaching terrorists "a lesson." Some cheerfully discuss on television where American planes should bomb, as if playing a video game. Such commentators should realize that decisions to engage in war taken impulsively, and without due consideration, will intensify the hostility toward the West felt by millions of people in the Islamic countries and poverty-stricken regions of the world—people living in conditions that give rise to feelings of humiliation and inferiority. It is neither Islam nor even poverty itself that directly engenders support for terrorists whose ferocity and ingenuity are unprecedented in human history; it is, rather, the crushing humiliation that has infected the third-world countries.

At no time in history has the gulf between rich and poor been so wide. It might be argued that the wealth of the rich countries is their own achievement and should not affect the concerns of the poor of the world; but at no time in history have the lives of the rich been so forcefully brought to the attention of the poor through television and Hollywood films. It also might be said that tales of the lives of kings are the entertainment of the poor. But far worse, at no other time have the world's rich and powerful societies been so clearly right, and "reasonable."

Today an ordinary citizen of a poor, undemocratic Muslim country, or a civil servant in a third-world country or in a former socialist republic struggling to make ends meet, is aware of how insubstantial is his share of the world's wealth; he knows that he lives under conditions that are much harsher and more devastating than those of a "Westerner" and that he is condemned to a much shorter life. At the same time, however, he senses in a corner of his mind that his poverty is to some considerable degree the fault of his own folly and inadequacy, or those of his father and grandfather. The Western world is scarcely aware of this overwhelming feeling of humiliation that is experienced by most of the world's population; it is a feeling that people have to try to overcome without losing their common sense, and without being seduced by terrorists, extreme nationalists, or fundamentalists. This is the grim, troubled private sphere that neither magical realistic novels that endow poverty and foolishness with charm nor the exoticism of popular travel literature manages to fathom. And it is while living within this private sphere that most people in the world today are afflicted by spiritual misery. The problem facing the West is not only to discover which terrorist is preparing a bomb in which tent, which cave, or which street of which city, but also to understand the poor and scorned and "wrongful" majority that does not belong to the Western world.

War cries, nationalistic speeches, and impetuous military operations take quite the opposite course. Instead of increasing understanding, many current Western actions, attitudes, and policies are rapidly carrying the world further from peace. These include the new visa restrictions imposed by many Western European countries on travelers from outside the EU; law enforcement measures aimed at impeding the movement of Muslims and of people from poor nations; suspicion of Islam and everything non-Western; and crude and aggressive language that identifies the entire Islamic civilization with terror and fanaticism. What prompts an impoverished old man in Istanbul to condone the terror in New York in a moment of anger, or a Palestinian youth fed up with Israeli oppression to admire the Taliban, who throw nitric acid at women because they reveal their faces? It is not Islam or what is idiotically described as the clash between East and West or poverty itself. It is the feeling of impotence deriving from degradation, the failure to be understood, and the inability of such people to make their voices heard.

The members of the wealthy, pro-modernist class that founded the Turkish Republic reacted to resistance from the poor and backward sectors of society not by attempting to understand them, but by law enforcement measures, prohibitions on personal behavior, and repression by the army. In the end, the modernization effort remained half-finished, and Turkey became a limited democracy in which intolerance prevailed. Now, as we hear people calling for a war between East and West, I am afraid that much of the world will turn into a place like Turkey, governed almost permanently by martial law. I am afraid that self-satisfied and self-righteous Western nationalism will drive the rest of the world into defiantly contending that two plus two equals five, like Dostoevsky's underground man, when he reacts against the "reasonable" Western world. Nothing can fuel support for "Islamists" who throw nitric acid at women's faces so much as the West's failure to understand the damned of the world.

—*Istanbul, October 18, 2001;*
translated by Mary Isin

REPORTS

PANKAJ MISHRA

The Making of Afghanistan

1.

IT IS HARD to imagine now, but for students at Kabul University, 1968 was no less a hectic year than it was for students at Columbia, Berkeley, Oxford, and the Sorbonne. A king, Mohammad Zahir Shah, had been presiding over the many ethnic and tribal enclaves of Afghanistan since 1933. But he knew enough of the world elsewhere to attempt, cautiously, a few liberal reforms in his capital city, Kabul. The university had been set up in 1946; a liberal constitution was introduced in 1964; the press was technically free; women ran for public office in 1965. By the Sixties, many students and teachers had traveled abroad; and new ideas about how to organize the state and society had come to the sons of peasants and nomads and artisans from their foreign or foreign-educated teachers.

In the somewhat rarefied world of modernizing Kabul, where women were allowed to appear without the veil in 1959, communism and radical Islam attracted almost an equal number of believers: to these impatient men, the great Afghan countryside with its antique ways appeared ready for revolution. It was from this fledgling intelligentsia in Kabul that almost all of the crucial political figures of the next three decades emerged.

Less than five years after 1968, King Zahir Shah was deposed in a military coup by his cousin, the ambitious former prime minister Mohammad Daoud.[1] Daoud initially sought help from the Communists, whose influence in the army and bureaucracy had grown rapidly since the 1960s: together, they went after the radical Islamists, many of whom were imprisoned or murdered for ideological reasons. But when Daoud, wary of the increasing power of the Communists, tried to get rid of them, he was in turn overthrown and killed. In April 1978, the Communists—themselves divided, confusingly, into two factions, Khalq and Parcham, that roughly corresponded to the rural–urban divide in Afghanistan—assumed full control of the government in Kabul, and in their hurry to eliminate all potential opposition to their program of land redistribution and indoctrination— an attempt, really, to create a Communist society virtually overnight —inaugurated what two decades later still looks like an ongoing process: the brutalization and destruction of Afghanistan.

Within just a few months, 12,000 people considered anti-Communist, many of them members of the country's educated elite, were killed in Kabul alone; many thousands more were murdered in the countryside. Thousands of families began leaving the country for Pakistan and Iran. Many radical Islamists of Kabul University were already in exile in Pakistan by 1978; some of them had even started a low-intensity guerrilla war against the Communist government. Several army garrisons across the country mutinied, and people in the villages, who were culturally very remote from Kabul, began many separate jihads, or holy wars, against the Communist regime.

Earlier this year, in the Pakistani city of Peshawar, I met Anwar,

---

1. Since then Zahir Shah, who is eighty-six years old, has lived in exile near Rome. The regimes that followed him now make his forty-year-long reign appear a golden age in the country's history, and he is much respected by an older generation of Afghans. He has been talked about recently as a possible alternative to the present Taliban regime. See "Secret Memo Reveals US Plan to Overthrow Taliban," *The Guardian*, September 21, 2001.

whose father and uncle were among the earliest Afghans to take up arms against the Communists. They weren't Islamists. Anwar's father, a farmer, lived in a village north of Kabul, near the border with what is now Tajikistan, and, although he was a devout Muslim, knew little about the modern ideologies of Islam that had traveled to Kabul University from Egypt, Pakistan, and Iran. It was Anwar's uncle, an officer in Zahir Shah's finance ministry in Kabul, who was a bit more in touch with them. He was friendly with Gulbuddin Hekmatyar, one of the prominent radical Islamists at Kabul University, who sought refuge in Pakistan in the mid-1970s after a failed uprising against Daoud and the Communists.

In the beginning, the Soviets were busy with consolidating the Communist hold over Kabul and securing the country's main highways, and they seemed very far from rural Afghanistan, which in any case had had for years relative autonomy from the government in the capital city. But later, with the aggressive campaigns of land reforms and Marxist indoctrination emanating from Kabul, resistance built up swiftly throughout the country. Anwar's father and uncle joined one of the Mujahideen groups that, though equipped only with .303 Lee Enfield rifles, managed to keep their region free of Communist influence. Then, in December 1979, the Soviet army entered Afghanistan in order to protect the Communist revolution, which was also being threatened by factional fighting among Afghan Communists and rebellions by the army; and the position of Anwar's family became more precarious.

In 1983, Soviet planes bombed the villages Anwar and his relatives lived in, in retaliation for attacks on Afghan army convoys by the Mujahideen. Although Anwar's father and uncle stayed back to fight and look after the animals and fields, there was no choice for many of the women and children but to leave.

Anwar, who was seven years old at the time, couldn't recall too many details of the long walk that brought him and his mother and young brother to Pakistan. He did remember that it was very cold. There was snow on the ground and on the hills, and Anwar and his family walked all day and rested at night in roadside mosques. The 350-mile-long road to Pakistan swarmed with thousands of refugees, but they had to avoid moving in large groups, which the Russian helicopters buzzing ominously overhead liked to fire upon. They also had to stay as close as possible to the main road, for there were mines in the fields and on the dirt tracks—these were the tiny "butterfly mines" that floated down from the helicopters and then lay in wait for unmindful children and animals.

I still heard about the mines when I traveled this past spring on the road that links Kabul to Pakistan, through Ningrahar province.[2] Dust-spattered refugee families from northern Afghanistan stood hopefully by the side of the eroded tarmac, where the Toyota pickups of the Taliban—young turbaned men and guns crammed in the back —were the new sources of fear. The land seemed vacant, the high surrounding mountains concealed behind a haze, and the stubborn bareness of rock and desert was relieved only occasionally by a green field and a black-tented encampment of nomads.

There is emptiness now, but in the days of Zahir Shah this land was reclaimed, with Soviet assistance, for cultivation; and orchards and fields, watered by broad canals, sprang up. In a half-abandoned village, rusty padlocks hanging from the doors of bleached wood set into long mud walls, an old Afghan was startled when I mentioned that time. Rasool had been in his late teens then; had known some of the prosperity that came to the region; and could even, with some prompting by me, remember the white men—Russian experts—traveling through the fields.

---

2. A recent UNDP report reveals that although 1.6 million explosives have been cleared, it will take another seven to ten years to turn Afghanistan into a mine-free place. See *Dawn* (Pakistan), July 1, 2001.

Unlike Anwar's father and uncle, Rasool wasn't a Mujahideen: he hadn't revolted against the Russians or the Communists; he had been content to tend his land. The jihad had almost bypassed him; and he had known hard times only when, sometime in the mid-1980s, Russian planes bombed the canals that brought water to his land. There had been another recovery after the Soviet army withdrew in 1989, when white men, this time from the UN, came and supervised the repair of the canals. By then, the local Mujahideen commanders were in charge. They taxed all the traffic on the roads; they took over the land which once belonged to the Afghan state and made the farmers grow high-yield poppy.

There was no point for Rasool to defy the commanders; he wouldn't have got any cash credit from the traders in the town for anything other than opium. Not that the poppy-growing had improved his circumstances. It was the Mujahideen commanders who had grown very rich from converting the poppy into heroin and then smuggling it across the border into Iran and Pakistan.

And then, suddenly, before he had even heard of them, the young soldiers of the Taliban arrived from the southern provinces, chased out the Mujahideen commanders, and took over the checkpoints. They supervised, and profited from, the drug business until 1999, when they abruptly banned the cultivation of poppy, leaving most farmers with no sources of livelihood, and the option only of migrating to Pakistan.

Rasool lived in the vast, now arid land, after being taken, in just three decades, through a whole fruitless cycle of Afghan history. The long reign of Zahir Shah was no more than a faint memory. All the slow, steady work of previous generations was canceled out; Afghanistan was even further back from its tryst with the modern world.

2.

But then, like many Muslim countries suddenly confronted in the nineteenth century with the rising power of the West, Afghanistan's route to modern development could only have been tortuous. The Afghan empire of the eighteenth century had reached as far as Kashmir in the east and up to the Iranian city of Mashhad in the west. Like present-day Afghanistan, it contained many different ethnic groups, the dominant Pashtun tribes in the east and south, Tajiks and Uzbeks in the north and west, and the Shia Hazaras in the central provinces. Almost all of them were Sunni or Shia Muslims. Fiercely autonomous and proud, they had successfully resisted the British attempt to extend their Indian empire up to Kabul; but after two Anglo-Afghan wars, 1838–1842 and 1878–1880, the Afghans had been subdued enough to serve as a buffer state between the expanding empires of Britain and Russia.

The British were content to exercise influence from afar without troubling themselves with direct rule. It was under their supervision that the present-day boundaries of Afghanistan were drawn, leaving a lot of Pashtun tribes in what is now Pakistan. The British also subsidized the Afghan army. Until 1919, when the Afghans won complete independence from the British, the ruler in Kabul reported to Delhi in matters of foreign policy, which essentially involved keeping the Russians out of Afghanistan.

The British-backed rulers of Afghanistan in the nineteenth and early twentieth centuries were insecure and ruthless, obsessed with protecting their regime from any local challenges as well: Afghanistan's continued isolation was in their best interests. During the twenty-one-year rule of Amir Abdur Rahman (1880–1901), one of Afghanistan's more pro-British rulers, only one school was built in Kabul, and that was a *madrasa* (theological school). Condemned to playing a passive part in an imperial Great Game, Afghanistan missed

out on the indirect benefits of colonial rule: the creation of an educated class such as would supply the basic infrastructure of the post-
colonial states of India, Pakistan, and Egypt.

Afghanistan's resolute backwardness in the nineteenth and early
twentieth centuries was appealing to Western romantics: Kipling,
who was repelled by the educated Bengali, commended the Pashtun
tribesmen—the traditional rulers of Afghanistan, and also a majority
among Afghans—for their courage, love of freedom, and sense of
honor. These clichés about the Afghans—which were to be amplified
in our own time by American journalists and politicians—also had
some effect on Muslims themselves.

One of them was Jamal al-Din al-Afghani, a polemicist of the
nineteenth century, who sought to alert the Muslim peoples to their
growing subjugation to the imperial powers of the West. The radical
Islamists I spoke to didn't remember that in 1968—while student
groups at Kabul University were organizing large demonstrations
against one another, distributing fiery pamphlets, and fighting one
another on the streets—a huge mausoleum for al-Afghani went up
inside the campus, to honor someone who, although born in Iran and
educated in India, adopted the pen name "al-Afghani" and even
began to tell other people that he was from Afghanistan.[3]

The increasing influence of the West, and the related undermining
of Muslim power, was the inescapable event of al-Afghani's lifetime;
he witnessed it more closely than most Muslims during his long stints
in India, Iran, Egypt, France, England, and Turkey. But Afghanistan
had hardly been affected by the lifestyles and new knowledge of
Europe, by the passion and energy of white men from the West that
were transforming old worlds elsewhere in the nineteenth century.
This resistance to Western-style modernization would have impressed

---

3. For an interesting discussion of al-Afghani, see Albert Hourani, *Arabic Thought in a Liberal Age, 1798–1939* (Oxford University Press, 1962).

al-Afghani, who, while stressing the need to modernize Muslim societies, disapproved of the wholesale adoption of European ways of the kind Kemal Atatürk would impose upon Turkey just two decades after al-Afghani's death in 1897.

Al-Afghani failed to see how even small but strategically placed countries like Afghanistan were being drawn into the great imperial games of nineteenth-century Europe, and then sentenced to isolation and backwardness as buffer states. Behind his romantic attachment to Afghanistan lay fear and defensiveness—his painful awareness, shared by many other educated people in once-great Asian societies, that they had fallen behind, and that they not only had to catch up with the West, but also had to keep in check its increasing power to alter their lives, mostly for the worse.

For many educated people in pre-modern societies, communism offered a way of both catching up with and resisting the West; and the ideology had a powerful, and often generous, sponsor in the Soviet Union. But the hasty, ill-adapted borrowings from Soviet communism—the simplistic notion, for instance, of Afghans as feudal people who had to be turned into proletarians—more often than not imposed new kinds of pain and trauma on such a traditional society as Afghanistan; and helped to push the country even further away from the modern world.

The Soviet Union had supported the Communist coup of 1978 in Kabul, and so had grown concerned about the clumsy and brutal way in which the Khalq faction of the Afghan Communist Party, led by the fanatical ideologue Hafizullah Amin, a one-time student at Columbia University, had hijacked the coup, and then had tried violently—and, as spontaneous revolts across the country proved, disastrously—to weld the incoherent ethnic-tribal worlds of Afghanistan into a Communist society. As the records of Politburo conversations reveal, the aging leaders of the Soviet Union at first resisted military intervention in Afghanistan. But they feared that the United States, unsettled by the fall of the Shah of Iran, was trying, with the help of the wily Amin, to find an alternative anti-Soviet base in Afghanistan. They suspected Amin of being "an ambitious, cruel, treacherous person" who "may change the political orientation of the regime."[4]

This sounds like cold war paranoia. It wasn't softened by the mutinies against the Communist regime by Afghan military garrisons, one of which, in the city of Herat, ended in the killings of several Soviet and East European advisers. In the last days of 1979, when the Communist regime looked close to collapse, a contingent of Soviet soldiers flew into Kabul, stormed Amin's palace, and killed him. A more moderate leader, Babrak Karmal, who belonged to the urban-based Parcham faction, took his place and attempted to avert the collapse of the Afghan state and bring an end to the brutalities.

Karmal was only partly successful in restoring order to Afghanistan. In 1986, the Soviets replaced Karmal with Mohammad Najibullah, the head of KHAD, the Communist intelligence agency. Najibullah, known so far for his role in the execution and torture of anti-Communists, tried even harder to win the Afghans' support. He toned down the Communist rhetoric, emphasized his faith in Islam, and began reaching out to the refugees and Mujahideen, speaking all the time of compromise and national reconciliation. But his government couldn't possibly acquire legitimacy among Afghans while being beholden to a foreign power. And in any case, things were out of his control: Afghanistan had already begun fighting in a new proxy war that would kill a million or more Afghans over the next decade, many of them from Soviet bombing of civilians, including fleeing refugees.

---

4. "Abstract, Politburo, Central Committee, USSR," *Journal of South Asian and Middle Eastern Studies*, Vol. 17 (Winter 1994), pp. 54–55.

3.

By the late Seventies, proxy wars between the United States and the Soviet Union were already being fought in Angola, Somalia, and Ethiopia. That is why the revelation made three years ago—by Zbigniew Brzezinski, national security adviser to President Carter—that small-scale American aid to the Afghan Islamists based in Pakistan had begun some months before the Soviet army arrived in Afghanistan is not surprising. In July 1979, President Carter signed the first of the directives for the clandestine aid that Brzezinski later said had the effect of drawing the Russians into "the Afghan trap." "We didn't push the Russians to intervene," Brzezinski said, "but we knowingly increased the probability that they would." This secret operation explains his exultant tone in the letter he claims to have sent to President Carter on December 27, 1979, the day the Soviet army entered Afghanistan. "Now," he said, "we can give the USSR its Vietnam War."[5]

Brzezinski's enthusiasm was shared by William Casey, a veteran of the OSS and the director of the CIA under President Reagan. In the mid-1980s, Casey committed CIA funds to the even grander plan of organizing the Muslims of the world into a global jihad against Soviet communism. By the mid-1980s, the CIA office in Islamabad, Pakistan, had become second in size only to the headquarters in Langley, Virginia; and American assistance to the Afghan Islamists, channeled

---

5. All quotes are from an interview Brzezinski gave to *Le Nouvel Obsérvateur*, January 15–21, 1998, p. 76. When asked in the same interview if he regretted "having supported Islamic fundamentalism [*intégrisme*]" and given "arms and advice to future terrorists," Brzezinski said: "What is most important to the history of the world? The Taliban or the collapse of the Soviet empire? Some stirred-up Muslims or the liberation of Central Europe and the end of the cold war?" That some stirred-up Muslims were a minor price to pay for the collapse of the Soviet empire cannot but seem now an especially cynical and wrongheaded bit of *Realpolitik*.

through the CIA and the Pakistani intelligence agency, the ISI, was running into billions of dollars.[6]

The military dictator of Pakistan, General Zia ul-Haq, was more than eager to place his country in the avant-garde of the jihad. Since April 1979, two years after his coup and after he had hanged his former prime minister, Zulfikar Ali Bhutto, he had been urgently seeking both money and respectability from the United States. By promoting radical Islamists in Pakistan and Afghanistan he also hoped to suppress Bhutto's party, the Pakistan People's Party, and the intellectuals, journalists, and human rights activists agitating for the restoration of democracy. Somewhat similar local reasons prompted President Sadat of Egypt to offer cheap arms to the CIA for use in Afghanistan. The most generous support of the jihad among other pro-American governments came from the ruling family of Saudi Arabia, which was concerned about the growing influence of its traditional Shia rival, Iran, since its Islamic revolution.[7]

The Saudis saw the jihad in Afghanistan as a way of exporting Wahhabism—an especially austere Saudi version of Sunni Islam, whose

---

6. Casey's and the CIA's dabblings in Afghanistan have been described in Bob Woodward, *Veil: The Secret Wars of the CIA, 1981–87* (Simon and Schuster, 1987). Lawrence of Arabia met James Bond in many of the fantasies that bloomed in this expensive but relatively under-reported battle of the cold war. Casey wanted the ISI to involve the Muslims of the Soviet Union in the jihad; and he wasn't satisfied with the ISI-arranged smuggling of thousands of Korans into what is now Uzbekistan and Tajikistan, or with the distribution of heroin among Soviet troops. Brigadier Mohammad Yousaf, a senior officer of the ISI, got Afghan Mujahideen to mine and bomb military installations a few kilometers deep inside Soviet territory; but plans for more such attacks were hastily dropped after the Soviet Union threatened to invade Pakistan. The story is told by Yousaf and Major Mark Adkin in *The Bear Trap* (London: Leo Cooper, 1992).

7. Zia did make himself unassailable through his partnership with the CIA. Many of his political opponents stayed in prison, and while promising elections and democratic rule all the time, he remained the dictator of Pakistan until his death in a plane crash in 1988. The present military ruler, General Pervez Musharraf, was offered a similar partnership by the US

promoters in the early nineteenth century attacked Mecca and Medina and purged them of the Sufi-style venerations which involved idolatry as well as dancing and music. They matched the American assistance to the Afghan Islamists dollar for dollar. Prince Turki, the head of the Saudi intelligence agency, worked closely with the CIA and the Pakistani ISI, and sent a rich Saudi businessman, Osama bin Laden, to organize the thousands of poor Arabs from the Middle East and North Africa who, attracted by promises of food and money, had traveled to Pakistan to enlist in the CIA-backed jihad against communism.[8]

Thus many separate ambitions and strategies powered the Afghan struggle against communism. The diverse agenda of its sponsors and prime agents meant that little attention was paid to organizing the highly fractious Afghans into a cohesive resistance movement that in time could replace the unpopular and discredited Communist government in Kabul—which by Najibullah's own admission had lost control over 80 percent of the Afghan countryside.

One of the few things that united the five million Afghans in Pakistan and Iran and millions more in Afghanistan itself was their resentment of the Afghan Communists and their Soviet backers. Seven Afghan resistance "parties" came forward to receive the millions

---

government, which expects Pakistan to be a "front-line state" again, this time in a war against terrorism. But Zia's encouragement of the jihad in Afghanistan produced hundreds of thousands of radical Islamists who make Pakistan an unstable country; and Musharraf, who seems to realize well that cooperation with the US could endanger rather than consolidate his hold on power, has responded cautiously so far, agreeing to cooperate in intelligence and other ways, but resisting the presence of US troops there. Unlike Musharraf, the Communist-era despots of the Central Asian countries of Uzbekistan and Tajikistan ruthlessly persecute their relatively few radical Islamists, and have been quick to ally themselves with the United States.

8. These and other details about Osama bin Laden are to be found in Ahmed Rashid's *Taliban: Militant Islam, Oil and Fundamentalism in Central Asia* (Yale University Press/ Nota Bene, 2000).

of dollars' worth of arms and humanitarian aid that started flowing into Pakistan in the early 1980s. The parties represented the ethnic, linguistic, and tribal divisions within the Afghans; but many of their members had little or no connection with the Mujahideen commanders and soldiers in Afghanistan who were fighting a sporadically intense guerrilla war against the Soviets.

The CIA avoided direct contact with the Afghans in order to maintain the fiction of American noninvolvement; it used Pakistani intelligence (the ISI) for the important logistical tasks: the distribution of aid, the military coordination between Mujahideen outfits. But the officers of the ISI had their own favorites; they wanted to promote the pro-Pakistan men within Afghanistan's majority ethnic community, the Pashtuns. As a result, one of the most effective fighters who was neither led by the CIA nor coordinated by the ISI, the brilliant Tajik Mujahideen commander in northern Afghanistan, Ahmed Shah Massoud, received hardly any assistance. Massoud fought the Taliban for six years, until he was assassinated last month, two days before the attacks on the World Trade Center and the Pentagon, by two suicide bombers posing as Arab journalists, who were in all likelihood sent by Osama bin Laden and the Taliban. The largest beneficiary of foreign aid was the Pashtun Islamist Gulbuddin Hekmatyar, who amassed a huge arsenal in southern Afghanistan and most of the time avoided the battlefield.

Then there were the obvious instances of corruption produced by a prolonged war effort, bankrolled covertly with unaudited money, and controlled through several intermediaries: the proof of unrestrained plunder is all there in the mansions of ISI officers and Afghan resistance leaders you see in Pakistan. A large number of sophisticated weapons ended up in an arms bazaar near Peshawar or traveled elsewhere in Pakistan, stoking the various ethnic and sectarian conflicts that ravaged the country in the late 1980s and 1990s. Mujahideen leaders like Hekmatyar, indulged by the ISI, branched off into opium cultivation—for years a small-scale business in Afghanistan—and smuggling, and began a turf war against other Afghans.[9]

4.

The Soviet army withdrew from Afghanistan in early 1989, three years after Mikhail Gorbachev had declared the decade-long losing war there a "bleeding wound" for his country. In a matter of months, the Soviet Union began to fall apart; the cold war seemed at an end; and although the Communists still held Kabul and would hold it until 1992, American assistance to the Afghans dwindled.[10]

On the day the last Soviet soldier left Afghanistan, William Webster, the new director of the CIA, hosted a champagne party in Langley, Virginia. Aside from the Soviet withdrawal, there wasn't much to celebrate in Afghanistan itself. The destruction of roads and agricultural land and the flight of more than five million people (the largest refugee population in the world) created a political and economic void which the Mujahideen commanders filled. Long subsidized by the United States and Saudi Arabia, they now had to be "self-financing." It was around this time that Afghanistan became the biggest producer of opium in the world. Farmers forced by local

---

9. In fact, Hekmatyar, who inaugurated his career as a radical Islamist by assassinating a left-wing student at Kabul University in the late 1960s, is held responsible for the murder of many rival Mujahideen as well as some of the liberal-minded Afghan intellectuals who had fled Kabul for Pakistan after the Communist coup in 1978. Hekmatyar's rocket attacks on Kabul during the civil war in 1994 killed more civilians in the capital city than had died in ten years of anti-Communist jihad.

10. Britain's Tony Blair was addressing a distrust and bitterness many Afghans feel toward their former Western sponsors when he claimed recently in an interview to the Pashto section of BBC Radio that the West would not repeat the mistake of walking away from Afghanistan after achieving its immediate aim.

Mujahideen commanders to cultivate poppy, however, received only a fraction of the wealth that the cash crop created as it moved along the supply line.

Smuggling was rampant: Pakistani military trucks that brought supplies to the Mujahideen during the jihad often went back loaded with drugs or consumer items. In Ningrahar province, the local Mujahideen commander operated his own airline: planeloads of TVs and air conditioners arrived from Dubai and were then trucked by him into Pakistan. Much money was to be made in controlling key trading routes and checkpoints; and so little battles kept erupting between different Mujahideen groups, whose leaders became known as "warlords." In the early 1990s, many of them were running clashing opium and smuggling empires across Afghanistan.

An economy built around predation could only lead to a moral breakdown, especially in the rural areas where the institutions of the Afghan state had barely existed, and where traditional codes of honor and justice, enforced by tribal and religious leaders, had so far governed daily life and conduct. There was at least a semblance of administration and law in the western and northern provinces controlled by the Mujahideen commanders Ismail Khan and Ahmed Shah Massoud. But things were very bad in the southern provinces, where the old tribal and religious elite had been rendered impotent by many different warlords who exacted toll taxes from traders and smugglers, fought with each other, and raped young children and women at will.

One day in early 1994—so the Taliban claims—in a village near the southern city of Kandahar, a Pashtun man in his thirties called Mohammad Omar heard about two women who had been abducted and raped by some local commanders. Like many young Pashtuns from his village, Omar, the son of landless peasants, had participated in the jihad against local and foreign Communists. He had been wounded several times and had lost his right eye. After the Soviet withdrawal he had gone back to teaching at his village *madrasa*. He was deeply aggrieved by the degenerate Mujahideen and the anarchy around him, and often spoke with his friends in the village about ways to deal with them and establish the law of the Koran.

The Taliban's version has it that the news of the raped women incited Omar into action. He went out to the local *madrasas* and raised a band of thirty Talibs, or students, for a rescue mission. The students mustered about sixteen rifles among themselves. They then went and freed the girls and hanged the commanders from the barrel of a tank. A few months later, there was another incident in which two commanders fought a gun battle in the streets of Kandahar over a boy both wished to rape. Once again, Omar showed up with his students and freed the boy and executed the commanders.

This is the romantic legend surrounding the rise of the Taliban and their reclusive, one-eyed supreme leader, Mullah Mohammad Omar. It goes on to describe how the young, motivated students had in just two years brought most of Afghanistan under their control (Herat in 1995, Kabul in 1996), captured the arsenals of the warlords, done away with their terror, and made secure the life and property of ordinary Afghans.

Such accounts are also meant to make the Taliban seem like the Muslim armies of early Islamic history pacifying the intransigent tribes of Arabia. They are part of the careful self-presentation of their leaders, who have been at pains to distinguish themselves from the previous generation and to justify the drastic restrictions imposed on the dress, movements, and education of women. They go with the stylish new black turbans, the beards with the mandatory length of eight centimeters, the freshly designed flag, and the grander name—the Islamic Emirate of Afghanistan—for the country.

The stories almost conceal the fact that the Taliban—consisting mainly of students, former Mujahideen like Omar, and the rural clergy—have come from the Pashtun tribes in the east and south of the country. The secretive leadership consists almost entirely of

Mullah Omar's friends and associates in Kandahar. As such they have been regarded with suspicion by the ethnic minority groups in the northern, central, and western provinces, the Persian-speaking Tajiks and the Shia Hazaras—a distrust that settled into animosity after the repeated massacres of them by the Taliban in their continuing war against the Hizb-e-Wahdat (Islamic Unity Party), a Shia Hazara party, in the central highland region of Afghanistan.[11] Though militarily underequipped, the Shia Hazara party and the forces of the late Ahmed Shah Massoud, which control the northern Tajik-majority province of Badakhshan, are, with ethnic Uzbeks, the main components of the Northern Alliance against the Taliban, whom they accuse, not inaccurately, of imposing a backward-minded Pashtun dictatorship over the ethnic mosaic of Afghanistan. In the last five years, this civil war has flared up every summer, after the snows in the high mountain passes melt, but petered out in late autumn, with little territory gained or lost on either side.

What the legend leaves out is the contribution to the Taliban's early military success by traders and smugglers in Pakistan and Afghanistan who were fed up with paying endless toll taxes on Afghan routes controlled by the Mujahideen warlords and welcomed the Taliban. Disaffected former Mujahideen and even officials of the former Communist regime helped the Taliban take on the warlords, and tens of thousands of Pashtun students in Pakistan joined them as the news of their victories spread.

Most importantly, the Taliban received a lot of support from Saudi Arabia and from Benazir Bhutto's government in Pakistan. The Saudi royal family had fallen out with Osama bin Laden by then; but they gave money and support to the Taliban independently of the private charities and donations that went from Saudi Arabia, some through

---

11. See *Massacre of Hazaras in Afghanistan* (Human Rights Watch, February 2001) and *The Massacre in Mazar-i-Sharif* (Human Rights Watch, November 1998).

Osama bin Laden, whose Arab fighters gave strong support to the Taliban. Bhutto and her ministers expected the student militia to bring stability to Afghanistan, and open up the possibility—which inspired the early, if brief, American approval of the Taliban—of trade routes and oil and gas pipelines to the newly created Central Asian republics. Bhutto and her colleagues also wanted to diminish the sinister power that the ISI and its officers had acquired over the Pakistani state during its collaboration with the CIA.[12]

The Taliban's connection with Pakistan went even deeper. Just as Kabul University had in the 1960s supplied the ideologists and activists of the next decades, so the theological schools in Pakistan known as Deobandi *madrasas* had in the 1990s produced among its refugees many of the young soldiers and leaders of the Taliban.

The name "Deobandi" came from the original *madrasa* that had been set up in 1867 in a small Indian town near Delhi called Deoband. The *madrasa* came out of an insular Indian Muslim response to British rule in the nineteenth century: the work of men who feared that Western-style education of the kind proposed by the British, and embraced by the Hindus, was going to uproot and fracture Muslim culture, and who were convinced that training in the fundamentals of the Koran and the *sharia* would shield Indian Muslims from the corruptions of the modern world. The Deoband *madrasa* has issued about 250,000 fatwas on various aspects of personal behavior.

In the early twentieth century, the missionaries of Deoband had begun to set up *madrasas* close to what was then the Indian border with Afghanistan. In the 1980s and 1990s, among the two to three million Afghan refugees in Pakistan, the poorest had gone to these madrasas. Some of the most senior leaders of the Taliban had been educated at the Darul Uloom Haqqania near Peshawar, which still

---

12. Bhutto had special reasons to be wary of the ISI, whose officers had conspired to bring down her elected government in 1990.

follows the Koran-oriented curriculum created at Deoband in India a hundred and fifty years ago.

Although it is the biggest of the Pakistani *madrasas* near the border with Afghanistan and quite famous, the *madrasa* had, when I visited it in April this year, the somewhat lowering appearance of a poorly financed college in an Indian small town: peeling paint, dust-clogged stairs, broken chairs, unfinished buildings bristling with rusting iron girders, and shabbily clad students. In one corner of the compound was a separate hostel for boys between the ages of eight and twelve—a courtyard lined with curious fresh faces under elegant white caps—who read nothing but the Koran, which they were expected to memorize. In one tiny room at the hostel for older students, many of whom were from Afghanistan, Uzbekistan, and Tajikistan, there was the unexpectedly moving sight of six young men sleeping on tattered sheets on the floor, their turbans respectfully arranged in a row next to the door.

The kitchen consisted of two dingy rooms, their walls stained black from the open wood fires; almost an equal number of flies hovered over the stagnant yellow curry in exposed drains and the freshly chopped mutton on a wide wooden table. Things were no better in the smaller *madrasas*. But food and lodging were free. And the orphans and sons of poor Pashtuns in the refugee camps—members of a powerless majority of rural Afghans—who went to the *madrasas* in the 1980s and early 1990s wouldn't have had many options, as opposed to the many CIA-sponsored Mujahideen leaders, who lived in style in a posh suburb of Peshawar. Living amid deprivation and squalor, and educated only in a severe ideology, a new generation of Pashtun men developed fast the fantasies of the pure Islamic order that they as the Taliban would aggressively impose upon a war-ravaged country.

—*October 17, 2001*

(This is the first of two articles; see also "The Afghan Tragedy," pp. 203–232.)

CHRISTOPHER DE BELLAIGUE

The Perils of Pakistan

1.

ON OCTOBER 5, 2001, two days before the US started to bomb Afghanistan, Tony Blair, the British prime minister, came to Islamabad, Pakistan's capital, to thank General Pervez Musharraf for his "courage and leadership" in committing his country to support George Bush's war on terrorism. It could not have been easy for Musharraf to do what he did. According to a Gallup poll of Pakistanis in urban areas, 83 percent sympathize with the Taliban rather than the US and 82 percent consider Osama bin Laden a holy warrior, not a terrorist, although 64 percent also believe the attack on the US was an act of terrorism. Behind the attacks of September 11, some claim to detect a nefarious Israeli plot, designed to elicit global support for more brutality against the Palestinians.

General Musharraf says he does not share such views; but he cannot admit openly that the Taliban rose to the top of the Afghan heap thanks to Pakistan—and, in particular, thanks to the military organization that Musharraf now heads. According to Ahmed Rashid, the author of the standard work in English on the Taliban, between 1994 and 1998, more than 80,000 Pakistani militants trained and fought with the Taliban—most of them ethnically Pashtuns, like most of the Taliban and some 40 percent of the Afghan population.[1] By now agreeing to provide moral and logistical support, intelligence, and Pakistani airspace for allied aircraft—but nothing more—Musharraf has said in effect he was sorry for helping to create the environment in which Osama bin Laden has thrived. This, so far, has been quite enough to stave off America's wrath.

Pakistan's self-styled chief executive, who in June added the presidency to his impressive list of military and civilian positions, has made a tricky U-turn. In the view of most of Pakistan's generals, America is to blame for the mess in Afghanistan. Following the 1979 Soviet invasion, America used the government of General Zia ul-Haq, Pakistan's last military dictator, as a conduit for some $2 to $3 billion worth of covert aid that was transferred to the Mujahideen, the "holy warriors" then struggling to expel the Soviet invaders from Afghanistan.[2] In backing the war against the Soviets, the US benefited from the expansion of religious seminaries inside Pakistan, especially those that inculcated the values of the jihad against the Communists. After the Soviet withdrawal from Afghanistan, in 1989—and, particularly, after the collapse of the Soviet Union two years later—American interest in Afghanistan dried up, leaving Pakistan, in Musharraf's own words, "high and dry."

Having cooperated in the struggle against communism, the Pakistanis were left to deal with a neighboring country awash with arms, disputed by despotic warlords, and disfigured by the same religious fanaticism that had served the anti-Communist cause. Naturally, Pakistan wanted a friendly Afghan regime to its west to help

---

1. Ahmed Rashid, *Taliban: Militant Islam, Oil and Fundamentalism in Central Asia* (Yale University Press, 2000).

2. See the special report put out by Human Rights Watch on foreign interference in Afghanistan, "Crisis of Impunity: The Role of Pakistan, Russia and Iran in Fueling the Civil War," Vol. 13, No. 3 (July 2001). This details not only Pakistani interference in Afghanistan, but also US, Iranian, Russian, and Central Asian meddling.

counterbalance India, the hostile power that lies to its east. So, in 1994, after their initial protégé, Gulbuddin Hekmatyar, had been defeated militarily, the Pakistanis turned to the nascent Taliban, whose combination of religious zeal and Pashtun ethnicity suggested that they had a good chance of bringing stability to the country. This the Taliban had succeeded in doing by the end of the 1990s, although pockets of Afghanistan remained in the hands of opposition groups that are members of the Northern Alliance. Pakistan's defense of the Taliban's right to diplomatic recognition did not waver even when the Taliban announced that some religious minorities should wear distinguishing symbols and demolished two ancient monumental reliefs of the Buddha. After he seized power from Nawaz Sharif, the now-exiled former prime minister, in 1999, Musharraf continued to plead the Taliban's case internationally. Pakistan continued to give aid and military advice to the Taliban government and consult with its representatives in Islamabad.

In his long television speech soon after the bombing started, Musharraf justified his decision to side with the US by talking of a choice between "two adversities"—of which he was obliged, as Islamic law prescribes, to choose the lesser. When he told a press conference on October 8, 2001, that Pakistan had never armed the Taliban, he simply ignored UN evidence clearly implying that it had.[3] What is more, it was the military, and the military-run Inter-Services Intelligence (ISI), that steered this policy. An unstable and geographically narrow country, vulnerable to attack on its flanks, Pakistan regarded the Taliban's Afghanistan not only as an ally—albeit an unruly one—

---

3. A UN secretary-general's report of 1997 cites "reliable eyewitnesses" who described the delivery of arms to the Taliban that, it is generally understood, came from Pakistan; see "The Situation in Afghanistan and Its Implications for International Peace and Security," Report of the Secretary-General, S/1997/894 (November 14, 1997), para. 18. See also Rashid, *Taliban*, and Human Rights Watch, "Crisis of Impunity"; both sources discuss Pakistani military aid to the Taliban.

but also as a sort of backyard, where unsightly detritus of Pakistan's military adventures could be hidden from view. After the Soviet withdrawal, camps and arms depots left over from the resistance movement were incorporated into another war, this time between Pakistan-backed fighters and the Indian army in the state of Jammu and Kashmir, where, in 1989, Muslim militants activated a long-dormant campaign for self-determination.

Pakistan could hardly take the political and military risk of participating overtly in an insurgency directed at its powerful neighbor. Instead, it encouraged links between Afghanistan and Kashmir—links that brought together fighters from dozens of Islamist organizations based in Pakistan and Kashmir, of varying sectarian persuasions. All the organizations were involved in the training and indoctrination of the Kashmir Mujahideen, the distribution of arms, and the launching of attacks on Indian forces in Kashmir. Among the fighters have been thousands of guerrillas trained in Afghanistan.

During the US military campaign to capture or kill bin Laden, and to dislodge the Taliban, there have been increasingly violent protests in Pakistan. These demonstrations have been larger and angrier than those that had preceded the attacks—at least eleven people, including five policemen, have so far been killed. The biggest demonstrations took place in Karachi, Quetta, and Peshawar—cities that have large Pashtun populations, and large numbers of Afghan refugees.

The consensus among most diplomats and foreign observers in Pakistan is that Musharraf has handled a tricky situation deftly. By retaining diplomatic contact with the Taliban, and sending mediators, some of them clerics, to Kabul, he can claim to have done more than anyone else to try to get the Taliban off the Osama bin Laden hook. Middle-class Pakistanis I have talked to refer self-pityingly to Pakistan's "Talibanization" in recent years, approve of Musharraf's view that Pakistan's policies have to change according to circumstances, and approve of his contention that the crisis has given the country a chance to "reemerge as a responsible and dignified nation." It is possible that the anti-US demonstrations that preceded the US bombing attacks actually helped the general; although few of them were very big, Western journalists obligingly made much of them, lending weight to the impression, already prevailing abroad, of a courageous leader refusing to buckle under pressure.

According to Musharraf, the initial allied assaults used Pakistani airspace and intelligence, although not airfields. Later, US aircraft landed on at least one Pakistani airfield, although the Pakistani authorities say they will not be used for attacks. The general has done Bush other favors as well. On October 4, the foreign ministry announced that evidence that had been provided by the US to Pakistan would be sufficient to secure bin Laden's conviction in court. This was worth a great deal more to the US than similar assertions from European countries. Musharraf has been more outspoken than most of the other Muslim leaders. The general braved Islamist opinion at home by freezing the bank accounts of four Islamist organizations that, according to the US, have links with al-Qaeda.

In return, the general got some payoffs of his own. At the end of September, Bush lifted the sanctions that had been imposed after Pakistan (following India's example) detonated nuclear devices in 1998. Congress is now working to lift the sanctions that were imposed after the suspension of democracy during Musharraf's October 1999 coup. Some debt payments owed to the US were quickly rescheduled. Tony Blair came to shake the hand of a dictator whose country has been suspended from the Commonwealth. The West has put aside its previous concern for Pakistan's democracy; the Western coalition-builders are convinced that no elected Pakistani prime minister could have supported the US in the way that Musharraf has. It is fortunate for them that he is answerable only to his fellow generals and not to the Pakistani public.

Still, at the beginning of the US-led offensive, the top Pakistani generals seemed more threatening to Musharraf than the protesters on the streets. On October 7, the day the offensive began, Musharraf abruptly fired two important members of the junta that had brought him to power, and who were influential when it came to important decisions: they were Ahmed Mahmoud, the director-general of the ISI, and Muzaffer Usmani, the deputy chief of the army staff. Mahmoud had been particularly tainted by his close association with the newly discarded pro-Afghanistan policy, and by his personal ambition. Talat Masoud, a former lieutenant-general, told me that he expects Abdul Aziz, Mahmoud's replacement, "to make the ISI subservient to the army"—i.e., to Musharraf's orders. Usmani, for his part, was a reluctant convert to the new Afghanistan policy, perhaps not a convert at all. He is an ideologically committed Islamist of the kind that Zia favored, and Musharraf, who attended staff college in Britain, does not.

Their replacements, and the other men whom Musharraf subsequently promoted in his reshuffle, may not all be as critical of the Taliban as Musharraf has become. The important thing, however, is that they owe their positions to Musharraf, and they will be beholden to him, not the other way around. The *News*, a pro-Musharraf English-language daily, said the new men held "moderate views and life-styles" —euphemistic talk for their having wives with uncovered heads, and for favoring a glass of whisky, not milk, after dinner.

For all that, the timing of the reshuffle suggested a case of the jitters on Musharraf's part. It was almost coincidental with a US offensive that seemed certain to unsettle Pakistanis, not to mention the country's more than two million Afghan refugees. Musharraf may have felt that, in the event of a breakdown in law and order, and an intensification of pressure from the religious right, Mahmoud and Usmani might turn against him. Talat Masoud expects the purge to continue, especially in the ISI. But maintaining law and order now depends as much on what happens in Afghanistan as it does on the resolve of Pakistan's armed forces and police.

Contrary to some early predictions, Musharraf now has a very good chance of surviving; the US, certainly, will do all it can to ensure that he does. The questions now are whether a new Afghan regime will emerge and what form it might take. Back in the 1980s, General Zia ul-Haq, in encouraging the Taliban, hitched Pakistan's Afghanistan policy to his own policy of domestic Islamization. His successors, and their ISI chiefs, hitched these to a third policy, aggressive action in Kashmir; when they were combined, these policies defined what Pakistan stood for in the 1990s. It is impossible to uncouple one from the other two; now that Afghanistan policy has changed, the others will have to change, too. The future actions of Musharraf, and the US, will determine whether this change further weakens Pakistan or invigorates it.

2.

The Dar ul-Uloom, or House of Learning, in the Pakistani village of Panjpir, in the Sawabi district of the North-West Frontier Province (NWFP), is an important place on the local political and social map. The school not only dominates the economic and social life of Panjpir, but also of the surrounding area, where seminarians preach in dozens of small mosques. Koran courses held during the fasting month of Ramadan attract up to nine thousand men and more than half that many women; the visitors stay in local mosques, or in private houses near the school. Maulana Muhammad Tayyab, the seminary's spiritual leader, has followers on both sides of the Afghan border, most of them Pashtuns. Thousands of them are affiliated with the other seminaries that are run in his name. Most of the seminarians, even those who are not Pashtun, admire the Taliban.

Tayyab's own political colors are more elusive. When Nawaz Sharif was prime minister, cabinet ministers from Sharif's Pakistan

Muslim League (PML) were regular visitors to Panjpir. One current seminarian is the son of Sufi Mohammad, a tribal leader who has waged a lengthy struggle, intermittently violent, for Taliban-style government in Malakand, an unruly frontier region. But the Maulana is also in close touch with Gulbuddin Hekmatyar, Pakistan's former Afghan protégé, who is a Dar ul-Uloom alumnus. Before the US started its offensive against Afghanistan, Hekmatyar, who now lives in Iran, said he would support the Taliban. Tayyab said that his students would wage jihad on behalf of "whoever has been oppressed."

There are more than four thousand registered seminary schools in Pakistan, with hundreds of thousands of students; many more seminaries are unregistered. Most such schools survive on voluntary contributions, rarely charging fees, and are exempted from paying tax. Few have ever been visited by a government inspector inquiring about the curriculum. They range in size from the eight-thousand-student Jamiat ul-Uloomi Islamiyyah, on the outskirts of Karachi, to countless huts in villages across the country, where often poorly educated teachers give rudimentary instruction in the Koran and the sayings of the Prophet, and nothing else, to a handful of small boys. A lot of seminarians come from very poor families that can't afford the school uniform and writing paper needed for their children to attend a state-sponsored school. Not all seminarians emerge as religious fanatics; thousands of young Pakistanis attend seminary classes for a few hours each week, after classes at their regular school are over. Some seminaries educate well-versed imams for the mosques. Many more, however, are organized to produce recruits for jihad.

In fact, the importance of Maulana Fazl ul-Rehman, and Pakistan's other cleric-politicians, derives not from elections but from their power over education. Ul-Rehman's branch of the divided Jamiat-Ulema-Islam party (JUI)—the Islamic Ulema Party—is rich and influential beyond the two parliamentary seats (out of 204) that it won in the last general election, in 1997. Ul-Rehman controls hundreds of seminaries around the country, many of them funded with Saudi money. These places, like British public schools, have an impressive old-boy network. It is an open secret that, through this network, the JUI has cultivated good relations, if not working links, with the Taliban, and also with *jihadi* and other religious organizations that are active in Afghanistan, Pakistan, and Kashmir. A few days before he was put under house arrest at the beginning of the US offensive, ul-Rehman boasted of the "constant contact" he had with Taliban leaders; he was more circumspect when it came to discussing rumored organizational links between the JUI and groups like Sipah-e-Sahaba (the Army of the Friends of the Prophet), a militant organization suspected of murdering Shias in Pakistan and Afghanistan, and the Harakat ul-Mujahideen—or the Movement of Mujahideen, a *jihadi* organization on America's list of terrorist groups, which has sent Mujahideen as far afield as Kashmir and Bosnia. India suspects the Jaish-e-Mohammad, or Army of Mohammad, an offshoot of the Harakat ul-Mujahideen, of carrying out the October 1 suicide attack on the Jammu and Kashmir state legislature, in which at least thirty-eight people were killed. As a consequence of that attack, the US is investigating the Jaish-e-Mohammad—which has hastily changed its name, to Tehrik ul-Forqan, the Movement of Those Who Can Distinguish Between Good and Evil—and may add it to its list of terrorist organizations.

Watching the Islamist protests that have followed the US strikes, a visitor might conclude that the JUI's two main branches, along with the Jamaat Islami (JI), or the Party of Islam, Pakistan's other big Islamist party, are doing all they can to bring down the government. It seemed at first that their demonstrations were intended to embolden Islamists in the army and that a putsch might follow. But the opposition mounted by ul-Rehman and the others is self-limiting. A drive along the road toward Pishin, about twenty-five miles north of Quetta, where the JUI's black-and-white standard flies from mosques, seminaries, and shops, illustrates how visible the JUI's followers have become, and how much a government crackdown would hurt the party. Many of the JUI's rich benefactors, furthermore, rely on the complicity of the authorities to conduct a vast smuggling operation, much of it in electrical appliances made in China and the Far East and sent via the Gulf States and Iran to Afghanistan and then into Pakistan. Ul-Rehman himself is as much a deal-maker as an ideologue. In 1993, he found ways to justify his joining, as a junior coalition partner, the second government of the Pakistan Peoples Party (PPP) of Benazir Bhutto, who could be described as a Westernized neo-secularist. Bhutto—who now lives in self-imposed exile in London—even appointed ul-Rehman chairman of the national assembly's standing committee for foreign affairs. Until the 1999 coup, the JUI was a coalition partner in the government based in Quetta that ran the province of Baluchistan, whose population is around 50 percent Pashtun.

With this in mind, it is not surprising that, a few days before his arrest, when his criticisms of the government's "hypocritical" policy of cooperation with the US reached their peak, ul-Rehman still spoke with caution. He carefully drew a distinction between a jihad against the US in Afghanistan—which the Musharraf government could merely deplore—and a jihad launched against the Pakistani government; that, the general has made clear, would provoke a tough reaction. Ul-Rehman made it clear that he understood this. "Unless the government itself takes action against the Taliban," ul-Rehman said, "the jihad will not take place inside Pakistan." A few days after the US bombing began, most of the country's Islamist parties and groups had declared jihad against the US, not against Musharraf, and some would-be Mujahideen were crossing the border to join the Taliban. Ul-Rehman's prestige, because he had defended the Taliban more stoutly than anyone else and been placed under house arrest, has risen considerably.

I met some of Ul-Rehman's followers in an impoverished suburb of Quetta called Qila Abdullah. Here posters exhort passers-by to join al-Badr, a *jihadi* group. Among the mud-brick houses, you come upon a half-built seminary inhabited by a dozen students whom locals identify as members of the Sipah-e-Sahaba. Across a dried stream bed, a mixed population of Afghan and Pakistani Pashtuns live in great poverty—but probably more comfortably than their kinsmen across the border, thirty-eight miles away. In the streets, there is not a woman to be seen. Most boys attend seminaries—their fathers work in the bazaar. Among people here, I learned during discussions with local residents, faith in the intervention of the divine in all things is strong: the belief that the martyred Mujahideen have achieved heavenly repose exercises a powerful hold over the imaginations of young people. Some other residents I talked to say they regard themselves as Muslims first, Pashtun second, and Pakistani or Afghan last. Religious politicians like ul-Rehman have great opportunities to exploit popular sentiment here.

3.

Even on October 12, when rumors were circulating that US combat troops had arrived at Pakistani airports, antigovernment protests held after Friday prayers were not particularly impressive except in Karachi, where some 20,000 people gathered, and there was some violence. In some places, especially near the Afghan border, religious leaders had gone into hiding, fearing arrest. Security was very tight. Whatever their fury at the US and their sympathy for the Taliban's spirit of defiance, many Pakistanis declined to associate themselves with a protest movement that had been orchestrated by religious parties they do not support. Neither the PML nor the PPP— which the regime allows to exist, but forbids to hold meetings or participate in elections—came out in support of the protests. Furthermore, many Pakistanis, understanding the pressures and payoffs that led

Musharraf to support the US coalition, continued to accept that decision.

The longer the conflict in Afghanistan goes on, and the greater the number of civilian casualties, the more such views favorable to Musharraf will be challenged. Musharraf has tried to reassure the Pakistanis that if there is to be a new government in Afghanistan, it will not be dominated by the component parts of the Northern Alliance, which Pakistanis regard as hostile. They have no affinities with ethnic Tajiks or Uzbeks or with the Iran-backed Hazaras. When Musharraf said he was open to proposals that Zahir Shah return to lead his nation, this was another u-turn; Pakistanis remember Afghanistan's deposed king for his attempts to keep Pakistan out of the UN. Musharraf is willing to be flexible about him because he is Pashtun at least, and he is not likely to exercise much power in any case. And many Pakistanis, although they have turned against the Pashtun-dominated Taliban, regard the Pashtuns as their natural allies in Afghanistan. If the King does not return, Musharraf will try to find another Pashtun to support.

Much could go wrong. What if, for example, the Northern Alliance, helped by the US, manages to take over Taliban-controlled regions and starts butchering Pashtun civilians? What if Musharraf's often expressed concerns that a future government include Pashtuns friendly to Pakistan are disregarded? At best, Pakistanis will regard Musharraf as a dupe, at worst, an accessory to murder. They will despise themselves for placing their trust, once again, in the treacherous US. If Musharraf falls because a new Afghanistan government seems unsatisfactory to Pakistanis, the military leader who replaces him will find it hard to resist the temptation to undermine Afghanistan's new government. Disgruntled ISI officers will line up to help him, and Pakistan's future will become more uncertain than ever.

Apart from Afghanistan, Pakistan has more to lose from the current American strategy than any other country. Nonetheless, several well-placed observers I talked to think the crisis will force Musharraf to try to reform his nation. The perverse rationale that sustained Pakistan's former Afghanistan policy cast a shadow over Pakistan's entire political life; it gave Pakistan's own *jihadi* groups, and their backers, much more power than their relatively small public support entitled them to. Since these groups were supposedly furthering Pakistan's interests in Afghanistan and Kashmir, they were permitted great liberties on Pakistani soil. In 1994, after the Pakistan–Taliban alliance was formed, the army, the ISI, and important parts of civilian governments competed with one another for the favor of, and control over, the religious parties and their *jihadi* affiliates. To criticize this policy openly was to criticize Pakistan's support for the Pashtun people, as well as the sacred obligation of jihad in Kashmir. This three-way policy involving Afghanistan, Kashmir, and the *jihadi* did Pakistan great harm. It radicalized millions of Pakistanis, and gave the country the image of a supporter of brutality and murder.

Afghanistan made this policy possible. It served as a physical refuge for the Kashmiri *jihadi* groups, and a moral refuge for Pakistan's rulers, in that it allowed them to disclaim responsibility for the *jihadi* groups they covertly supported. That refuge will probably disappear. If there is a new Afghan government, especially one that is watched over by the UN, it is unlikely to allow *jihadi* groups with Pakistani members to maintain camps and supply depots on Afghan soil. Having declared a war on all terrorism, the US will find it hard to maintain its equivocal position toward Pakistan's unofficial support for *jihadi* groups in Kashmir. Musharraf has already shown he appreciates this—he took the unusual step of publicly regretting the October 1 attack on the Jammu and Kashmir state legislature.

Whatever immediate satisfaction they have taken from bin Laden's moment of success, most Pakistanis believe, in common with their coreligionists elsewhere, that there is a difference between jihad, exemplified by the freedom struggles being waged in Kashmir and

Palestine, and the kind of terrorist actions that destroy skyscrapers. The Indian government says that as far as Kashmir is concerned, there is no difference. This is a stale position; but only a serious diplomatic effort to bring about peace in Kashmir, an effort conducted amid a de-escalation of violence, could supersede India's argument, and open the way for a serious discussion of the Kashmir issue. This, in turn, cannot happen unless the US itself is willing to bring strong pressure on the Indians and the Pakistanis—as it also should on the Israelis and Palestinians. Most Pakistanis would welcome such a process. Musharraf would be a credible negotiator; it was he who ordered a dramatic incursion of Pakistani troops into an Indian-controlled sector of Kashmir in 1999. Signs of progress would marginalize *jihadi* groups, giving Musharraf the opportunity quietly to sever the establishment's support for them.

For Pakistan to become a "responsible and dignified nation," in Musharraf's words, the US and the rest of the industrialized world need to be far more deeply engaged in its problems than they have been in the past. Without a big aid package, Pakistan will be unable to develop the kind of economy in which Pakistan's young people can find work instead of turning to the proselytizing politicians of the JUI and JI. Without strong economic support, Pakistan will be unable to set up the public education system it needs if the stranglehold of the religious seminaries is to be broken, and Musharraf will continue, as he did in the first two years of rule, to vacillate before the threats of charismatic mullahs.

Before September 11 Musharraf's largest problem was that he was a dictator. Now it is his biggest asset. He intends to strengthen the president's powers before letting Pakistanis elect a new prime minister next October. The US will not object. Thanks in no small measure to a history of political interference by Pakistan's armed forces, Pakistan's very weak and flawed façade of a democratic system cannot assume the tasks that September 11 has thrust upon it, particularly the task of controlling the violent religious groups fighting in Kashmir. Musharraf, if the US strongly backs him—and, at the same time, does not undermine him by killing civilians in Afghanistan —at least has a chance to carry out some of the reforms Pakistan desperately needs.

—*Karachi, October 17, 2001*

EPILOGUE

When Lakhdar Brahimi resigned in 1999 from his post as the UN's special representative for Afghanistan, he had clearly lost patience with Pakistan and Iran. Both countries were—and remain—members of the group comprising the six states that border Afghanistan, along with Russia and the US, that was established to help bring about a peaceful conclusion to the war between the Taliban and the Northern Alliance. In 1999, Pakistan and Iran had solemnly pledged "not to provide military support for any Afghan party." It was an open secret, however, that both countries were violating the letter and spirit of these undertakings. Pakistan's military backing for the Taliban, and Iran's for the Northern Alliance, had become part of a broader rivalry between the two nations, and a major impediment to the resolution of the Afghan war.

The rivalry was evident when I visited Herat, western Afghanistan's commercial hub, following its liberation by the Northern Alliance in mid-November. The city's residents—who are mostly Persian-speaking Tajiks, and include both Sunni and Shia Muslims—seemed almost as delighted by the departure of Pakistan's consul general as they were by the flight of the Taliban. The diplomat in question, a local politician told me, had exercised great influence over Herat's affairs. A few days after his departure, less than a hundred yards up the road, Iran's consul general moved back into the consulate he had been forced to abandon, out of fear for his life, earlier in the year. Among the events that forced him to leave was the murder of an outspoken Iranian dissident, a Sunni cleric whom the Taliban had granted asylum in Herat. Rumors spread that the killing had been carried out at Iran's behest. A Taliban-inspired mob marched on Iran's consulate.

From my conversations in Herat, it was clear that the meaning of these consular comings and goings had not been lost on the local residents. The very day he returned to the city, Iran's consul general helped mediate a dispute that had arisen between Ismail Khan, the Sunni Tajik who, as a member of the Northern Alliance, had taken control of most of western Afghanistan, and the Shia leaders who had fought the Taliban alongside him. The Iranian envoy was politely received; both Khan and the Shias have benefited from Iran's military, diplomatic, and financial largesse. Nonetheless, Khan made it clear that, while he was grateful for Iran's help, he remained suspicious of its intentions toward western Afghanistan. During the meeting, which was held in the presence of four unidentified Iranian officials, Khan asked the Iranian consul why, despite his country's support for the Northern Alliance, Iran had also supplied fuel to the Taliban. There was an awkward silence.

Iran's policy toward the Taliban was more complex than it seemed. Some Iranian conservatives, whatever their antipathy for the Taliban's Sunni orthodoxy, appreciated Mullah Omar's anti-Americanism, a sentiment they correctly fear is on the wane in their own country. There were practical reasons, too, for avoiding absolute hostility. Before September 11, Iran had accepted more than two million Afghan refugees. (When most of northern Afghanistan was liberated from Taliban rule, that number started to decrease.) More than two million Iranians were addicted to Afghan opium and, increasingly, heroin. Farmers in the Iranian province of Sistan-Baluchistan suspected that the Taliban had dammed the Helmand River before it flowed into Iran, worsening the effects of a severe drought. The way to solve such problems, Iranian pragmatists said, was to do business with the Taliban. Selling fuel oil to the Taliban—in what quantities, it is almost impossible to find out—was reward for the Taliban's enforcement of a ban on poppy cultivation, which cut production by 96 percent in a year. In the months preceding September 11, the price of opium soared in Iran.

As long as international attention is focused on it, Iran's policy toward a post-Taliban Afghanistan will have to be more clearly and openly defined. Iran has two fears. The first is that the return of Muhammad Zahir, the former king, will encourage monarchism inside Iran. The second is that there will be an open-ended deployment of foreign troops, especially American troops, on neighboring soil. Iran regards western Afghanistan as lying within its sphere of interest, and would like to be commercially and politically influential there. Iran's leaders have indicated, however, that they appreciate that a stable Afghanistan, even if they can't control it, is the best guarantee of Iran's security. Musharraf's Pakistan seems to have reached the same conclusion. This, in turn, has had interesting diplomatic ramifications. Little-noticed amid the missiles, food drops, and the search for bin Laden, Afghanistan's two most interfering neighbors have started to get on better with each other.

Brahimi, who took back his old job after the September 11 attacks, has had a hand in this rapprochement. There has been unprecedented contact between the foreign ministers of both countries. At the beginning of November, Musharraf even paid a brief visit to Tehran. These are encouraging signs. If new policies toward Afghanistan are to emerge from Pakistan and Iran—a prerequisite for the solution of Afghanistan's problems—the world's gaze needs to be focused not only on Kabul, but also on Tehran and Islamabad.

—*November 30, 2001*

TIM JUDAH

War in the Dark

Khoja Bahaudin, northern Afghanistan

A FEW WEEKS ago President George W. Bush said something to the effect that he didn't want to fire off $2 million missiles to hit $10 tents in Afghanistan. Well, I think he said that, but I can't check, because now I am living in a $10 tent in northern Afghanistan. There is no electricity, no clean water, no paved roads, not much food, and it is only the aid agencies that are staving off famine here. In this part of opposition-controlled northern Afghanistan, close to the border with the former Soviet republic of Tajikistan, it has barely rained for three years and choking dust swirls everywhere, entering every pore.

I arrived in the early hours of the morning after a five-day journey from London. On the banks of the Amu Darya, the Oxus River of legend, which marks the frontier between Tajikistan and Afghanistan, Afghan and Russian officials pored over everyone's documents. Although Tajikistan has been independent for more than a decade, it has fought a war against Islamic insurgents and thousands of Russian troops help guard its frontiers. On the other side, after more document checks, and haggling with pickup-truck drivers, my colleagues and I got to the little town of Khoja Bahaudin. There we were directed by Afghan officials of the anti-Taliban Northern Alliance to spend our first night in the country on the concrete veranda of a small building.

When I woke up I noticed that the windows of half the building were boarded over and that the ceiling was black. In fact it looked as if there had been a fire or explosion inside. My suspicions were quickly confirmed. I was sleeping just outside the room where the first deaths of this new war had happened. On September 9, two Moroccans posing as journalists had set up their television camera inside the room to interview the legendary Afghan Mujahideen commander Ahmed Shah Massoud. One of the Moroccans asked, "When you get to Kabul what will you do with Osama bin Laden?" Massoud took a breath to answer but before he did so the Moroccan set off the bombs strapped around his waist; he was shredded, and body parts were scattered around the room. The second suicide bomber survived and ran down to the nearby river, where he was killed.

According to one version, Massoud died in a hospital six days later. Another has it that he died within hours but that his death was covered up for six days so as to ensure a smooth succession. Of course it is impossible to prove a link between the murder of Massoud and the attacks on New York and Washington two days later, but people here have few doubts about it. Osama bin Laden, they feel sure, was giving his Taliban hosts the head of their most implacable foe before moving on to bigger things.

1.

Ahmed Shah Massoud, an ethnic Tajik, was born in 1956, the son of a military officer. He attended Kabul's French-run Lycée Istiqlal. In 1975 he fled to Pakistan because he had been involved in trying to begin an Islamic movement along with others, such as the engineering student Gulbuddin Hekmatyar. After the Soviet invasion in 1979 he became one of the founders of the Mujahideen resistance along with Hekmatyar and others. With Western backing, they were able to force the Soviet occupiers to retreat and thus played a major part in the collapse of the Soviet Union. Following the Soviet pullout the Russian-backed regime of President Mohammad Najibullah clung to power until 1992, when Massoud made a deal with General Rashid Dostum, a powerful ethnic Uzbek in Najibullah's army, to switch sides and join his troops to Massoud's against Najibullah. After that Kabul fell.

Michael Griffin, a British writer and journalist who is the author of the excellent *Reaping the Whirlwind: The Taliban Movement in Afghanistan*, quotes from an interview given to a US reporter by Najibullah just before the end:

> We have a common task—Afghanistan, the USA and the civilized world—to launch a joint struggle against fundamentalism. If fundamentalism comes to Afghanistan, war will continue for many years. Afghanistan will turn into a center of world smuggling for narcotic drugs. Afghanistan will be turned into a center for terrorism.

The rival Mujahideen commanders and their armies now turned on one another. In 1993 the new president, Burhanuddin Rabbani, an Islamic scholar and poet, opposed Hekmatyar. Between January 1994 and February 1995 Massoud fought Dostum and Hekmatyar for control of Kabul, which had not been seriously damaged during the war with the Soviet Union but parts of which were now turned to rubble. Some 50,000 people are estimated to have died in these battles. By the autumn of 1996 Massoud had formed a new alliance with Dostum and others because they had a new common enemy, the Taliban. By September their advance had forced Massoud to retreat from Kabul to the heartland of his support, the Panjshir Valley, the southernmost tip of which lies roughly thirty miles north of the capital. Rabbani also fled north from the Taliban.

According to Ahmed Rashid, the widely respected Pakistani journalist and author of *Taliban: Militant Islam, Oil and Fundamentalism in Central Asia*, Massoud's reputation was at its peak in 1992, but "four years in power in Kabul had turned [his] army into arrogant masters who harassed civilians, stole from shops and confiscated people's houses, which is why Kabulis first welcomed the Taliban when they entered Kabul." The Taliban sprang from the *madrasas*, or religious schools, which flourished among the Afghan refugees in Pakistan during the years of the Soviet occupation and indeed ever since. "These boys," writes Rashid,

> had no memories of their tribes, their elders, their neighbours nor the complex ethnic mix of peoples that often made up their villages and their homeland. These boys were what the war had thrown up like the sea's surrender on the beach of history.... They were literally the orphans of war, the rootless and rest-less.... Their simple belief in a messianic, puritan Islam which had been drummed into them by simple village mullahs was the only prop they could hold on to and which gave their lives some meaning.... Ironically, the Taliban were a direct throwback to the military religious orders that arose in Christendom during the crusades to fight Islam.

The main Taliban leaders came from the southern city of Kandahar. The driving force behind them was Mullah Mohammad Omar, who lost his right eye fighting the Soviets. Born in 1959, he came from a family of landless peasants and supported his family after his father died by becoming a village mullah and opening a *madrasa*. Different legends circulate about how Omar founded the Taliban because he was outraged by the sexual behavior of Mujahideen commanders; but we will probably never know exactly what prompted him to gather the religious students into a fighting force of their own, which would then go on to seize most of Afghanistan and subject it to its extreme version of Islam. What is clear is that religion here is entwined with the delicate ethnic politics of Afghanistan, which in turn is a factor manipulated by the country's neighbors and others.

Today there are probably some 23 million or so Afghans, but of course, after twenty-two years of war no one can be sure. According to the 1973 census, the last to be carried out, 43 percent were Pashtuns (also known by the anglicized name of Pathans), mostly Sunni Muslims, who live mainly in the south. The border, known as the Durand line, which was drawn in 1897 to demarcate the frontier with the then British India, now of course Pakistan, divides the Afghan Pashtuns from their Pakistani brothers. Pakistani governments have always felt the need to keep their Pashtun population of some 20 million happy; their enduring nightmare is a revival of Pashtun nationalism, which would seek to carve a Pashtun state out of Pakistan and Afghanistan.

Curiously, in view of the fact that Britain's Royal Air Force has been bombing Afghanistan "shoulder to shoulder" with the US, it was this border question that was the reason for Britain's last bombing of Afghanistan, in 1919. After an Afghan-inspired attempt to raise a revolt among Pashtuns over the border, the RAF bombed Jalalabad (near the present Pakistani border), while a single plane made it to Kabul and bombed the royal palace and an arms factory. Martin Ewans, a former British diplomat who is the author of a highly readable new primer, *Afghanistan: A New History*, quotes a letter that an Afghan leader sent in 1919 to the viceroy of India; it sounds curiously reminiscent of the statements of Taliban and other Muslim leaders today:

> It is a matter of great regret that the throwing of bombs by Zeppelins on London was denounced as a most savage act and the bombardment of places of worship was considered a most abominable operation, while now we can see with our own eyes that such operations were a habit which is prevalent amongst all civilized people of the West.

Pashtun ethnic loyalty continues to be strong in Afghan politics today. The Taliban themselves come from the Pashtun heartlands and all but a few of their leaders are Pashtuns, some of whom do not even speak Dari, the Persian lingua franca of Afghanistan. Many ordinary Afghans, of whatever ethnicity, at first supported the Taliban because, after years of war and mayhem, they expected them to bring peace and law and order. But after the fall of Najibullah it had rankled Pashtuns that the new authorities in Kabul were dominated by Massoud and Rabbani, who were both Tajiks, and by an Uzbek general, Dostum, while Hekmatyar, the main Pashtun Mujahideen, had lost out.

According to the 1973 census, Tajiks, whose language is close to Persian, made up 24 percent of the population. They are concentrated in the north, where the old border of the tsarist Russian Empire had cut them off from their cousins in what is now Tajikistan. Uzbeks make up 6 percent of the population, and are likewise cut off by the old Russian and then Soviet border from their cousins in what is now Uzbekistan. The next-largest ethnic group are the Hazaras, who live in the center of Afghanistan, and who are set apart from most other Afghans in that they are Shia Muslims, like Iranians. Their broad faces and slanting eyes also make it clear that their origins must lie far to the east, and some believe they are, at least in part, the descendants of Genghis Khan's Mongol Hordes. Other Afghans have tended to look down on the Hazaras, and in turn there is no love lost between them and the Pashtuns in particular. In 1995 Massoud drove the Hazaras out of Kabul.

Even if Afghanistan did not have strategic importance for all of its neighbors, it is clear that these ethnic and religious links would have drawn the surrounding states into the country's politics anyway, either for their own reasons or to help their ethnic or religious kinfolk. Iran has helped the Hazaras. Tajikistan and Uzbekistan have helped the Tajiks and Uzbeks, and still do. And of course Pakistan wants to support the Pashtuns. Russia too has its interests; its chief concern has been to stop the spread of Islamic fundamentalism. Iran has made it clear it wants a weak and divided Afghanistan, which could not threaten it. Pakistan has wanted Afghanistan to have a strong central government, dominated by Pakistan of course, which would then ensure open trade routes to Central Asia and allow the building of valuable gas and oil pipelines across Afghanistan and then into Pakistan. These were major considerations when Pakistan's security services, the Inter-Services Intelligence (ISI), poured money and arms over the border to build up the Pashtun Taliban.

2.

What the Taliban did when they took Kabul and indeed some 90 percent of Afghanistan is by now well known. They prevented women from working, closed schools for girls as well as many nonreligious schools for boys. They debated whether homosexuals should be killed under falling walls or whether another type of punishment was appropriate. They banned music, television, and just about any other type of entertainment. They also played host to Osama bin Laden, the rich Saudi dissident who had fought with the Mujahideen and who, after US troops were stationed in Saudi Arabia, declared a jihad against the United States. Bin Laden is believed to have been a major source of funding for the Taliban, along with Pakistan and Saudi Arabia. But until last spring the Taliban also financed themselves through the production of opium for heroin, which was deemed acceptable because only infidels, i.e., non-Muslims, became heroin addicts. (For their part, the health authorities in Pakistan say that their country has a major heroin addiction problem.)

As the Taliban took towns that lay outside Pashtun areas they became more and more brutal, committing massacres against civilians, especially Hazaras and Uzbeks. In return, thousands of Taliban prisoners were treated badly. The Taliban hope was not just to take all of Afghanistan, but to foment Islamic revolution throughout Central Asia and beyond. For this reason they welcomed thousands of Arab fundamentalists, as well as Chechen rebels and extremists from Uzbekistan and Tajikistan, and from among China's Muslim minorities.

However, even with their foreign legions, the Taliban were never able to dislodge Massoud. They chased Dostum from his base at Mazar-e-Sharif, less than fifty miles from the Uzbekistan border, but could not crush resistance there either; nor could they defeat several other groups connected with the Tajiks and Uzbeks in at least half a dozen enclaves. Over the last year the front lines have not moved much, but these groups fight under the common banner of what is widely called the Northern Alliance, although technically they should be known as the United Front. Most of these groups are not Pashtuns. When Massoud was killed, the Taliban's leaders must have hoped that the troops led by the man they dubbed the Lion of the Panjshir would be so demoralized that the Northern Alliance would no longer be able to resist a knockout blow. What they had not bargained for then was that the events of September 11 would set in motion a series of events that seem, thus far at least, to have had precisely the opposite effect.

3.

While you can see Massoud's picture everywhere up here in the north, the curious thing is that people don't talk about him unless you ask. After he was killed, a *shura*, or traditional council, of his commanders was called. They decided that they had to carry on the struggle or face death. Massoud's successor as minister of defense for the Northern Alliance is his former deputy, General Mohammad Fahim, a man who had fought by his side since the days of the war with the Soviets. By all accounts, and by appearances here, Fahim is doing a good job coordinating all the disparate semiautonomous commanders and their troops that make up the armies of the Northern Alliance.

If the World Trade Center and the Pentagon had not been bombed then perhaps things would have been different. As it is, these small forces fighting in faraway Afghanistan are now being courted by the United States, with Russia and the Central Asian states all promising more aid. The US is mounting daily air strikes against their mortal foes. And just because Massoud has gone, this does not mean the Northern Alliance is unable to take advantage of the new situation. Evidence of preparations for an offensive are everywhere. By the banks of the Amu Darya, I came across hundreds of soldiers who had just been brought north from the Panjshir Valley to prepare to fight up here.

I went to Ai Khanoum, a majestic natural escarpment at the confluence of the Amu Darya and the Kokcha rivers. In 1963 French archaeologists discovered the remains of a fabulous and wealthy Hellenistic city, complete, Martin Ewans writes, "with a citadel, palace, temples and a gymnasium," that "appears to have been sacked and burnt at the end of the second century BC." It is once again in the middle of a war. Soldiers wait for the offensive to begin while a tank, dug into position, fires off odd rounds at the Taliban about a mile away. This is a rear position, but significantly the soldiers here, as everywhere else along these front lines, are both Tajik and Uzbek plus a sprinkling from other Afghan ethnic groups, including Pashtuns who have turned against the Taliban. They also include old enemies. I met former members of Mujahideen groups who were now fighting next to Afghans who had themselves years ago fought with the Soviets against the Mujahideen.

I caught a ride on the back of a truck loaded with soldiers going to their positions. Some were in uniform but others were wearing baggy pajama-style outfits, with pinstriped or checked waistcoats. The sturdy Russian truck lumbered across the Kokcha River and took us first to another escarpment at Kuruk. Here a spotter with a walkie-talkie was directing fire on Taliban positions from artillery on another hill. "Down a hundred meters! That's it!"

Then I drove for miles down the dusty track that lies behind the Kalakata hills. Here the front line is strung along the hilltops. It was eerily quiet except for the desultory exchange of the odd tank or artillery shell. It was also clear that almost everything was now in place for a major push to try to break Taliban lines. In otherwise empty mud-brick villages hundreds of soldiers were living in small barracks compounds that would not have looked out of place on the set of a 1920s film about the French Foreign Legion.

At the barracks of the Mazar-e-Sharif 01 ("zero-one") Brigade, the soldiers, refugees from Taliban-controlled territory, were making eight-foot-long rakes. When the offensive comes, the first troops to advance will be armed with these, which they will use to clear Taliban mines lying in their path. All of these men are full-time soldiers. They are housed and fed and paid between $12 and $20 a month.

As dozens of his soldiers crowded around General Abdul Manon, the leader of the 01 Brigade sat cross-legged on the floor. "We have been fighting the Taliban and terrorism for six years, but the world did not know about their dangers. Now we hope that the UN and the whole world will fight against them and soon peace will come." On the wall behind him a slogan was written in charcoal: "We are waiting for tomorrow's victory over the Taliban! Our Taliban brothers, the traitors, have sold our country to the foreigners!"

General Manon said that his hope was that the US air strikes would "destroy their army—then only bin Laden will be left. He will be alone and have nowhere to hide." General Manon, who fought on the side of the Russians during the Soviet war, said he believed that desertions were diminishing Taliban ranks, a statement that was of course impossible to verify. "They want to fight America," he said, "but they don't have antiaircraft guns or good enough weapons."

Ten minutes' walk from his headquarters, his men have set up positions at the top of a very steep hill. They have dug trenches and sandbagged their bunkers in readiness for action. Peering across the valley, you can see a landscape pockmarked with shell craters.

Less than a mile away two figures could be seen moving on the top of a facing hill. "*Dushman! Dushman!*" (Enemy! Enemy!) the soldiers shouted before loosing off rounds from heavy machine guns. Barely a minute later the Taliban fired back. As I sprinted for shelter and fell into the deep dust of the trenches, the crowd of thirty or so accompanying soldiers broke out in hysterical laughter, before taking cover themselves. As the firing died down they ran back down the hill to safety, whooping and screaming like kids plunging down a roller coaster at a funfair.

If they survive the coming storm General Manon says that he and his men, some of whom, like himself, have been fighting for the last twenty-two years without a break, want to go home to Mazar-e-Sharif. And then, he says, "if people agree, I hope we will have a good government. Our people are hungry for peace. We hope that then we will be able to put our guns away and grow food, build roads, build schools, and build hospitals."

4.

For the last few weeks there has been speculation by Western analysts about whether the US and Britain will try to invade Afghanistan, using bases in Uzbekistan and Tajikistan. An invasion with sizable ground forces seems unlikely and may be doomed to repeat the lessons of history, which in this part of the world can be summed up as "Don't invade Afghanistan." I met a man who said, "Are your soldiers coming here to Afghanistan? They can help us for a while, OK, but not if they come to live here." A well-informed Afghan intellectual, who asked not to be named, said, "I don't think these soldiers will come. It would completely change the dynamic of the situation and it would bring people together to fight the foreigners." Before I left London I had called Tom Carew, who led missions into Afghanistan for Britain's special forces, the SAS, during the war with the Soviet forces, and asked him about the prospects of US and British troops. Carew is the author of the highly readable and revealing book called *Jihad: The Secret War in Afghanistan.* He said, "You can't even look at an Afghan woman so you can imagine what it would be like bringing in your average squaddie [ordinary soldier] to Afghanistan! All the Afghans would go: 'Whoa! Here come the infidels again,' and all get together and jump on them."

Chris Stephen, a friend of mine who writes for *The Scotsman,* and who shares the $10 tent with me, has been saying, "This is the first postmodern conflict because we are definitely at war but we don't know who the enemy is." If the aim of the war is to get rid of the Taliban, as opposed to trying to shut down Osama bin Laden's network and camps, and arrest him, then it would seem that the Northern Alliance members are the West's strategic allies. The Alliance is clearly ready to fight; but it is not certain if it is strong enough to take on even a weakened Taliban army spread out across the country. After all, the last time the people who lead the Alliance were in control, the country descended into bloody chaos, a fact that worries Western planners too. As for the size of the Northern Alliance forces, the estimates I heard—including one of ten thousand soldiers—are unreliable. Everyone over fourteen years old seems to have a gun; there is no clear distinction between soldiers and civilians. In any case, no one can say how many fighters are being added to the expanding local units.

What the Alliance leaders and at least some of the Western strategists are hoping for is that after a couple of military defeats Taliban commanders will begin to defect with their troops, either because they want to be on the winning side in the war or because they would be well paid. Throughout the last decade money has had as important a part as force of arms in determining who wins and who loses. Once one or two commanders defect, runs the theory, then their fellow commanders will follow like dominoes. Indeed the hope here is that once that happens, the northern territories will fall first, followed by much of the rest of the country, where there will be no major fighting at all; there would instead be local coups to overthrow the Taliban leaders and take over each province.

According to the Northern Alliance, this is already starting to happen. On October 13 I got through to General Dostum by satellite phone. He is fighting south of Mazar-e-Sharif, far away across Taliban territory. He claimed that within the last twenty-four hours a Taliban commander called Qazi Abdul Hai had defected to him, bringing his four thousand men with him. This is probably a highly inflated figure. Still, if it proves to be true then it is possible that the strategy is working. If Mazar-e-Sharif falls, it is widely assumed that the Alliance will take control of the rest of the north, including the north–south road leading from Kabul to Uzbekistan, where US and British troops are reportedly being deployed.

"Of course," says the Afghan intellectual I've mentioned, "when it is all over no one will admit to having been a Taliban. It is easy to shave off your beard and take off your turban. Actually I know several people who were not mullahs but who grew beards and now they are big mullahs."

The opposition and the West could face a disaster if the Taliban are willing to continue fighting and don't collapse; or if the Taliban are forced to retreat from non-Pashtun areas but stand firm in their ethnic heartlands, bolstered by support from the Pakistani Pashtuns. If that happens it is impossible to predict what the outcome might be, but then, as my Afghan intellectual source says, "It is impossible to predict what is going to happen in this country in an hour."

5.

Who is running the Northern Alliance and what would happen if they did take over the country? In mud-built Khoja Bahaudin you will not find much by way of a reasoned answer. The Northern Alliance is, formally at least, the legitimate, internationally recognized government of the "Islamic State of Afghanistan," which just happens to have been kicked out of Kabul in 1995. It still controls the country's UN seat and most of its embassies abroad. Officially Burhanuddin Rabbani is still president, living in Faizabad, about forty miles from the Tajikistan border, but he is seldom heard from. On October 11, however, he said at a press conference in Dushanbe, the capital of Tajikistan, that representatives of all of Afghanistan's peoples should help determine the nation's fate, "except terrorists and those who are up to their elbows in blood," i.e., bin Laden and his organization and his Taliban allies.

Rabbani did not say so, but we often hear of the plan for a future government headed by the former king of Afghanistan, Zahir Shah, who is eighty-six, was overthrown in 1973, and lives in Rome. He is keen to return, and, crucially, he is a Pashtun, although his first language is Dari. There is a chance that this might work, especially now that Massoud, who loathed the monarch and was opposed to his having any political position, is dead. Zahir Shah's advantage is that he can claim to be above politics and is not associated with the internecine bloodletting of the past decade.

In mid-October Northern Alliance officials gathered in the Panjshir Valley to select sixty delegates to attend a *shura* with sixty partisans of the King; this meeting is supposed to select delegates to a Loya Jirga, or grand council, that would discuss the future shape of any post-Taliban government. The Northern Alliance now says that it is holding the door open to collaborating with at least a part of the Taliban if they defect now. What the Northern Alliance resists however is pressure from Pakistan, which in turn is pressuring the US, to accept what Pakistani President Pervez Musharraf wants, which is a broad-based government "including moderate Taliban elements." Pakistan is of course terrified that a hostile Northern Alliance government will come to power in Kabul and take revenge on Pakistan for supporting the Taliban.

When, on October 16, Dr. Abdullah Abdullah, the urbane Northern Alliance foreign minister, came to Khoja Bahaudin, he said there was no such thing as a "moderate Taliban element," adding: "Their objective is terrorism and fanaticism so who could expect us to join such a government with such people? This is against the objective of the international alliance against terrorism." But Dr. Abdullah accepted that a future government did have to have a broader base than the Northern Alliance, which is code for saying that it did need to include some significant Pashtun representation.

Another senior leader in northern Afghanistan is General Atiqullah Baryalai, the deputy minister of defense. He says the "original" Taliban, that is to say Mullah Omar and his cronies, can have no say in the future of the country because they are nothing but Pakistani agents. "They brought foreigners here to kill Afghans. They educated boys of thirteen or fifteen in Pakistan to destroy our history, our museums and our archives." Like the Afghan intellectual I met, General Baryalai believes that there are many who became Taliban for opportunistic reasons and, especially if they defect now, they should be able to participate in decisions on how the country should be run.

Of course it is difficult to divine what will happen from Khoja Bahaudin, but it is possible that the UN will be drawn into a diplomatic process by which it would oversee a transitional phase in Afghanistan just as it did in Cambodia. The UN, which has its own special representative for Afghanistan, has formed a task force to consider this and other possibilities, but it is too early to say whether foreign governments would commit troops to bolster any such operation. The Afghan intellectual told me he was "quite optimistic" about the prospects of the Northern Alliance leaders. As for the slaughter they committed when they were in Kabul, which leaves their popularity in doubt, he said: "I think now they understand very well. If there is no cooperation [with Pashtuns and other groups] they will lose everything."

I saw Dr. Syed Kamil Ibrahim, who is the acting minister of health. He told me: "Our aim is an Islamic democracy. It is freedom for the Islamic religion, but not by force. Yes, we will have *sharia* [Islamic] law but not like the Taliban. Women will have rights to study and work. They will be equal." This was echoed by Dr. Abdullah, who claimed that women would have a say in determining the future of the country.

Here in the north of Afghanistan, however, women are not equal. They have no part in decision-making. But girls go to school and they can work. In this deeply conservative society you rarely see women outside their homes and when you do they are veiled. In the camp of Lalla Guzar, which houses ten thousand refugees from Taliban-controlled territory, I visited a new school, which was built by a French aid group called ACTED and funded by the Turkish government. It has space for fewer than half of the children in the camp, but it is a start. Boys go to school in the morning, girls in the afternoon. When I went I saw four classrooms full of eager girls chanting the alphabet, doing arithmetic, and having a religion class. I asked them what they wanted to be when they grew up and almost all of them said they wanted to be either a teacher or a doctor, the only jobs they ever see women doing. They also knew that in Taliban-held territory girls are banned from school and women not allowed to work. Lalimoh, aged twelve, said that girls were being prevented from going to school in Taliban-held areas because the Taliban "are not educated and that is why they don't allow schools."

I wanted to ask if anyone wanted to become an astronaut, but the director of the school said that this was absurd since "they don't know what an astronaut is." In this land without electricity there is no television either. Everyone lives in tents or mud huts, yet despite their tough life these refugee girls were full of energy and smiles. Bucking the trend among her schoolmates, Zokira, aged ten, said: "If I try, I will become a minister!"—she meant in a future government. Such are the glimmers of hope in northern Afghanistan.

—*October 17, 2001*

Bolak Kushlaq, northern Afghanistan

IN THE AFGHAN fashion we sat around the edge of the room while a small banquet of rice and mutton was served. We were in Dasht-e-Qala, a village five miles south of the border with Tajikistan. My host was Alam Khan, the leader of hundreds of refugee soldiers from Mazar-e-Sharif, which Northern Alliance forces hope to take. When the meal was over, sweets were served as dessert. One of Alam Khan's aides is Faziludin, who lost his right arm fighting in Kabul many years ago. His wife and children are still living in a village near Mazar-e-Sharif and he has not seen them since the city fell to the Taliban three years ago. I asked him what he would do when he got home. As he sucked his coffee-flavored hard candy, he thought a while, shrugged, and said: "I will kill Pakistani, Arab, and Chechen Taliban but not Afghan ones because they are my brothers."

In 1997, just after the Taliban first entered Mazar-e-Sharif, approximately two thousand of them were massacred before they were forced to withdraw. Some 1,250 of them were crammed into containers and left to bake to death in the blistering sun. When the containers were opened the bodies were found to have turned black. Paik Chong-Hyun, a UN special rapporteur who investigated the deaths of the Taliban, wrote in his report that many of them were tossed down deep wells, then hand grenades were thrown in, and then the wells were bulldozed over. In 1998 the Taliban retook the city and massacred some six thousand people in revenge.

Alam Khan has been fighting for the last twenty-two years, first against the Soviet Union and then in the various civil wars that followed. Most people in Afghanistan are exhausted by war, so I asked this famous warlord if he was, too. "Not only am I not tired," he said, "but I want to fight Pakistan." Alam Khan's antipathy toward Pakistan, which supported his fellow Mujahideen fighters during the war against the Soviet Union, springs from his feeling and that of his fellows that, after the Communists fell, Pakistan then tried to dictate who would govern Afghanistan and finally sponsored the Taliban. "I don't want to attack Pakistan," said Alam Khan, "but I don't want Pakistan to attack our country."

Here in Afghanistan and in Pakistan, in Iran, in Russia, and in the West diplomats and policymakers are frantically trying to put together some form of broad-based government that they hope will form the first post-Taliban administration. None of them is optimistic. A friend of mine who is a senior official at the United Nations in New York told me, "This makes Bosnia look like a kid's game."

1.

Since Western journalists cannot go to Taliban territory it is hard to know what Taliban leaders are thinking. Still, that does not mean that we have no idea what some of them are thinking. Here in northeast Afghanistan all the commanders of the Northern Alliance that you meet tell you that they are in touch with Taliban commanders on the other side and that they are involved in discussions with them about defecting. Until now, however, there has been little hard evidence of such talks.

In one Northern Alliance military headquarters I came across such evidence. The local commander introduced me to a man who looked distinctly uneasy. He wore an elegant black turban with a broad pin-stripe design surrounding a colorful cap, but he clicked his worry beads nervously. The man was an envoy sent across the front line by three Taliban commanders who wanted to jump ship. We say "don't shoot the messenger," but in Afghanistan they just might. The Northern Alliance commander set a condition for my talking to the messenger. I could not reveal the names of anyone involved or the location of the meeting, nor could I take photos. Since no deal had been made and the Taliban obviously did not know that this man was here, this seemed fair enough, especially since it was a question of life and death, and not just for the messenger.

The offers to defect that he carried were handwritten on small scraps of paper, which looked like restaurant receipts. I asked the messenger why the offers had not come before the current crisis, and he shifted uncomfortably and said: "Six months ago was not a good time for us, now it is." In other words, Afghan commanders want to end the war on the winning side.

In the mid-Nineties, as the Taliban moved through Afghanistan taking territory, there was, in many places, no fighting at all. The Taliban simply paid opposition commanders to switch sides. I asked General Baryalai if he was doing the same now and he simply became angry and denied any such thing was happening. But he denied it in a way that made me think I'd hit a nerve. Still, other Afghans I have talked to don't think money is a principal factor today. It's all or nothing, which means "join us or die."

Although it is clear that many commanders from the Taliban side in northeast Afghanistan want to defect, this does not mean that similar talks are taking place throughout the country. This messenger came from three ethnic Tajik commanders and the Northern Alliance forces ranged against them are also mostly ethnic Tajiks. The Taliban are dominated by Pashtuns, Afghanistan's largest single ethnic group. Like a man making a sales pitch the messenger said: "Because we are Tajiks it is very difficult for us to live with their regime. That is why I was sent."

The messenger's three Taliban commanders had written that between them they had four hundred men that they could bring with them. If similar such numbers are being discussed along hundreds of miles of front line, then this may explain why the Northern Alliance has not yet begun a major push from the east. It may be waiting to see how many commanders from the other side are prepared to defect first, and whether their offers are genuine or made simply to extricate themselves from a difficult but temporary military situation. Two weeks ago the Northern Alliance announced that in a region close to Mazar-e-Sharif a commander called Qazi Abdul Hai had defected with four thousand men. A few days later they admitted that he had now switched back to the Taliban; but they claimed that some of his men had remained with the opposition. Whether Qazi Abdul Hai had ever really defected or whether he actually has four thousand men is, of course, unverifiable since he is fighting in a region inaccessible to journalists.

2.

Messengers are not the only men crossing the front lines. The town of Farkhar is one of the most inaccessible spots on this jagged front. It lies several hours' drive from the place where the meeting with the messenger was held. Here boys of military age from the nearby Taliban-held town of Taloqan have been arriving in droves. They are fleeing the Taliban press gangs. A couple of days after the US bombing of Afghanistan began on October 7, Shukib, aged eighteen, had just begun his Pashtun language lesson when the Taliban came to call.

Three pickup trucks roared into the school playground and armed men leaped out. They made straight for the main building of Taloqan's best school, the Abu Osman High School, named after a distinguished poet, and burst into the classrooms. "Six of them came in and they were all shouting at the same time. They pushed my teacher out of the way and they pointed their guns at us."

Shukib knew immediately what they wanted. For some days Taliban soldiers, desperate for recruits, had been cruising the streets of this small town picking men at random. They were being sent to the south for rudimentary military training before being thrown into units in Kandahar and Jalalabad, which lie in the Taliban's Pashtun heartlands. The Taliban fear that putting these men into local units near Taloqan will mean immediate desertion. "They chose the boys who looked the strongest," said Shukib. "Nobody said anything. When you have a gun pointed at you, what can you do? They said: 'You must do jihad and fight against the Northern Alliance.'"

By the time they had finished, some twenty young men had been marched off at gunpoint to be sent to war. With the school in turmoil some boys slipped out through the back of the building and ran home. There are of course no girls in school in Taloqan since the Taliban have forbidden education for girls.

That night, after talking to their families, Shukib and his friend Suliman, aged seventeen, decided to escape into the hills close to the front line. There they made contact with local guides who know the tracks through the minefields and over the front lines. They paid them an $8 fee, which is the going rate to get across to opposition-held territory, and then walked through the night to Farkhar.

Their story is evidence of weakening Taliban morale and strength in northern Afghanistan. But it should not be a guide for the whole of the country since Taloqan is inhabited mainly by ethnic Tajiks. When they got to Farkhar, Shukib and Suliman met up with their friend Said Bismillah, also aged eighteen, who had fled the press gangs a few days

before them. "I was at the mosque in a religion school," Said
Bismillah said. "There were about five hundred of us. The Taliban
came and asked: 'Who wants to do jihad against the Northern
Alliance? America wants to start a war against us!' Everyone was
afraid so we all put our hands up. I went home to speak to my family
and my father said I could not go there again. He did not allow me to
do jihad and I did not want to do it."

The next day Said Bismillah slipped away to begin the all-night
trek to cross the front lines. Fearful that someone might report on his
intentions, he did not tell any of his classmates what he was planning
to do. However he said that in the three weeks since he had arrived, of
his class of twenty-five at the Abu Osman High School, "ten or eleven
are now here." Even though Said Bismillah is blind in one eye he says,
"I have decided 100 percent to go into the army. Afghans don't want
a terrorist regime."

According to Said Bismillah and his friends the Taliban were desperately short of men, which is why they were resorting to press
gangs. Until now every mosque in the Taloqan region was forced to
provide one able-bodied man for Taliban forces for a six-month
stretch. Since the beginning of the conflict with the US they were now
demanding that mosque councils provide up to ten men per mosque
and that every household also provide one man.

Idle unless they join up, the boys all say that they'd like to leave
Afghanistan and come to London. The problem is that, unlike the $8
they paid to the guides to get them across the front lines, the trip to
London will cost them $8,000, an almost unimaginable sum here.
Still, many do manage, somehow, to scrape the cash together, often
because families club together to contribute, hoping that when they
get to London or wherever else they succeed in getting to, their relatives will then start sending money home.

"First you pay $1,200 to get to Tajikistan," explained Abdulrioz,
aged eighteen, a boy who says he would like to make the trip. "The

dealers use the same passport twenty times to get people there, changing the photo every time. After that a Tajik woman will get you documents as her son, and you go to Moscow." After that there are several different onward routes. Generally the trip takes six months, with money being paid out along the way, and most of those who flee this parched and war-ravaged land are successful in getting out.

Unless this war ends quickly, the numbers of people now surging out of the country are likely to soar. Shukib told me that so many boys had now made the first leg of the journey from Taliban-held territory to Farkhar that the Abu Osman High School has had to close.

3.

Apart from the fact that ethnic Tajiks don't want to die for the Taliban, there are several other good reasons why the Taliban can't find enough volunteers, at least in this part of the country. When night falls the Northern Alliance attacks their lines with volleys of three-meter-long rockets fired from truck-mounted BM-21 Soviet-era rocket launchers. The roar is deafening and it leaves the inner core of your body vibrating like a tuning fork. Once the rockets have streaked into the night sky, curving over the mountain range that here divides opposition from Taliban territory, what remains, amid the curling smoke, is exactly the same smell that hangs over a display of fireworks, except that here dozens of people on the other side of the mountain may be dead.

According to Said Mohammad, the officer in charge of the BM-21 at Chosmai Sangi, three miles or so west of Farkhar, the rockets are aimed at targets nine miles away. Targeting is done in coordination with a spotter on the front line but an accurate report of what is being hit only comes the next day from agents operating inside Taliban territory. The next morning Bashir, an aide to Commander Daoud, who is in charge in Farkhar, said: "Last night the rockets took out three Datsun pickup trucks and killed eight Taliban."

Once the rockets have roared off, the silence over the pitch-black front lines is broken only by the menacing sound of invisible American helicopters. The sound conjures up images of *Apocalypse Now*. The sound fades, then returns, then disappears. Where the helicopters are going or what they are doing is anybody's guess. In the wake of the first raid by Special Forces on the Taliban headquarters town of Kandahar, no Taliban commander can be certain that American or British troops won't be paying them a visit. No wonder that many commanders, up here at least, far from the Taliban heartlands, are reconsidering their loyalties.

4.

One of the reasons why peace will be so hard to achieve in Afghanistan is precisely because the country has been at war for so long. In 1979, the year of the Soviet invasion, the country was already desperately poor and divided by all sorts of tribal, clan, and ethnic rivalries. What twenty-two years of war have done is to throw the country back to an era that Westerners can only recognize by what they know of their own history, that is to say, by recalling the centuries of the crusaders, of religious fanaticism, and of feudalism.

The core of Taliban forces and their foreign legions of several thousand Arabs, Pakistanis, Chechens, and others can be compared to the crusaders. On the opposition side, where Islam is of course also very important, it is clear that feudal relationships play a central part in the way society works and soldiers are recruited.

I understood this when I was invited to spend the night at the compound of Mohammad Aqa Humayun Khadim, an ethnic Uzbek commander who has a private army of three hundred men, six tanks, and a BM-21 rocket launcher. His soldiers, based in the village of Bolak

Kushlaq, three hours' drive northeast of Farkhar, hold part of the front line facing Taloqan. None of this would be particularly remarkable, except that Humayun, as he is known, is only fifteen years old. He has never shaved but he is married.

With a row of silent elders at his right hand, ready to give counsel if asked or scamper off to buy cigarettes, Humayun held forth for several hours on questions of war and politics, while plowing through a banquet of meat and potatoes. His father, who first recruited Bolak Kushlaq's village militia during the war against the Soviet Union, died in a Taliban rocket attack three months ago. "I have three hundred soldiers. They were my father's soldiers and now they belong to me." Conversation was frequently interrupted by calls coming in from his commanders on the front.

When he left the room to say his prayers an elderly retainer leaned forward and whispered: "All the people loved his father, so after he died they called a council and then chose Humayun." Humayun's father was grooming him for succession and would leave him in control when he was away. So that is the way it works here. Humayun's family are big landowners and their fief covers a region, which includes twenty-six villages and hamlets. If, when his father died, someone from outside the family had challenged the family for control of the district, then their power and influence would have come under attack. So with the blessing of Ahmed Shah Massoud and Burhanuddin Rabbani, Humayun succeeded his father. But, just as young kings in medieval Europe would have their power circumscribed by a regency council, the same applies in Bolak Kushlaq.

Humayun's council is headed by two of his uncles. The next morning, while Humayun was posing for photos in front of his rocket launcher, one of his uncles, Mohammad Yaqub, told me: "He does not have the experience but this is not such a problem because he has advisers who do. He is also very intelligent but he must accept our advice. We are trying to train him."

Humayun is a boy worth watching. He speaks with the confidence of a natural leader and can hold his own at the same level as commanders who were fighting years before he was born. But there is a difference. Unlike them he shows an interest in the world outside Afghanistan. He says that when he is older he would like to become president of Afghanistan, but, in the meantime, he needs to study more. "Now the situation is not good but I must find a good English teacher. Rabbani told me that when it was safe in Afghanistan he would send me to London to study. Do you think my bodyguard will have problems with the gun? If I have a pistol would that be okay?"

He also wants to know: "How many Muslims have you got in your country? Did they suffer any revenge attacks after what happened in New York and Washington? How many people can read in your country? Can women get married in your country if they are not beautiful?" To this he adds: "Here it is beauty that counts but if a woman can do things like weave a kilim then she'll be okay."

At first sight the story of Humayun would seem to illustrate the problem of child soldiers in Afghanistan. In fact, although there are such soldiers in Afghanistan, this is not a problem that is particularly widespread, as it is in, say, West Africa. There is also the question of how you define a child. While some countries define children as anyone under the age of eighteen, and technically this is the age accepted by the authorities in northern Afghanistan, in fact, boys are really considered to have reached full maturity here at the age of sixteen.

According to Eloi Fillion, a delegate of the International Committee of the Red Cross in northern Afghanistan, the case of Humayun highlights other fundamental problems. "On both sides of the front lines, you have a 'government' and an 'administration' but, in fact, outside the cities, there is no administrative control at all. This case reflects the reality of Afghan problems. You'll have the leading family of an area, the father dies and he is replaced by the eldest son, so that's it. It is like the succession of a king."

An official at the UN's Children's Fund, UNICEF, told me: "Twenty years of conflict have made all children experts at war in Afghanistan. It is a hard life and those that do become child soldiers actually have to support their families. Another problem is that there is not enough to do. There is a lack of schools and activities and playgrounds. If they had these things they would not think so much about war."

Humayun first went to the front with his father when he was thirteen. "I have been to the front line many times. It is my duty." Asked about moves in the West and other parts of the world to end the use of child soldiers, he thought a moment and said: "You in the West have the wrong idea. Children make great soldiers. They are strong and fast and they are very brave."

I called my friend who works at the UN in New York and told her about Humayun. She said that she had told the man coordinating the UN's response to the Afghan emergency that she wanted to be part of any forthcoming UN peacekeeping mission here. He said to her: "What mission?" Here in opposition-controlled Afghanistan, meetings are taking place to choose delegates for a *shura*, or council, which in turn, at some date yet to be decided, will meet with delegates who are partisans of Zahir Shah. But there have also been other meetings outside the country, notably in Peshawar in Pakistan, a region with a large Afghan refugee population. Some of these meetings have supported the King, some have not. Some support the Northern Alliance but some do not, fearing that if it comes to power in Kabul it will not have the support of Pashtuns and hence cause a new chapter in the conflict to begin.

In Pakistan, which supported the Taliban until now, all sorts of machinations have begun in an attempt to salvage something from the catastrophe. Unverifiable reports speak of secret US- and Pakistani-sponsored meetings in which attempts are being made to break up the Taliban by attempting to lure so-called moderates into dropping Mullah Omar and handing over Osama bin Laden. Names such as

Wakil Ahmad Mutawakil, the Taliban foreign minister, are allegedly being proposed as possible Taliban "moderates" who might participate in a new broad-based government, while names such as that of Maulana Jalaluddin Haqqani, the minister of frontier regions, are being singled out as examples of those who would be unacceptable.

Since no decisions have been made, Northern Alliance officials prefer not to talk until they know what the party line is. One such official who did speak, on condition of anonymity of course, gave me a typical on-the-fence response when I asked him whether some "moderate" Taliban members might be included in any new government. He said: "Well, the Taliban as a system is not acceptable for the future of Afghanistan but some people may be. If it is possible that there are some people, they would have the right to participate."

From my own talks, I suspect that the Northern Alliance leaders are not in the mood for deals yet. As of the end of October, their front lines in the northeast and above Kabul had still not moved an inch. They claim to have made advances around Mazar-e-Sharif but extended supply lines and a lack of ammunition had stopped that offensive from going forward. The US has announced some air drops of ammunition to the Northern Alliance and the arrival of some US troops to coordinate air strikes, and at the end of October it intensified the bombing. But, in view of Pakistani fears, the US apparently does not want to help to such an extent that if the Taliban collapse, the Northern Alliance would take over, and feel no need to make concessions to Pashtuns. By contrast Northern Alliance thinking may well be that sooner or later the north of Afghanistan will fall to them so there is no need to make any political concessions until this happens.

In the meantime some US officials have floated the idea of a UN peacekeeping force for a postwar Afghanistan. This has sent shudders through UN headquarters. "What have they got in mind?" said one UN source. "For how long? What would the mandate be? The US would like to move quickly and declare a situation where the UN takes over, but we are saying this cannot be rushed. The conditions are not there to think of deploying troops, let alone anything else. Who is going to give the troops? Africans? Is the US going to put its troops in harm's way? That is no joke. "

Apparently taking account of such reactions, Colin Powell, the US secretary of state, said on October 25 that a UN force is unlikely. But he also put forward the idea that a UN action could be somewhat similar to the UN's mission in Cambodia, when it supervised elections there in May 1993. A peace process became possible in Cambodia because the great powers and Cambodia's neighbors all concluded that the conflict in that country had gone on too long, that they now all had other interests, and so it was time to impose a solution. This consensus meant that they were able to compel the leaders of the Khmer Rouge, the Vietnamese-backed government, and Prince Sihanouk, the former monarch, to make a deal. Following that agreement a UN peacekeeping force was sent into Cambodia alongside UN administrators who then ran the country until elections were held. According to a report in the October 25 *Washington Post*, Powell foresees the United Nations playing an important role should the Taliban fall, in particular providing help with public administration until the new institutions of government begin functioning. He said the UN has considerable experience playing this role in other places emerging from war, such as East Timor and Cambodia.

Superficially there are resemblances. The great powers, and all of Afghanistan's neighbors, want an end to the conflict, and, if the top Taliban leaders are eliminated, they probably have the power to compel the warring factions to come to the table. Afghans are exhausted by the war just as Cambodians were. And, just as a former monarch presided over the transition in Cambodia, Afghanistan's former king could play a similar role. That is where the similarities end. A crucial difference is that in Cambodia the conflict did not involve deep ethnic divisions. And, for the moment at least, as the UN source points out,

"In Cambodia you had a framework for peace. In Afghanistan you don't."

Kofi Annan has recently reappointed Lakhdar Brahimi, a former Algerian foreign minister, as his special envoy for Afghanistan. Brahimi had the same position once before, but in 1999 he resigned in disgust at the lies and dissimulations of the Taliban. At UN headquarters an emergency group, officially called the Integrated Mission Task Force, has been formed to coordinate a UN response to the war. One insider told me that Annan and Brahimi had told the Security Council "that a UN peacekeeping force is not feasible and should not be considered, anyway not in the short term. Most of the players have accepted this. A UN force could not be mobilized before three or four months. There would be great difficulty in trying to find troop contributors and the whole history of foreign forces in Afghanistan gives us great cause for concern."

Instead of such a force other ideas now being considered are, first, a multinational "coalition of the willing," which would include British and American troops, or "an Afghan security force, which might be one of the outcomes of a political process." Some reports have talked of Mr. Brahimi acting as a UN "proconsul" in Kabul while a provisional government establishes itself in power. But my UN source in New York told me that the UN is "not planning a UN administration [as] in Kosovo or East Timor. Rather we are thinking in terms of enhanced UN activities in the humanitarian area and a very big reconstruction effort." He said he has little optimism "because one of the key things needed to happen is the construction of some kind of political authority and I don't see that happening soon, and until that happens you can't return the country to any form of normalcy." So, he adds, "I foresee more bombing and a very difficult humanitarian situation. The Taliban have proven themselves to have far more staying power than anticipated."

—*October 31, 2001*

Kabul, Afghanistan

"DO YOU LIKE my jacket?" asked the man who got in the car. It was still barely seven o'clock in the morning on November 13. "I was fighting all night. I got it off a dead Arab. Look." He was pointing at the Champion label. "If he was dead," I asked, "then how come there isn't any blood on it?" He paused before beginning to speak rapidly. "Because he wasn't dead when I got it off him. He was speaking in his own language, I don't know what he was saying, he was wounded, he was young, about twenty-four or twenty-five." I asked, "Was he pleading for his life?" The man said, "I told you, I couldn't understand what he was saying, but I suppose he was." I have seen this before. It is the time to get worried. Men high on war, crazed even, and these situations can quickly turn nasty.

In the front of the car, the driver was moaning. "Is it safe? What happens if the Taliban shoot my car? Anyway I want more money, you didn't tell me we were going this far!" I said, "Look, there are people walking on the road, just keep going." Another car passed us. "Follow that car!" The driver slowed to check with soldiers by the side of road. "Go, go, go!" they shouted. We were now well past what had been the Taliban front line for the last three years. As we went past their trenches, we could see their blankets and teapots where they had left them when they fled. By now, we had two more soldiers in the back of the car. They were pretty quiet. They were returning to their unit at the front after having taken the body of a friend back to Charikar, the nearest Northern Alliance–held town, some twenty-five miles north of Kabul.

Then we found the last defenders of Taliban Kabul. They lay in the middle of the road just where they had been shot. There were five of them. The man with the new coat was jumping around, saying,

"Look, two Pakistanis and three Arabs." Their bodies hadn't been badly damaged and since their corpses were fresh I caught myself looking at one and thinking, "Why don't you just get up?" We got back in the car and five miles farther on we hit the traffic jam. Hundreds of Northern Alliance troops, tanks, armor, the works were clustered, all waiting for orders.

We were at the top of a pass called Khair Khana Kotal. Kabul was down the hill and right around the corner. We got out of the car and began to walk. "You can't go any further," shouted a Northern Alliance commander. So we milled around and wondered what would happen next. There seemed to be quite a few men also milling around at the bottom of the pass and some were now walking toward us up the hill. "Oh, he just came from Kabul," said Sayed Ibrahim, my translator, as he chatted with a teenage boy on a bicycle. Then a yellow taxi drove up the hill, then another. Then more men, some now embracing the soldiers and friends they had not seen, maybe for years. "OK, let's go," I said. We grabbed our stuff and began walking down. Seeing us, the men walking up were laughing and smiling. "Welcome to Kabul City!" shouted one in English.

1.

Kabul, Day One. People were gathering in large crowds talking about the latest news. The Taliban had simply packed up and left. They got in their pickup trucks, some stopping to rob the men who change foreign currency, and then they were gone. All but a few of them. In Shahr-i-Naw Park, we saw five bodies of men who didn't get away. They were lying in a ditch. One had his identity photo stuffed in his mouth, one had a rolled-up banknote sticking out of a nostril, and one had a banknote sitting inside his now half-empty, shattered skull. The crowd said that one of them had tried to climb a tree to escape. Exactly who killed the men and what the banknotes signified were uncertain. Since I had only been in the city an hour or two, I wasn't yet sure how safe I was either.

A mile away we saw the charred and twisted remains of four Arabs. Next to them were the charred and twisted remains of their truck. Some local people kicked and poked at their bodies, and told me that their car had been hit by a rocket fired by an American jet. Most shops were shuttered and bolted. Looters were dragging furniture from buildings that may have been occupied by the Taliban. There were crowds outside police stations, curious to see their new occupants. They were Northern Alliance men in gray uniforms whom we had seen training up in the Panjshir Valley only a few weeks before. Cars with other armed men were driving around, but they weren't in uniform. "This is turning nasty," I thought. Now truckloads of soldiers were fanning out across the city. Within hours, they had moved into all of Kabul's main buildings. They could be seen at all the city's main intersections and began patrolling the streets. The looting stopped.

For weeks, the leaders of the Northern Alliance had said they would not send troops into the city if it fell. The US and its Western allies made it clear that they preferred that there be a political settlement before Alliance troops entered the city. In the days before they did so, an increasingly desperate-sounding Pakistani President Pervez Musharraf was saying that the Northern Alliance should not enter the city. But the Northern Alliance doesn't care for Pakistan, regarding it as the main sponsor of the Taliban. The Alliance leaders said they had to send their troops in because the Taliban were leaving a power vacuum and law and order were in danger.

As we passed the bolted gates of the sacked US embassy, I thought it might be a good idea to call on the Pakistani embassy. Soon after September 11 its diplomats had been recalled to Islamabad, but Pakistan remained the only country in the world to recognize the Taliban regime. The embassy guards invited us to climb in through a window into the guardhouse. Both the residence and the embassy had been sacked a few hours earlier. In the residence, the ambassador's socks and books were strewn about on the floor. One of the books was *The Great Game*, by Peter Hopkirk, which recounts the subterfuge and scheming of the British and Russians in the nineteenth century as they vied for control of this part of Central Asia during the heyday of their imperial ambitions.

Scattered in the street outside the embassy were its papers and files. One caught my eye—a piece of paper listing gifts given to top Taliban officials by Pakistan on the Feast of Eid, at the end of Ramadan last year. Mullah Omar was given "eight meters cloth + four meters turban silk cloth, black." I thought, "cheap," considering that the promotion of the Taliban was a main plank of Pakistani foreign policy and now that policy, like the inside of the embassy, is wrecked.

Over at the ghostly buildings of Kabul Airport a man was taking down the Taliban flag. From the top of the tower, you could see the wing tips of the Taliban's old MIG fighter jets. Between the tips, there was just a big black mark and a few chunks of metal where the American bombs had hit them. An Ariana Afghan Airlines plane also suffered the same fate.

Not far away was Macroyan, a decaying Soviet-built housing development, of the type the Soviets cloned from Bucharest to, well, Kabul. In front of one of its blocks was a huge hole. According to the block manager, Ghulam Destegir, a six-year-old girl died when this American bomb went astray. She was one of perhaps hundreds of civilians—nobody knows the figures yet—who died during the bombing. But he showed no rancor, saying only, "It was a mistake. America is not our enemy and we are glad they have got rid of the Taliban because we were their hostages." Everyone we saw seemed happy that the Taliban was gone. A small crowd was pressing against me, eager to talk. But my eye caught little Ruhina, aged nine. I asked her what she hoped for now. She said simply, "I want to go to school."

On Day One, most barbers' shops were locked, but outside the ones that were open, crowds of men were lining up for a shave or a trim. "This is the busiest day of my life," said a barber named Parwana, as he clipped off yet another beard. The requirement that every man must have a beard and never trim it was enforced by the Taliban's feared and loathed men from the Ministry for the Prevention of Vice and Promotion of Virtue.

On the way over to the ministry we stopped to view the control panel and a wheel of an American helicopter that had crashed or been shot down and was now on display under a kind of elevated traffic control box, near the Hotel Ariana. In 1996 it had been used as a gibbet for the body of Najibullah, the former Communist president of Afghanistan, and his brother. They, too, had rolled-up banknotes stuffed up their nostrils.

At the ministry building the guards seemed eager to show us around. But all the doors were padlocked. I arrived at the same time as a man from a British tabloid. He kept saying, "Where did they torture people? Where did they beat them?" Apparently, they did neither in the ministry building. He was disappointed. We raced up the stairs and he said, "Where is the minister's office?" He was disappointed again. The minister, like all the other Taliban leaders, issued decrees from Kandahar, 350 miles from Kabul, the birthplace and home of the Taliban. Orders were administered by the minister's deputy, one Salim Haqqani. We got to his office, which was also padlocked. An Italian photographer whipped out a penknife and began fiddling about with the lock. He couldn't open it and the frustrated tabloid reporter kicked the door in. Yet more disappointment. The prim little office had little of interest in it. On the deputy minister's desk was a small Taliban flag (which the tabloid man took with him), along with an Islamic calendar, a green pencil sharpener, and a Scotch tape dispenser. The banality of evil, I suppose.

2.

It was getting dark, and there were soldiers everywhere. They were stopping cars and checking them. At a traffic circle, some of them sat on top of sacks of grain and flour. "What's all that?" I asked. "Oh, we stopped the looters," they said.

The next morning we went to Faroshgar Street, which is where all the best music stores in Kabul can be found. Crowds of people were waving fistfuls of money at the shopkeepers, who could barely keep up with demand. Music, of course, was banned under the Taliban so now it was blaring from every shop. The loudspeakers were playing Afghan music performed by singers who now live in exile, as well as Western disco music and Indian Hindi pop, which they love here.

Inside every shop we went to, they were wiping out the Taliban. Quite literally. Under the Taliban the only entertainment permitted was a monotonous religious chanting without instruments. So now, as customers eager to get their hands on something new waved their money, the shopkeepers were slapping cassette after cassette into their double recorders to dub the new stuff over the Taliban's dirges. Of course, this is not to say that there was no music being sold before, but it was sold at high prices strictly under the counter. A shopkeeper named Mohammad Jawed showed off a row of cassettes with the names of Taliban singers written on the spine. But not all of them contained Taliban music. Black-market music dealing was a risky business here. During the last five years Mr. Jawed served three one-month sentences in jail after being caught selling banned music. The other music sellers I talked to had similar tales.

Now that music was suddenly legal, I asked whether the prices would come down. I had forgotten the basic laws of supply and demand. Precisely because music was now legal prices had shot up by 50 percent because everyone wanted to hear music and, besides, with the Taliban still controlling the road to Pakistan, new cassettes would be harder to get.

For the people I saw in Kabul, the end of Taliban rule has been greeted with a mixture of joy, relief, and apprehension. If women want to take off the burqa, the tent-like veil they wear, they may do so, but during these first days I saw only a few that had. Still, the difference is between wearing the burqa for reasons of custom and tradition and being forced to wear it by law. The apprehension was best summed up for me by Feridoun, a twenty-five-year-old teacher of computer science. (Under the Taliban there was no Internet connection.) "For a while it will be calm," he said, but if the members of an inclusive national council do not agree, "then there will be fighting again." Since this country has been at war for twenty-two years Feridoun has no memory of peace, but he does have a lot of experience of war. And, of course, since Kabul has now lived under four different regimes during the last nine years, nobody can summon up much optimism. After all, they welcomed the Taliban in 1996 because they believed that they would put an end to the bloody infighting of the former Mujahideen, who now form a large part of the Northern Alliance.

The problem now is that there is no National Council, or Loya Jirga, as they call it. For the last two months there has been intense diplomatic pressure for all the Afghan parties and ethnic groupings, except the Taliban, to come together in a Loya Jirga to help form a transitional government. It is clear that if there is to be lasting peace, all of Afghanistan's ethnic groups, especially the largest of them, the Pashtuns, must be represented.

The plan of the Northern Alliance was to flush the Taliban out of the northern non-Pashtun areas of the country where the mostly Pashtun Taliban were regarded as little better than foreign occupiers. But they knew that if their troops entered Pashtun lands, they would become the occupiers. Therefore, they said, they would rely on Pashtun uprisings. By November 14, it looked as though their game plan was working. We heard reports of an uprising in Jalalabad and challenges to Taliban authority in Kandahar; but there was already talk of a future guerrilla war.

3.

How and why did the Taliban crumble so quickly, at least in the north? The single most important factor, of course, was the US bombing. When it began it was relatively light. The theory was that if it were too heavy, the Northern Alliance would sweep into Kabul before some broad-based transitional authority was set up. But that didn't work, because the bombing wasn't heavy enough to dislodge the Taliban. The policy changed on October 31 when the heavy B-52 bombings of the Taliban front lines began.

An hour after they started I stood in the ruined control tower of the Bagram air base, thirty miles north of Kabul, with General Baba Jan, the local commander of the Northern Alliance. Until the offensive of November 13 they had held the actual air base, from which, of course, no planes had flown for years, while the Taliban held its eastern and southern perimeters. The plump, former Communist general sat on a chair in the middle of the ruined octagonal control tower and, as each American bomb fell, he said little but jotted down the times and locations of the strikes on a small slip of blue paper. He reminded me of a judge at a figure-skating contest.

At a nearby barracks soldiers whooped with joy as they raced up a ladder to the top of their lookout post to see the planes bomb positions that they said the US had not hit until now. But not all of them. Many were engrossed in a volleyball match that you could watch while the sky beyond them was streaked with plumes of smoke and dust from across the front line. While the carnage went on a few miles away, we saw families packed into little horse-drawn traps; the horses sported outlandish red and blue bobble decorations on their harnesses, and trotted up and down the main road, close to the air base.

In his tiny shop at Bagram, decorated with a designer's drawing of a Soviet fighter plane, Haji Zainuddin told me, "So long as they don't kill civilians I am happy about it, but it does give me a headache." Between raids an eerie silence settled on the base, one that was broken only by the wind rustling softly through the trees and by fallen leaves swirling between its shattered buildings.

This air base was once the biggest in Afghanistan. It was built with Soviet money loaned to the Afghans as far back as 1955. The Russians lent them the money with a view to their own future strategic interests. In 1979, on the eve of the Soviet invasion, Moscow might have had reason to believe this had been a very wise investment. Just before the invasion began the Soviet military pre-positioned key units here. Then, on January 1, 1980, they used Bagram to fly in Babrak Karmal, the leader of what was to be their client state. He was then taken to Kabul inside a tank. Until the Soviets were evicted in 1989, Bagram played an important part in the Soviet occupation, with planes and helicopters taking off from here in the Russians' doomed bid to subjugate the country.

Now, after a decade of fighting between Afghans, Bagram's buildings are bombed-out shells. Wrecked tanks and old fighter jets lie strewn around like discarded toys. In the control tower, equipment is in ruins; there is no glass in the windows and a shell hole in the roof. Unlike some of his soldiers, General Baba Jan appeared to be in no mood to celebrate the beginning of the B-52 strikes. Before the Soviets were driven out he fought alongside them in the Afghan army against the Mujahideen. "This is still not enough to make the Taliban run," he said. "They need to do more. We have had twenty-two years of war and we Afghans are used to it." Then he got up, put his piece of blue paper in his pocket, and drove off. For Baba Jan, the carpet-bombing of his enemy by the world's most powerful bombers was the equivalent of just another day at the office. In the distance, we could see the trails of dust rising behind the Taliban's trucks speeding to and from the front. Perhaps they were picking up the wounded. To give credit where credit is due, they had to have been very brave.

For the following two weeks the strikes continued but varied in intensity. Some days they were heavy and some days there were virtually none. We guessed that there were a limited number of bombers available and that every day they bombed in several different places. In the days leading up to Friday, November 9, we heard that there were heavy strikes on the Taliban near Mazar-e-Sharif. However, no one was expecting too much since the Northern Alliance forces there —under the command of General Dostum, and the younger but widely respected General Ostad Mohammed Ata—had complained of a lack of ammunition. But the Americans were dropping ammunition to them along with fodder for their horses and donkeys.

All of a sudden the Taliban lines cracked. Northern Alliance forces poured forward while the Taliban ran for their lives. Over that weekend large parts of the north fell to the Northern Alliance while the Taliban stopped fighting and fled. Early in the morning of November 12 thousands of Northern Alliance troops were gathered at Bagram and other front-line positions north of Kabul. That day artillery and tank fire pounded the Taliban in evident close cooperation with the US Air Force. Fighter-bombers wheeled and dived in the sky above, while the attacks from a B-52 were awesome. After one pass, a giant cloud of dust and earth erupted along a thousand-meter-long stretch of Taliban front line. Then, at four o'clock in the afternoon, the tanks and the infantry made their move. After some resistance, the Taliban collapsed. Already weakened during the last twenty-four hours by the defection of hundreds of unwilling conscripts and others, they abandoned their trenches and fled. That evening panic spread among the Taliban in Kabul. The Northern Alliance did not expect to take Kabul without a fight but the Taliban had not expected

their front line to crumble so quickly. So they packed up their pickup
trucks and moved out.

4.

Before I left London at the beginning of October, I thought that all
Taliban were hard-line religious zealots. I also took seriously all those
maps in the newspapers, full of color and showing swooping arrows
tailed with boxes giving troop strengths, numbers of tanks and planes
and aircraft carriers, and that sort of thing. But when the history of
this war is written the military and other historians who dare to tell
the truth will have to admit that a key to understanding this conflict
was the donkey. What the maps should have showed was arrows with
donkeys. Depending on how many crossed the front line, you could
tell whether the Taliban in any particular location were hard-core—
or Taliban-lite.

Money makes the world go round, but in Afghanistan nothing goes
anywhere except by donkey. You may be a former head of NATO and
now a well-paid pundit, but unless you have eaten anything here you
cannot grasp some of the essential truths of the Afghan wars, and the
very first one of these is that it is all down to donkeys. Before the fall of
Kabul I was staying in Jabal Saraj, thirty-eight miles north of Kabul.
To get there I drove over the Anjuman Pass on the Hindu Kush. When
the jeep got stuck behind a truck blocked in the snow we walked until
it was freed. The next day the pass was closed completely.

Until the Taliban were driven out of northern Afghanistan there
was only one road from the north down to here, through the Panjshir
Valley. So you might expect everyone to have been very worried that
the gleeful Taliban would now use this golden opportunity to starve
the Panjshir as well as such places as Jabal Saraj, Bagram, and indeed
the entire region into submission. Not a bit of it. Every day hundreds

and perhaps thousands of donkeys were trotting over from Taliban territory laden with food, staples, fuel, and indeed almost everything except for fresh food, which you could buy in the area's well-stocked markets. And if the products didn't originate in Taliban territory then they came through it. From Taliban-held parts of the country came staples like wheat, beans, rice, and sugar, not to mention sweets and rugs. From Iran came biscuits, soft drinks, cigarettes, and tea. From Pakistan came fuel, clothes, textiles, and medicines. From China came radios, batteries, and lanterns. The trade was highly market-sensitive, so the arrival of foreign journalists meant that boxloads of exotic products such as Austrian processed cheese, Heinz tomato ketchup, and bottled water were being strapped onto the poor donkeys.

In principle, the Taliban could have throttled the area by stopping the donkeys, but here money talked, not the ultimate victory of Taliban-style Islam. The sheer volume of goods on the market was so vast that it was clear that this was not a clandestine smuggling operation. It was just a huge money-spinner for Taliban commanders and was highly organized. Goods came by road from Kabul to Giobah, which is four hours' drive from Jabal Saraj, although only about twenty miles southeast as the crow flies. After one paid a Taliban toll of $10 per donkey, the goods were loaded onto the donkeys, which then crossed the front line. On the other side they were loaded back into vehicles. According to Abdul Wakil, a trader who commuted back and forth to Kabul, there were up to five hundred donkeys working the Giobah crossing.

You don't have to be very good at arithmetic to work out that the local Taliban commanders were making a fortune here; and indeed, there were also unconfirmed reports that much of the trade was actually organized by them, as opposed to their simply taxing it.

One of the more intriguing questions was just how much fuel was pouring across from Taliban country. With the only road north closed it would be fascinating to know whether the Taliban commanders here were so greedy that they sold the fuel which the Northern Alliance army used to take itself to Kabul.

The donkey story is not just one of those amusing if grotesque tales of war. It is crucial for understanding "the Taliban." What it underlines is the fact that there are (or were?) two types of Taliban. At Giobah the business was obviously controlled by men who fought under a Taliban flag of convenience rather than a banner of belief and who, when the time came, would switch sides. In fact, on the morning of November 13, I saw a whole group of them going to pay court to a Northern Alliance commander at Charikar. They were not prisoners; they had simply defected when they realized the Taliban were done for. They could expect no punishment for their behavior because that is the way war is done here, and it is quite possible that they had been told not to defect earlier because of their valuable services as purveyors of food and fuel to the Northern Alliance.

However, by no means were all the front lines controlled by such amenable, business-friendly Taliban. For those moving goods across to enemy territory where Taliban true believers controlled the front lines, this was a serious business of life and death. Every morning, in Farkhar, which lay just across the front lines from Taloqan, which was until November 11 in Taliban territory, dozens of donkeys could be seen trotting through the mist and into the market. Here I met Braoud, who still had the blood of his friend Najibullah on his clothes. Two nights before, while bringing food across from Taliban country, Najibullah had stepped on a mine. "We were walking very quietly," said Braoud. "He was five meters in front of me. I saw him put his foot on the mine. It just exploded." He died a few hours later on Braoud's back. Najibullah, who was thirty-five, had five children. His wife, in Taliban territory, still did not know that her husband was dead. Braoud said, "Yesterday a donkey was killed and another man injured. It happens every week. The Taliban are planting mines to stop us coming but we still have to do it."

In Farkhar's hospital, I met Suleiman. About fifty years old, he contemplated the stump of his newly amputated leg. He and three of his friends had been surprised by a Taliban patrol as they made the nighttime crossing. His friends got away but the patrol confiscated his donkey along with his goods. Then the Taliban ordered Suleiman to "walk" straight into a mine, where they left him for dead. His friends were too scared to come back but they paid a man to rescue him. Now we know that there were more people who just went along with the Taliban than there were hard-core believers. What we don't know yet is whether the hard-core are doomed or whether they will manage to rally their troops.

—*November 15, 2001*

Kabul, Afghanistan

AS THE WAR winds down I have a theory. This is that the village of Bagram, some thirty miles north of Kabul, may be the center of the world. On October 31 I had stood in the ruined control tower of the Bagram air base and watched as US B-52s began their first day of pulverizing carpet-bombing attacks on Taliban lines on the perimeters of the base.[1] At the time I thought there was something spooky about this. After all, the base had been constructed with Soviet money during the 1950s, and had then been the center from which the Soviet Union had run most of its air war during its occupation of the country from 1979 to 1989. The Soviets had full and murderous command of the air until the US supplied the Afghan Islamist Mujahideen with Stinger missiles, which utterly changed the strategic situation, hastening the Soviet retreat from the country and, in no small measure,

1. See pp. 150–152.

contributing to the collapse of communism and the Soviet Empire. Strewn around the air base is the detritus of that war, rusting old MIG fighters and long-dead tanks.

On November 26, almost two weeks after the fall of Kabul to Northern Alliance forces, I came back to Bagram. We drove north from Kabul and, as we passed the area that I had earlier watched being bombed, we saw the incinerated remains of the Taliban's tanks and vehicles, which had, a couple of weeks before, been on the front line. But, in the view of the Taliban and Osama bin Laden and his followers, this hadn't just been any old front line. It was the front line in their very own clash of civilizations, of their brand of fundamentalist Islam against, as they call us, "the Crusaders and the Jews" and so on.

I knew of course that since the collapse of the Taliban in the north, one hundred or so British Special Forces had arrived in Bagram, along with some Americans. This seemed to reinforce my theory that Bagram is the epicenter of world history. In November 1841, a British imperial force had been annihilated in the next-door village of Charikar, but the following year the British returned. They flattened Kabul's bazaar, went on a killing, looting, and raping spree in another nearby village called Istalif, flattened parts of Charikar, and then beat a hasty retreat back to British India.

On the runway on November 26 was a large Russian cargo plane. Next to it was a column of Russians dressed in blue uniforms with military vehicles—being greeted by, yes, American Special Forces. Officially, the Russians, who flew in twelve cargo loads of equipment that day, were back as part of Russia's contribution to the mounting humanitarian aid mission to Afghanistan. But if this is a clash of civilizations, and Bagram is the epicenter, then the Russians are surely laughing at this particular twist of fate. In the battle against fundamentalism, the Americans have done for the Russians in two months what the Russians failed to do in twenty-two years—ever since Bagram was the front line of their war in Afghanistan.

So in recent history Bagram has seen troops fighting for the British Empire and the Soviet Empire; and in the last few weeks it has seen troops fighting for a would-be Empire of Islam and for the United States, an empire in all but name. But here's the curious twist. Since the most ancient times, thanks to its geographical location, Bagram has been on the front lines of empire, culture, and civilization. Just before World War II archaeologists working at Bagram discovered a fabulous horde in two small rooms. The guidebook of Kabul's National Museum says of the collection: "Here are Chinese lacquers, Graeco-Roman bronzes, plaster plaques, and vessels of porphyry and alabaster, Roman glassware and exquisite ivories from India. Together they form the most spectacular archaeological find of the twentieth century." Perhaps the second century AD was a happier time when, as the guide notes, "the Caesars of Rome and the Han Emperors of China avidly exchanged their most exotic products while bargaining for the spices, gems, and cosmetics of India and Ceylon and the gems and furs of Central Asia."

Of course, today's "clash of civilizations" means that the museum is nothing but a virtual shell now. The Taliban smashed a large part of its contents because Islam does not approve of representations of the human figure. Much of the rest of its collections were stolen and spirited off to dealers in Pakistan who probably sold most of the treasures, such as the famous Bagram ivories carved with pictures of busty and sinuous Indian girls, to wealthy collectors from the Far East, Europe, and America.[2] The second century AD was a golden age of liberalism in Afghanistan compared to now.

---

2. A group called the Society for the Preservation of Afghanistan's Cultural Heritage (SPACH) has been working hard to publicize and halt the pillage and destruction of the country's monuments, museums, and archaeological sites. It is based in Pakistan and can be contacted at spach@comsats.net.pk; or at Suite 13, Block 19, Allah-dad Plaza, G-8/Markaz, Islamabad, Pakistan; or by telephone/fax: 0092-51-2253082. See also their Web site: www.col.com.pk/~afghan.

1.

When I suggest that Bagram is once again at the center of history, some may say I am exaggerating, although after September 11 it is hard to see why. I have heard it suggested that just as Pol Pot and Enver Hoxha were the nadir (or apogee) of fundamentalist communism, after which there was only retreat, so will the Taliban and al-Qaeda come to be seen when the history of fundamentalist Islam is written. We have to hope this is the case. But some of the evidence I have seen suggests that the ideas they stand for are far from finished. While the US has been bombing terrorist training camps across Afghanistan, the really frightening work, which could threaten much of the world, has not been taking place in inhospitable camps in the desert but in ordinary houses in the center of Kabul.

Following a lead, I went to a house in Wazir Akbar Khan, the wealthiest district of Kabul and an area with many foreign missions and NGOs. Next door to Save the Children is a nondescript house that, until the Taliban fled, was occupied by the representative of a Pakistani charity called Ummah Tameer-e-Nau, or Islamic Reconstruction (UTN). Its president is Bashiruddin Mahmood. He is one of Pakistan's leading nuclear scientists and a specialist in plutonium. In March 1999 he was decorated by the president of Pakistan in recognition for his thirty-seven years of work on Pakistan's nuclear program.

In public, UTN's work in Afghanistan included supplying medicine for major hospitals, helping an artificial limb–manufacturing unit at a Kabul hospital, and studying the country's mineral potential, including uranium. According to their neighbors, the Pakistanis who lived and worked here fled Kabul along with the Taliban. But the evidence they left behind suggests that they were working on something rather different from worthy projects to help needy Afghans. It suggests that they were planning to build an anthrax bomb.

An upstairs room of the house had been used as a workshop. What appeared to be a Russian rocket had been disassembled and a canister labeled "helium" had been left on the worktable. On the floor were multiple copies of documents about anthrax downloaded from the Internet, and details about the US military's vaccination plans for its troops. The fact that there were so many copies of each document suggests that seminars were also taking place here.

One of the photocopied documents downloaded from the Internet featured a picture of the former US Defense Secretary William Cohen holding a five-pound bag of sugar. It noted that he was doing this "to show the amount of the biological weapon anthrax that could destroy half the population of Washington, D. C."

On the floor was a small bag of white powder and in the living room were boxes of gas masks and filters. More than likely the bag contained nothing more deadly than sugar, but sugar could be ideal for demonstrating to students how to scatter anthrax spores from a great height over a whole city. On the desk was a cassette box labeled "Jihad" in the center and with the name of Osama bin Laden handwritten along the spine. In another room were pictures celebrating the terrorist strike in Yemen against the USS *Cole*, in which seventeen US sailors died.

On a white board on the wall were a mass of calculations and drawings in felt pen. There were also designs of a parachute and several for a long, thin balloon resembling a weather balloon. Arrows and lines suggested that the balloon should be flying at a height of six miles. "Flying" toward the balloon on the board was a sketch of a fighter plane alongside which someone had written in English: "YOUR DAYS ARE LIMITED! BANG." In a cupboard was a child's blow-up model of a jet fighter, which had presumably also been used in demonstrations.

Since UTN was run by one of Pakistan's top scientists, a man with extremely close links to the Taliban and, to judge by newspapers found at the UTN office, very close ideological affinities with Osama bin Laden, this circumstantial evidence points to the conclusion that those who worked here were designing an anthrax bomb which would be floated above its target by balloon. It could then either be detonated or, if it was shot down by a fighter, would have exploded, showering deadly airborne anthrax spores over a wide area—as wide, say, as half of New York City or Washington, D. C.

The fact that seminars appeared to be going on here suggests that students were possibly being prepared before being sent abroad on their missions. If this is the case, then graduates of this particular course might well already be living among us.

In September Mr. Mahmood was arrested by the Pakistani authorities but was released soon afterward because the authorities said they had found "nothing objectionable" in his behavior. He has since been detained again along with another nuclear scientist, Chaudhry Abdul Majid, and at least five others from the aid group. On December 20 the Bush administration added UTN to its list of terrorist organizations along with the names of Mr. Mahmood and Mr. Majid.

2.

As I write, Kandahar, the Taliban's last stronghold, has fallen, but Osama bin Laden is still at large. He may well be caught, or more likely killed, very soon, but I suspect that one reason he has kept himself alive this long is that he has some fairly good intelligence sources at his disposal. One evening in early December I went to the village of Beni Hissar, on the southern outskirts of Kabul, which bin Laden had visited at the end of October, escaping death by less than three hours. At the edge of the village is a compound that used to be an al-Qaeda headquarters. The building in the center of the compound has been shattered by US missiles.

Not far from it I met Amin, a twenty-three-year-old Afghan recruit to al-Qaeda who, after September 11, had been sent to Beni Hissar. He told me about Bin Laden's visit. "There was so much secrecy that we were not even told it was him until afterward. All we were told was that we had to secure the whole village. He arrived in the night, it was after eight, he came in a big convoy of jeeps with 120 body-guards. When he came into our camp he was completely surrounded by a wall of very tall men. They were so close together you could not see him at all—they were arranged so they could fire in three different directions."

Until September 11 Amin had worked in the Taliban's Ministry of Education. After that he was sent to Beni Hissar with fourteen others so that the Arabs based here, part of a group of 850 of bin Laden's foreign legion, could all either fight or carry out other duties. The camp was run by a Sudanese called Abdul Aziz.

When bin Laden arrived he told Aziz that he would leave at eight o'clock the next morning. He had been expected to spend two days in Kabul. "But then," said Amin, "he got up at five, said his prayers, and left." Soon afterward everyone in the camp was ordered to get out "because we were told there was a cruise missile strike coming." The missiles hit at eight o'clock, targeting the house in the center of the camp compound. Immediately after the attack a witch hunt began. "They said we must have a spy in the camp but they could not find anyone," Amin said.

The fact that bin Laden left earlier than planned implies that he had received intelligence that the camp was about to be attacked. Amin said that the alarm in the camp sounded frequently to warn its occupants to evacuate when there was the threat of an air strike. Bin Laden's foreign legion was equipped with sophisticated Codan radios, of the type used by the UN and NGOs in poor countries such as Afghanistan, which lack ordinary communications, enabling them to be in touch with others across the country.

Although Beni Hissar had been used as a headquarters for up to four years, the number of Arabs here rose significantly after the US bombings began on October 7. However, fear of air strikes kept the Arabs and others constantly on the move. According to Amin the 850 soldiers who answered to Abdul Aziz came from across the Muslim world but most were Egyptians, Saudis, Lebanese, and Qataris.

He told me: "After twenty-five days we were joined by about forty Arabs who were living in Germany and Italy and who came via Iran." These Arabs never fought, however, because although they were well equipped and ready, they lost heart when they realized that much of the local population, which had supported the Taliban before, were now shifting their support to Zahir Shah, Afghanistan's exiled monarch. "They said it was not worth it." In the rubble of the building in Beni Hissar were ripped-up airline tickets, which, when you piece them together, appear to support Amin's claim. They show that the men had flown from Damascus to Iran on October 29. They presumably then crossed by land into Afghanistan. Until then al-Qaeda members had mostly come via Pakistan, but the war made this difficult and perhaps even impossible.

According to Amin one of the main jobs of the many hundreds of Arab fighters was to try to stop Afghan Taliban from fleeing from places like Bagram when the going got tough. When that began to happen it was the Arabs who were dispatched to stop them. "They ordered them to get back to their positions," Amin said.

Despite rudimentary military training given to him by the camp's second-in-command, a man named Tuaib, a Lebanese veteran of the Afghan struggle against the Soviets, Amin was detailed to work on camp finances. He was amazed by the amount of money he and the Arabs were paid. He was to be paid $120 a month and the Arabs received even more, while an Afghan university professor is paid $120 a year. Amin was even more impressed by the lavish meals laid on for the foreign legionnaires. For one week fifteen men were given four sheep, while a relatively well-off Afghan considers himself lucky if he gets two pounds of meat a week.

Unlike most of his colleagues, Amin chose not to flee with the Taliban after Kabul fell. He believes he has some measure of protection because his father had fought with Ahmed Shah Massoud and been killed in 1992. Like most Taliban Afghans, Amin is an ethnic Pashtun, but now, despite his hopes, he is a frightened man. He agreed to talk to me only in a moving car, so that he would not be seen talking to a foreigner. He told me that only his mother, his brother, and two friends, who had acted as intermediaries, knew he had worked with the Arabs.

I was not with Amin for long enough to know whether he really believes most of what he says, but even if he does not, it tells us something about the way bin Laden and his men view the world. Amin explained that because the ideology of the Taliban and al-Qaeda does not believe in national states, as opposed to a universal entity of Muslim believers stretching from the Atlantic to Indonesia, their rout in Afghanistan was not a defeat but just a withdrawal, which left its fighters free to fight another day. I asked him what he would have felt if bin Laden had been killed that day in Beni Hissar, and he said simply: "Everyone who works for Osama is like Osama. So after Osama it might be Abdul Aziz or someone else. Everyone loves him." Then I asked him whether he would be prepared to die as a suicide bomber, killing women and children in the West. He said: "*Inshallah*"—God willing—"I will go. It is our way, it is the way of Allah because these people are unbelievers."

3.

Sales of guidebooks to Afghanistan have not been strong during the last two decades, so the bookshop in Kabul's Intercontinental Hotel (no running water on most floors, and bring your own sleeping bag) still has plenty of copies of Nancy Hatch Dupree's 1977 *Afghanistan* left on its shelves. It is perhaps the most extraordinary guide I have ever read. It was published just two years before the Soviet invasion of this country began the cycle of recent wars. After no more than twenty-four years this has become a guide to a country that no longer exists, like the Austro-Hungarian Empire or British India. Once there were schoolgirls in miniskirts in Kabul. In two months I have never seen the face of a girl older than seven. Even in post-Taliban Kabul most women are firmly covered in their burqas.

After two months of war, I took a day off. Armed with Ms. Dupree's guidebook I went to the zoo. But here there is no day off, because the story of the zoo is the story—the tragedy really—of Afghanistan in miniature, but with animals for victims.

The zoo opened in 1967, and Ms. Dupree wrote admiringly about it: "A lion, a gift of Germany, has a regal run beside the Kabul river; the kangaroos from Australia have settled in nicely; the raccoons from the United States are raising a family. A three-year-old elephant presented by the Government of India arrived by air in June 1973."

The elephant died in a rocket attack eight years ago when the Mujahideen forces that had fought the Russians were fighting one another. The zoo lies in a district that was shelled and rocketed mercilessly by one faction led by Gulbuddin Hekmatyar. The elephant house remains a ruin; the elephant is buried nearby. The kangaroos and raccoons are long gone; either they died, escaped, or were killed. But the "German" lion is still here. His face is lopsided and he can barely walk. He is almost totally blind because a man threw a hand grenade at him after he killed his brother, who had climbed into his run to tease him. "There are crazy people everywhere," sighs Sheer Agha, the zoo's director. Two years ago another man went into his run and suffered the same fate—but that time, there was no revenge. Today nineteen species live among the ruins, including several monkeys, two porcupines, two wolves, some eagles, a wild cat, forty rabbits, a bear, and a deer. During the grim months when Hekmatyar's forces were rocketing Kabul, Mr. Agha and his fellow workers could not come to work. "But," he told me, "when the shelling died down, we would bring food and the guard who was here would give it to the animals. When we could not come he gave his own food to the animals."

Nancy Hatch Dupree writes glowingly in her guide about the zoo's "considerable collection of fish and reptiles from all over the world... added with the opening of an aquarium in July, 1974. In addition, there is a very fine Zoological Museum... which was reopened in May 1972 after two years of modification and expansion." The entire collection was destroyed by Hekmatyar's rockets—along with what little hope remained after the Soviet years, which had already snuffed out the spirit of the carefree city of the 1970s. Then it had become a magnet for Western hippies and also shared something of a glamorous reputation among Arabs, Indians, Pakistanis, and others—much like the similarly doomed Beirut.

It was during this bout of fighting that Mujahideen soldiers ate the deer and the rabbits, because, says Mr. Agha, "the guard could not stop them." I asked him if they also ate the elephant after it was killed and he laughed and said, "No, that is not permitted by our religion." But, surprisingly, Mr. Agha told me that he did not believe that the months of Hekmatyar's rocketing were the worst time the zoo ever faced. "It was the Taliban period," he says. "They were always bothering people and they were uneducated and threw stones at the animals. Once a Taliban commander came here and asked who was responsible. I said, 'I am,' and then he asked me: 'Is there one sentence in the Holy Koran which says we should have a zoo?' I said that there was not, so then he said, 'Please take all the animals out.' I went to the mayor, who was a little better, and he gave me a paper which I showed whenever we had any other problems." Mr. Agha reflected: "The Taliban were not at all sympathetic, they did not like scientists, only mullahs."

WAR IN THE DARK

After the Taliban fled Kabul on November 12, there was no money for food for the animals, so Mr. Agha was reduced to begging the market traders for credit. Now, however, he says that the new interim government has kept its promise and sent him cash. Still, the staff have not been paid for three months and very soon their numbers are going to grow. Women who worked at the zoo and were then banned will soon be coming back to their jobs. "They are very happy," says Mr. Agha, who is also hopeful that somehow he will find money to rebuild his zoo.

In one cage a bear has a bloody, unhealed wound on its nose, the result, Mr. Agha says, of his being beaten with a stick by a Taliban seven months ago. Mr. Agha said: "Please tell the world about our plight so that people can come and help us." He was, of course, only talking about the zoo, but he might have been talking about his country.

4.

On December 5 Afghans convened by the United Nations and meeting near Bonn in Germany agreed to form a transitional government that would take power on December 22. They also agreed that a UN-backed multinational force should be deployed in Afghanistan. However, what exactly it would do, for how long, and how big it would be remained unclear. Skeptics believe that the deal is untenable. They point to the fact that three of the most important jobs, the ministries of defense, interior, and foreign affairs, all go to three Tajiks from a small area of the Panjshir Valley who were all close to Ahmed Shah Massoud. It is also not yet clear whether the mainly Pashtun south of Afghanistan will relapse into the anarchy which plagued it in the years before the Taliban took over.

The leader of the transitional government is Hamid Karzai, a powerful forty-six-year-old Pashtun tribal leader, and a supporter of Zahir Shah, Afghanistan's former king. He is also well educated, Westernized, speaks good English, and was deputy foreign minister in 1992. He spent much of the 1980s living in the US and he is a man whose views have chimed well with those of the US in the recent past. On July 20, 2000, he gave evidence to the Senate Foreign Relations Sub-Committee on Near Eastern and South Asian Affairs, which was holding a hearing called "The Taliban: Engagement or Confrontation?" He told the committee that the terrorist presence in his country could not be removed without strong international support.

The coming weeks and months are Afghanistan's moment of opportunity. Its people are desperate for peace and normality and have no love for the warlords who have ruined their lives for so long. But it will take both Afghans and the "international community"— i.e., the US, the Europeans, and a few others, including Muslim countries like Turkey who could offer troops for peacekeeping forces—to make sure that the chance is not lost. Afghans need to compromise among themselves and put the interests of their country above their own narrow ethnic interests. The responsibility of Western countries is not to do what they did after the Soviet defeat, which was to lose interest in Afghanistan once their own concerns had been satisfied. By now these may be somewhat mundane observations—but it does not make them any the less true. We failed Afghanistan before and now we are paying the price. Future historians shouldn't have to look for the roots of a US decline in Bagram.

—*December 20, 2001*

TIMOTHY GARTON ASH

Is There a Good Terrorist?

Have you heard that Osama bin Laden is coming to Macedonia?
No. Why?
Because we've declared an amnesty for terrorists.

THIS MACEDONIAN JOKE, told to me recently in Skopje, invites us to reflect on one of the most important questions in the post–September 11 world: Who is a terrorist? It is a question to which the international community sorely needs an answer.

Slav Macedonian nationalists insist that they face their own Osama bin Laden in an Albanian Macedonian guerrilla leader called Ali Ahmeti.[1] Yet, they say, the United States and NATO have been making deals with this terrorist, and pressing the Macedonian government to grant him amnesty. Of course, nationalist regimes around the world have always played this semantic card—Russia denounces Chechen "terrorists"; Israel, Palestinian "terrorists"; China, Tibetan "terrorists"; and so on—with widely varying degrees of justification. In this

---

1. The point was made to me, vociferously, by a group of nationalist demonstrators outside the Macedonian parliament. A Macedonian Web site makes a tabular comparison of the two men (Occupation: Leader of a terrorist organization; Leader of a terrorist organization; Islamic? Yes; Yes; and so on). See www.realitymacedonia.org.mk.

case, however, it is not just the local nationalists who have taken a dim view of Mr. Ali Ahmeti.

On June 27, 2001, President George W. Bush signed an executive order freezing all US-based property of, and blocking donations to, a list of persons engaged in or supporting "extremist violence in the Former Yugoslav Republic of Macedonia" and in other parts of the Western Balkans. "I find," said the presidential order, "that such actions constitute an unusual and extraordinary threat to the national security and foreign policy of the United States, and hereby declare a national emergency to deal with that threat." Near the top of the list of persons thus dramatically stigmatized is "AHMETI, Ali, Member of National Liberation Army (NLA)," born in Kicevo, Macedonia, on January 4, 1959. The presidential order does not actually use the word "terrorist," yet it treats him as such. In May 2001, the NATO secretary-general, Lord (George) Robertson, described the National Liberation Army that Ahmeti leads as "a bunch of murderous thugs whose objective is to destroy a democratic Macedonia."

In mid-August, however, under heavy pressure from the United States, NATO, and European negotiators, representatives of the Slav and Albanian Macedonians signed a peace deal. In return for constitutional and administrative changes designed to secure equal rights for Albanian Macedonians in the Macedonian state, the NLA would stop fighting and hand in many of its weapons to NATO. As part of the deal, the Macedonian president, Boris Trajkovski, committed himself to giving amnesty to the insurgents, a commitment effectively guaranteed to Ahmeti by NATO. As President Trajkovski memorably explained to me: "I signed an agreement with the Secretary-General [of NATO] and the Secretary-General's representative signed an agreement with the terrorists."

I found some confusion among Western representatives in Skopje about the proper characterization of Mr. Ahmeti. One senior British military officer, who had spent years fighting the IRA in Northern

Ireland, told me with emphasis and passion that Ahmeti and his colleagues in the NLA are terrorists. "If you take the NATO definition of terrorism, they absolutely fit," he said.[2] Other senior civilian and military NATO representatives described the NLA action as an "insurgency" and expressed admiration for the restraint exercised by Ahmeti and his men in their astonishingly successful seven-month campaign. On paper, international organizations had characteristically taken refuge in a euphemism wrapped in an acronym. "EAAG," said the documents —short for Ethnic Albanian Armed Group.

I felt it might be useful to ask Mr. Ahmeti himself. So, with an Albanian driver and interpreter, I drove up high into the beautiful wooded mountains of western Macedonia, past Macedonian police checkpoints, past well-built hillside villages with gleaming minarets, past a makeshift road sign saying "STOP: NLA," to the village of Sipkovica. Dodging mules carrying great loads of straw up the steep and narrow cobbled street, we made our way to a large house guarded by young men in jeans and dark glasses. While we waited, they proudly pointed to a black Audi "captured" from the deputy speaker of the Macedonian parliament. Inside, Ahmeti, a weary-looking man with swept-back silver-gray hair and fingers heavily stained with nicotine, seated himself cross-legged on a weary-looking armchair and offered me what he called a "very good" whiskey—a fifteen-year-old Bowmore from the Scottish island of Islay. He drank some too. (In the Balkans, Islay trumps Islam.)

After a few minutes of preliminary conversation, I told Ahmeti that there was much discussion since September 11 about terrorism

---

2. But what is the NATO definition of terrorism? This officer could not remember exactly. Subsequent inquiries reveal that NATO does not have one, not least because its member states cannot agree on one—which again indicates the difficulties. Probably this officer was thinking of a working distinction made in British military doctrine between "terrorism" and "insurgency."

and that "some people would say *you* are a terrorist." How would he answer them?

As my question was translated, his bodyguards shifted slightly in their seats. Ahmeti replied calmly and quietly. I expected him to say words to the effect of "No, I'm a freedom fighter," but his response was more thoughtful. "That person cannot be a terrorist," he said, "who wears an army badge, who has an objective for which he is fighting, who respects the Geneva Conventions and the Hague Tribunal, who acts in public with name and surname, and answers for everything he does.... Someone who is aiming for good reforms and democracy in the country—and that people should be equal before the law."

Now of course one can't simply say, "Oh well, that's all right then!" One has to look at what the NLA actually did, and may still do. Nor should we retreat into the weary relativism of the phrase I have heard so many times in Europe over the last few weeks: "One man's terrorist is another man's freedom fighter." To be sure, on this matter there are blatant double standards throughout the world. The Kurds are freedom fighters in Iraq and terrorists in Turkey, or vice versa, depending on where you sit. To be sure, the kind of sudden shifts that we have often seen in Western policy and language invite cynicism. The banned terrorist Ahmeti becomes a valued partner in a peace process. The CIA-funded, heroic, anti-Soviet fighter Osama bin Laden becomes the world's most wanted terrorist. The former terrorist (or was it freedom fighter?) Menachem Begin wins the Nobel Peace Prize.

Yet it is also true that people change. They spiral downward into brutality like Conrad's Kurtz, or they reemerge from darkness as they conclude that their political purposes are best served by moving on from armed struggle, as did the former German terrorist Horst Mahler, the Sinn Fein leader Gerry Adams, and Nelson Mandela. It is also true that there are many different terrorisms, and not all forms of using violence to achieve political ends are properly described as terrorism. If we are not to lose the global "war against terrorism," proclaimed

by President Bush after September 11, we need a sophisticated understanding of the differences.

1.

Here are four things to look at in deciding whether someone is a terrorist, and, if he or she is, what kind of terrorist: Biography, Goals,
Methods, and Context. Only a combination of the four will yield an
answer. I will use the example of Ahmeti and the NLA, but the template can be used anywhere.

> BIOGRAPHY: Who are they, where are they coming from, and
> what do they really want? Why did fifteen of the nineteen assas-
> sins of September 11 come from Saudi Arabia? Does Osama bin
> Laden really want to destroy the West, to purify Islam, to topple
> the Saudi royal house, or merely to change the Saudi succession?
> The classic questions of intelligence work are also the first intel-
> ligent questions about any suspected terrorist. Biography may not
> be at the heart of all History—but it certainly is for this patch.

To anyone who has spent time in Kosovo and Macedonia, what we
know of Ali Ahmeti's life story feels quite familiar. He comes from the
village of Zajas, near the town of Kicevo, in the mountainous western
part of Macedonia that is largely inhabited by Albanians, but he studied at the University of Pristina, in Kosovo. (It was then all Tito's
Yugoslavia.) He was a student radical. Like many others at that time,
he combined Albanian nationalism and Marxism-Leninism. He was
imprisoned for a few months. He was, aged twenty-two, an active
participant in the 1981 uprising of Albanian students in Pristina.
Then he fled to Switzerland. Not having access to classified intelligence reports, I do not know exactly what his "studies" and "work"

in Switzerland consisted of, but he remained politically active. In exile he reportedly joined the Movement for an Albanian Socialist Republic in Yugoslavia, and formed a Macedonian subcommittee of the Marxist-Leninists of Kosovo. His style during our long conversation spoke to me of many hours spent debating revolutionary politics in smoke-filled rooms. He read many books, he told me, "for example, about psychology and guerrilla warfare."

While the rural population among whom he operates is largely Muslim, at no point in our conversation did he even mention Islam, let alone give any hint of fellow feeling for Islamic terrorist groups such as al-Qaeda. It is a reasonable assumption that a whiskey-drinking, ex-Marxist-Leninist, Albanian nationalist does not see himself as part of any Muslim international.

His movements during the 1990s are unclear. He told me that he was back in Macedonia in 1993, when he found his Albanian compatriots still hoping for peaceful recognition of their rights inside the newly independent Macedonia. An unconfirmed report speaks of him being in Tirana, the capital of Albania, in 1997, attempting to organize guerrilla groups. A great influence on him was his uncle, Fazli Veliu, a former schoolteacher from the same village of Zajas (and another name on President Bush's exclusion list of June 27). Ahmeti joined a small political party called the LPK, which Uncle Fazli had been instrumental in founding. The LPK was the main precursor of the Kosovo Liberation Army (KLA).[3] They also organized the Homeland Calling Fund, which raised money among Albanians living abroad for the armed struggle in Kosovo.[4] How much of that money derived

---

3. On this, see Tim Judah, *Kosovo: War and Revenge* (Yale University Press, 2000), and my review essay on the Kosovo war in *The New York Review*, September 21, 2000. I quote there US special envoy Robert Gelbard characterizing the KLA in February 1998 as "without any questions, a terrorist group."

4. The Homeland Calling Fund may be compared with the US-based NorAid Fund, which

from the drug trade, prostitution, or protection rackets we shall never know, but some of it certainly came from ordinary Albanians making patriotic contributions.

Obviously, the military campaign of the KLA in Kosovo in 1998–1999 was a formative experience for him. Ahmeti told me he was in Kosovo at that time, but did not actually fight. Other reports say he fought. Not accidentally, the Albanian initials of the National Liberation Army in Macedonia are the same as those of the Kosovo Liberation Army: UCK.[5] Some of the leading figures of the NLA came from the KLA. So did some of the weapons. But above all, there was the immediate example. I asked Ahmeti if he thought Albanian Macedonians would have been ready to fight for their rights in 1998. No, he said, "because of the situation in Kosovo." But after the West had come in to Kosovo and—as most Albanian Macedonians saw it—the KLA had "won" as a result, there were enough people ready to heed the call to arms in Macedonia at the beginning of this year. Most of the ordinary fighters of the NLA were Albanian Macedonians, many of whom had bought their own guns.

Summarizing what he told me, I would say that the now forty-two-year-old Ahmeti drew two main conclusions from the Kosovo war. First, you could win more by a few months of armed struggle than Albanian politicians had achieved in nearly a decade of peaceful politics. As in Kosovo, so in Macedonia. Second, that you could do this only if you got the West involved. That was the great tactical goal—and the great unknown. He told me that when the insurgency

---

raised money in the US for the IRA—except that the NorAid Fund was long tolerated by the US authorities. The Albanian-American vote was, of course, rather smaller than the Irish-American one.

5. The Kosovo Liberation Army is Ushtria Clirimtare e Kosoves (UCK); the National Liberation Army is Ushtria Clirimtare Kombetare (UCK). Thus, when my driver was asking for the location of Ahmeti's headquarters he asked, "Where is the headquarters of the UCK?"

took off in February, "I knew that without the help of the West we couldn't win. But we didn't know how much they would help...." So he had to do everything possible to bring the West in. That meant being deliberately restrained in both their goals and their methods. This was Albanian Macedonia's chance. This was Ali Ahmeti's chance.

> GOALS: Whatever the tangle of biographically conditioned motives—and human motives are often unclear even to ourselves—one also has to look at the proclaimed goals of a terrorist goal or movement. Sometimes, as in the case of al-Qaeda or the German Red Army Faction, the overall goals are so vague, apocalyptic, and all-embracing that they could never be realized in any real world. But sometimes they are clear and—as much as we deplore tactics that shed the blood of innocents—in some sense rational objectives, which may sooner or later be achieved in the real world. The KLA wants independence for Kosovo; the IRA, a united Ireland; ETA, independence for the Basque Country, and so on.

The NLA is remarkable for the clarity and relative modesty of its proclaimed goals. From the outset, its leaders insisted that they only wanted what Albanian Macedonian politicians had been arguing for since Macedonia became independent in 1991: equal status and equal rights for the Albanian Macedonians. Albanians should be recognized as a constitutive nation of the Republic of Macedonia. The Albanian language should be accepted as an official language, in parliament and the public administration. Albanians should have the right to higher education in their own language. Albanians should be proportionately represented in the bureaucracy, the courts, and, especially, the police, who should stop harassing them. There should be more devolution of powers to local government—with obvious implications for those areas with an Albanian majority. But Macedonia should remain a unitary, multiethnic state.

Compared with the demands of the KLA, Bosnian Serbs and Croats, the IRA, or the ETA, these look as if they were drafted by Amnesty International. Most Western representatives regard them as reasonable, and believe that the Macedonian state should have conceded most of them years ago. Now you may say: but these demands are tactical, designed to appeal to the West. Certainly they are. Altogether, I found Ahmeti guarded, elusive, even evasive on these political questions—which is to say, he spoke as a politician. Like the old Marxist-Leninist comrade that he is, he stuck firmly to the party line: equal rights in a unitary, multiethnic state, nothing more! But, it seemed to me, he did so with some personal conviction—and good arguments.

Why, I asked, could one not envisage a federal solution for Macedonia? He smiled: "In a country with just two million people and 25,000 square kilometers?" It would be ridiculous. Federalism would mean new territorial borders and competition between the constituent parts. How could you draw the lines in a country where Albanian and Slav Macedonians live so mixed up together? "Either we're in the twenty-first century and thinking of integration into Europe, or we do it as they did one hundred years ago...." Putting his hand on his heart, he said, "My country is Macedonia."

Not all his colleagues agree. I spoke to another NLA commander, Rafiz Aliti, known as "Teacher" because he was, until the spring uprising, the village physical education teacher. He told me that he favored the federalization and "cantonization" of Macedonia. A unitary state could not work. If the Macedonian side did not implement the mid-August "framework agreement," which on paper fulfills the Albanians' moderate demands, then they would go to war again. And this time it would be a war for territory. What territory? "The territory where Albanians live."

Yet there is a substantial body of evidence that most of the Albanian political elite in Kosovo and Macedonia have agreed that the medium-term strategic goal should be different in each place: independence for Kosovo, equal rights in Macedonia. And, incidentally, not Greater Albania for either. Not for the foreseeable future anyway.

There is a very good reason for Albanian Macedonians to take this gradualist path. According to the Macedonian authorities, some 23 percent of the Macedonian population is Albanian, but unofficial estimates put the number as high as 35 percent. The "framework agreement" provides for a new, internationally supervised census, and it will be interesting to see what figure it comes up with. Whatever the result, everyone knows that the Albanian Macedonians have many more children than the Slav Macedonians. At current birth rates, the Albanians will probably become a demographic majority in about 2025. And then the majority might elect the sixty-six-year-old Ali Ahmeti president of Macedonia...

METHODS: An old man who stands on a soapbox at Speakers' Corner in London of a rainy Saturday afternoon demanding that the Lord raze to the ground all branches of Marks & Spencer is not a terrorist. He is a nut at Speakers' Corner. The Scottish National Party has goals much more far-reaching than the NLA—it wants full independence for Scotland—but it works entirely by peaceful, constitutional means.

Does the individual or group use violence to realize their personal or political goals? Is that violence targeted specifically at the armed and uniformed representatives of the state, or does the terrorist group also target innocent civilians? Does it attempt to limit civilian casualties while spreading panic and disruption—as Irish paramilitaries have sometimes done, by telephoning bomb warnings—or does it aim for the mass killing of innocent civilians, as al-Qaeda plainly did on September 11?

Ahmeti and the NLA deliberately chose violence. The lesson they learned from Kosovo was: if you play your cards right, a little well-calculated violence achieves what years of nonviolent politics had not. Which, once again, it did. But, Ahmeti and others claim, they never targeted civilians. They observed the Geneva Conventions, were mindful of the Hague Tribunal, and so on. Most international observers agree that the NLA did much less harm to Slav Macedonian civilians than the KLA did to Serbian civilians in Kosovo. This was especially true in the areas most directly under Ahmeti's command. But Human Rights Watch and Amnesty International have documented several cases of kidnapping, torture, and abuse by members of the NLA.

I spoke with a group of young Slav Macedonian men who had fled from their villages in western Macedonia. However, they had done so—even by their own account—after themselves having taken up arms against the NLA. They told the dreadfully familiar story of how neighbors who had lived and worked peacefully together for years suddenly turned guns on each other (as in Kosovo, as in Bosnia, as in Croatia...). According to the Macedonian government, some 70,000 people fled or were expelled from their homes as a result of the fighting. International observers suggest the number is much lower. They also say that the worst damage to civilians was done by the Macedonian army and security forces. The guns of an incompetent army indiscriminately pounded rebel villages—the textbook way not to fight an insurgency. Paramilitaries called the Lions, working, as in Milosevic's Serbia, under the interior ministry, attacked Albanians in the shadows. And there is no doubt that ordinary Albanians have for years been subjected to harassment by a police force that is overwhelmingly Slav Macedonian.

Coming down from my mountain meeting with Ahmeti, our car was stopped by a man in the uniform of a police major and a paramilitary soldier with a large wooden cross around his neck. The major verbally abused my interpreter. When I tried to intervene, saying (rather pompously) that I had that morning spoken to President Trajkovski and I was sure the President would wish us to be given fair passage, he said to my interpreter, "Tell your man I don't give a fuck about the President." When I smiled, he said, "Tell him to stop smiling." This Macedonian policeman was a fine propagandist for the Albanian cause.

Afterward, my Albanian driver was physically trembling with rage. "You see how they treat us," he cried, in his broken German. "If I had not seen the policeman waving us down at the roadside, they would have shot us. That is not *korrekt*." Not *korrekt*, indeed.

This was a messy little low-level civil war, in which neither side was very *korrekt* and neither very brutal, by the low standards of the Balkans. The NLA started it, but the Slav Macedonian side behaved rather worse during it. This brings us to our last criterion: context.

CONTEXT: Basic Principle 1.1 of the Framework Agreement for Macedonia says, "The use of violence in pursuit of political aims is rejected completely and unconditionally." An admirable principle. But not to be taken too literally. After all, in bombing Afghanistan, America and Britain are pursuing political aims through the use of violence. You may say: but that is justified by all the time-honored criteria of "just war," and legitimated by international coalitions, organizations, and law. Anyway, to use political violence from inside and against a legitimate state is a quite different thing. But who decides if a particular state is legitimate?

Even within an internationally recognized state, there can be such oppression that armed resistance may be considered legitimate. This is the claim expressed with incomparable force in the words that Schiller puts into the mouth of Stauffacher in his *Wilhelm Tell*. When the oppressed man can find justice in no other way, says Stauffacher, then he calmly reaches up into the sky and pulls down his eternal rights that hang there, inalienable and, like the stars, imperishable. When no other means remains, then he must needs take up the sword.[6] Such, perhaps, were the Polish uprisings for freedom in the eighteenth and nineteenth centuries. Such was the American War of Independence.

It therefore matters hugely what kind of state you're in. It is one thing for groups like the IRA and ETA to use political violence in states like Britain or Spain, where the means of working for peaceful change are equally available to all in a mature democracy. It is another thing for Palestinian groups to use political violence against an oppressive military occupation in the Gaza Strip or the West Bank. Another again for the ANC against the South African apartheid regime. Yet another for the violently repressed Kosovo Albanians to take up arms against the Milosevic regime in Serbia. We may want to uphold the universal principle "No violence!" but we all know that these are,

---

6. I cannot resist quoting these marvelous lines in full:

> *Nein, eine Grenze hat Tyrannenmacht:*
> *Wenn der Gedrückte nirgends Recht kann finden,*
> *Wenn unerträglich wird die Last—greift er*
> *Hinauf getrosten Mutes in den Himmel*
> *Und holt herunter seine ew'gen Rechte,*
> *Die droben hangen unveräusserlich*
> *Und unzerbrechlich, wie die Sterne selbst—*
> *Der alte Urstand der Natur kehrt wieder,*
> *Wo Mensch dem Menschen gegenübersteht*
> *Zum letzten Mittel, wenn kein andres mehr*
> *Verfangen will, ist ihm das Schwert gegeben.*

in political fact and in moral content, very different things, and some violent political actions are—shall we say—less unjustified than others.

"So far as I know," President Boris Trajkovski smilingly informed me, "world leaders are all praising Macedonia." Well, I have news for President Trajkovski (who is a nice, decent, personally uncorrupt, and well-intentioned man, but not perhaps possessed of the world's strongest intellect or character). They're not. In private, many of them are cursing it. I remarked to a very senior Western negotiator who has had much to do with Macedonia that I had never encountered a more pigheaded, shortsighted political elite than the Slav Macedonian one. "Amen to all that," the negotiator said, "except that I would question your use of the word 'elite.'" Just as they fought the war against the NLA in a way that rebounded against themselves, so they are still—at this writing—pigheadedly holding out against amendments to the constitution that most international observers regard as wholly reasonable.

A particular sticking point is a wording in the preamble that refers (in my official English translation) to "the historical fact that Macedonia is established as a national state of the Macedonian people...." Understandably, the Albanians don't like this reference to a national state, especially since the word for "people" in this context is *narod*, implying ethnic community, rather than the broader and more civic *nacija*. The Slav Macedonian side agreed to a rewording in the summer peace deal, but now the parliament is threatening to renege on it.

Extraordinary Western pressure—almost weekly visits by the EU foreign-policy representative Javier Solana and NATO Secretary-General George Robertson (who might have a few other things on their minds), the withholding of international aid to the crippled Macedonian economy until the amendments are passed—seems incapable of budging them. The sledgehammer is defied by the nut.

And at lower levels, the bureaucracy, the army, and the police seem as stubborn, corrupt, and incompetent as their politicians.

There are explanations for all this. Looking back over the last decade one must have sympathy with Slav Macedonians too. There are peoples that aspire to statehood and peoples that have statehood thrust upon them. The Macedonians had statehood thrust upon them, as former Yugoslavia collapsed in 1991. Well into the twentieth century, all of the country's four neighbors had claims on its territory: Serbia between the wars treated it as part of southern Serbia, Bulgaria regarded it as part of Bulgaria (and the Macedonian language as just a dialect of Bulgarian), Albanian nationalists wanted great chunks of it for Greater Albania, and Greeks said Macedonia is really Greek.

None of these claims was fully, unambiguously laid to rest in 1991. Their already battered economy was then shattered and corrupted by Western sanctions on Milosevic's Serbia, and a Greek blockade of international recognition for Macedonia because, said the Greeks, there is already a Macedonia in Greece. (Hence the state's awkward international name, the Former Yugoslav Republic of Macedonia, though it calls itself plain Republic of Macedonia.) Then it had to cope with the vast Albanian refugee influx from Kosovo. Western promises of economic aid and investment have remained largely that—promises. Oh yes, and the Slav Macedonians will soon be a minority in their own country. A little existential *Angst* is understandable. This helps to explain, but it does not excuse. Most of the changes now being made (or not being made) under pressure from the NLA and the West should have been made years ago.

All that being said, the fact remains that the position of the Albanians in Macedonia at the beginning of this year was nothing like the one unforgettably evoked in Schiller's *Wilhelm Tell*. There were still possibilities for peaceful change. Established Albanian political parties were in the government as well as parliament (as they still are), and they were pressing for most of the same reforms. They were not getting there very fast (partly because both Slav Macedonian and Albanian Macedonian parties harbor impressive levels of corruption), but in time, with Western and especially European pressure, they would have got there. However relatively restrained the NLA was in its goals and methods, it willfully chose the path of violence when other paths were still open. As a result, it has accelerated the necessary reforms on paper, but it may also have impeded their practical realization. For the war has resulted in further alienation of the Albanian and Slav Macedonian communities, and political radicalization on both sides.

2.

So: was I drinking whiskey with a terrorist? Well, certainly with a former revolutionary politician and a guerrilla leader who deliberately reached for the gun when other means were available. Perhaps the moderation of his proclaimed goals, and the fact that he tried not to target civilians, pull him just the right side of the line. Just. Perhaps. Certainly, he has moved on to become an impressively consistent advocate of change through political negotiation inside an undivided, multiethnic state. So maybe it is all right to drink whiskey with a reformed terrorist? If it were not, the consumption of whiskey by world leaders would have been reduced by quite a few bottles over the last fifty years.

Will the United Nations give us some further guidance on this matter? For a long time, the UN has avoided any definition of terrorism. Recently, it has tiptoed toward one. A November 2000 report by the UN's Sixth Committee came close to a general definition when it declared:

> Criminal acts intended or calculated to provoke a state of terror
> in the general public, a group of persons or particular persons

for political reasons are in any circumstances unjustifiable, whatever the considerations of a political, philosophical, ideological, racial, ethnic, religious or other nature that may be used to justify them.[7]

But that is unsustainably broad. Isn't the Taliban a "group of persons" among whom we hope to provoke a state of terror? Who decides what is a criminal act?

Since September 11, support has been growing for a UN convention on terrorism. One wonders how useful any definition it comes up with can be, both because member states will have such widely differing views of what should count and because of the intrinsic difficulties for even the most neutral, independent analyst. Realistically, the best one can hope for may be that as wide as possible a spectrum of states, including states from different "civilizations," in Samuel Huntington's sense, may reach agreement on the description of as many particular cases as possible. At the very least, Europe and America should agree—which is by no means guaranteed, if one thinks of differing approaches to Iraq, for example, or to Israel and the Palestinian question. Even then, a common policy might not follow, but at least there would be a common analysis to start from.

To this end, my four headings—Biography, Goals, Methods, Context—may serve as a modest template, but the content in each case will be very different and there will be no universal guidelines for judging the combination. As the great Bishop Butler once unshallowly remarked, every thing is what it is and not another thing.

—November 1, 2001

---

7. I owe this quotation, and my summary of what the UN has done, to my Oxford colleague Professor Adam Roberts.

POSTSCRIPT

The international sledgehammer finally cracked the Macedonian political nut. The required amendments to the constitution were passed. But the situation in the country remained extremely tense, and Macedonian nationalists continued to insist that Ali Ahmeti and his colleagues were kindred spirits to Osama bin Laden. Meanwhile, Osama bin Laden said in a video interview, "The bad terror is what America and Israel are practicing against our people, and what we are practicing is the good terror that will stop them doing what they are doing." And President George W. Bush commented, in a speech to the UN General Assembly, that there is no such thing as a good terrorist. Had they been reading *The New York Review*?

—*November 30, 2001*

TIMOTHY GARTON ASH

Europe at War

IS THIS WAR a defining moment for Europe?

Since September 11, I have been exploring that question in nine European countries, through conversations with political leaders, intellectuals, officials, and so-called ordinary people (but they never *are* ordinary) in Madrid, Paris, Warsaw, and other capitals. To visit so many nations in so short a time is like using one of those flick-books some of us had in our low-tech youth, with a series of cartoon sketches drawn on successive pages of a notebook. Flick the edges with your thumb and you see a jerky moving picture.

Everywhere, I found a fundamental sympathy with the United States under terrorist attack. This may seem obvious, but it has hardly been true in all regions of the world. A great black banner across the Brandenburg Gate declared "*Wir trauern*—Our deepest sympathy." A working-class Parisian in a bar told me, "We're all under attack... the democracies. We're all the free world."

Yet every European country has its own war. For Spain, it is about fighting their own Basque separatist terrorists (ETA), as the Spanish prime minister, José María Aznar, very forcefully impressed upon me. For Germany, it is about domestic security (in Germany alone I found people feeling personally threatened, as they do in the US), and then about a post-post-Hitler Germany gingerly stepping up to play a military role in the wider world. In Macedonia, it is about their own terrorists—or alleged terrorists—and what this will do to US involvement in the Balkans. Under Tony Blair, Britain burnishes its special relationship with the United States ("Newest US Ambassador Is Prime Minister of the United Kingdom," said a memorable headline in *The Wall Street Journal Europe*), but wants to lead in Europe too. Bulgaria worries about the effects on its prospects for joining NATO and the EU. And so on.

This story of similarity and difference is one constantly repeated at all levels of the European experience. A street in Madrid suddenly reminds me irresistibly of a street in downtown Belgrade. Sit in a café in Sofia and you could be in Paris. Shops, smells, fashion, the way an intellectual smokes his cigarette, the toss of a girl's head, all transport you from one city to another. "Yes, this is Europe," you say: hard to describe, impossible to pin down, but it exists. Yet part of what defines this Europe is precisely the richness of its diversity in such a small space. How many cuisines, languages, wines, newspapers, styles of femininity, across just a few thousand miles!

"Unity in diversity" is the pat formula often used. Well, there is much similarity beside diversity. There is, I would say, *commonality* in diversity. But that is not the same as unity. Has there been a united European response to the events of September 11? Only if one uses the word "united" in a very loose sense. Is there a united European response to the way the war is being waged in Afghanistan? Only if one uses the word still more loosely. All European governments support the action, but with varying degrees of difficulty. Many European societies have been worried about it, but again, in varying degrees.

Have these events helped the process known in most European languages (though rarely in English) as "European unification"? In one important respect, it would appear so. With a dynamic European commissioner, António Vitorino, helped by energetic support from governments such as that of Aznar in Spain, the European Union is introducing new measures to combat terrorism. Besides increased cooperation between police forces and intelligence services, and new powers to cut off terrorist funds, the most important measure is an EU-wide arrest warrant. This will allow persons wanted in any member state to be arrested in any other, and handed over directly to the country in which they are sought. These are important steps against terrorism; they also serve to bring the countries of the EU closer together.

Still, that is not quite the same as "European unification." At best, it is the unification of part of Europe. What about the rest of Europe not yet in the EU, but knocking at its door? The French foreign minister, Hubert Védrine, was one of several people who suggested to me that the events of September 11 could actually impede the long-awaited eastward enlargement of the EU to include countries of the former Soviet bloc. Védrine pointed to these new, rigorous EU standards of police, judicial, and frontier control: here was yet another hurdle that countries like Poland would have to jump before being admitted. Védrine's comment was not merely an analytical contribution. If the French foreign minister says this to me now, it means that France (and others) might next year raise a specific objection to including this or that Central or East European state—many of which have weak and corrupt police forces, judicial systems, and customs services.[1] In this way, the effect of September 11 might even be to slow down the larger unification of Europe.

Has the attack helped to consolidate a European foreign policy? Not unambiguously. Yes, the EU's high representative for foreign and security policy, Javier Solana, is playing an active part in promoting peace talks in the Middle East. Yes, the leaders of Europe's three most

---

1. The prime minister of Bulgaria—who, in another example of Europe's rich diversity, is actually the former king, known in his current office as Mr. Simeon Saxe-Coburg Gotha—told me that he was shocked by the way in which whole trucks conveying contraband were being

important military powers, Britain, France, and Germany, have closely
coordinated their approach. But that has provoked resentment among
the rest. The increasingly operatic EU president, Romano Prodi, threw
a fit because the British, French, and German leaders held a private
meeting about the war immediately before an EU summit in Ghent.
This was not, Prodi suggested, the true community spirit.

When Tony Blair recently tried to hold a working dinner about the
war at No. 10 Downing Street, with just the German chancellor and
the French president and prime minister invited, the Italian prime
minister, Silvio Berlusconi, insisted on joining them. So Blair felt he
had to include his friend José María Aznar as well. Then the Belgian
prime minister, Guy Verhofstadt, invited himself, since Belgium currently holds the rotating presidency of the EU. That meant also having Mr. Solana, as Europe's Mr. Foreign Policy. Finally—to turn the
episode into pure Feydeau farce—the Dutch prime minister, Wim
Kok, tipped off by the Belgians, rang up to say it would be a "good
idea" if he came too, and arrived forty-five minutes late in the back of
a London police car.

The comedy of this dinner party illustrates the tension between
two versions of "European foreign policy." On the one hand, there is
the ideal of the 1992 Maastricht Treaty, that all fifteen member states
should speak with a single voice, through Mr. Solana or the government currently holding the EU presidency. On the other, there is the
reality in, for example, the Balkans, which is that the major European
powers—always Britain, France, and Germany; often Italy; sometimes Spain; in future perhaps Poland—make policy in close coordination with the United States, and the rest of the EU follows, with a
few adjustments at the margin. This tendency is strengthened by the

---

allowed through by Bulgarian customs officers. However, said the King (as everyone still calls
him informally) in his slightly old-fashioned English, he would not tolerate such "hanky-
panky" and had invited "some German chaps" to help sort it out.

Bush administration's preference for pick-and-choose "coalitions of the willing" in the present war. (Many are willing but few are chosen.) But some major European powers, especially Britain and France, also prefer it this way. "*Il y a une directoire*," a senior French diplomat said to me over lunch in Paris, with emphasis and approval, meaning, there is a directorate of the three major powers in the EU. The United States may be comfortable with that. Indeed, Henry Kissinger has suggested the rebirth of the nineteenth-century Quadruple Alliance, now to comprise the United States, Britain, France, and Germany.[2] Everyone else in Europe hates the idea.

Underlying these political struggles are deeper questions of identification and identity. Many Europeans do not identify with "Europe" as a political organization or force. According to the EU's own Eurobarometer polls, less than half those asked think EU membership is a good thing for their country. In the Taberna La Dolores, a tapas bar in central Madrid, Carlos Molinas, a twenty-eight-year-old unemployed lifeguard, explained: "People don't feel European; they feel English or Spanish." "Europe," he told me, "is a politicians' project. It doesn't reach down to the people in the street." Whereas, he said, the United States of America reaches down to virtually every household—as we've seen so vividly since September 11. He had the impression that every American home has its American flag, its pride, its sense of belonging to a larger political community.

Pro-European intellectuals put it differently. We have, they say, to ask the question "Why Europe?"—and find a good answer to it. One can view this questioning in two ways. One can see it as a symptom of crisis. Few Americans ask "Why America?" Until recently the British

---

2. American, British, German, and French ministers or officials already meet to coordinate foreign and security policy in an informal grouping known as the "Quad." There is also the "Quint," which includes Italy, and the Contact Group, originally set up to deal with the Balkans, and including Russia as well.

did not ask "Why Britain?" The anthropologist Mary Douglas once observed that the strongest institutions are the invisible ones. Similarly, the strongest political identities are the unquestioned ones. Ten years ago, in a dynamic period of the EU's development, few bothered to ask "Why Europe?" Now they do. More hopefully, one could regard this as a symptom of something in the making. We ask "Why Europe?" as Italians in the Risorgimento asked "Why Italy?" This being Europe, the reality is a bit of both, but rather more of the former.

Identities are usually defined not just by what you are for and who you are with, but above all by who or what you are against, or what you feel is against you. This is often an outright enemy, but it may just be a great rival—the other team, so to speak. In the jargon of identity studies, it is the Other. The deepest question posed to Europe by this war is: Who or what is Europe's Other? During the cold war, the answer was plain. Europe's Other was the threat from the Communist "East." Much of the integration of Western Europe in the European Economic Community can be understood as a response to that threat. There were other Others, too: Europe's own bloody past was a kind of historical Other, the United States a very important rival for Gaullists of all countries. But this was the main one.

Since the end of the cold war, Europe has been a continent in search of its Other. However, as I have recently argued, in the 1990s many European intellectuals, especially on the left, found the Other in the United States.[3] Europe was to be defined as the Not-America. This worked at several levels. At the most quotidian, Europe was to be about the defense of a certain way of life, with its traditional foods and drinks—the baguette, the cheese, the wine, the espresso, the schnapps—and the long lunch breaks to enjoy them, its old customs, and extraordinarily rich culture of living well. This idea is particularly strong in France. "To say it very simply," Hubert Védrine told

---

3. See my article "Odd Man Out," in *The New York Review*, November 1, 2001.

me, "Europe should be the best place in the world to live." Reminding me that in Germany, when one wants to convey that someone enjoys the good life, one says, "he lives like God in France," Védrine suggested that Europe should be about us Europeans all living like God in France. A rather self-congratulatory idea perhaps, and a little old-fashioned—for many young Europeans feel that God now lives in California—but one with resonance nonetheless, for millions of Europeans.

The underpinning for this way of life was to be found in a different model of the organization of a democratic capitalist economy and society, placing more emphasis than the United States on the state as welfare provider, on public services, solidarity, social justice, the environment, and quality of life. The EU was seen as a means to preserve this "social Europe" in a globalized world of brutal competition. Being big and united, Europe could enjoy the benefits of globalization without paying the price in the sort of stripped-down Americanization that a Polish friend complained to me is now spoiling his country. We could, as the French prime minister, Lionel Jospin, put it, have the market economy without the market society.

Finally, Europe was to be a counterweight to the crude, brash, only-surviving-superpower, with its misguided policy in the Middle East, its lamentable record on aid to the third world, and a general tendency to throw its weight around. Hubert Védrine famously coined the term *hyperpuissance*—hyperpower—to describe this American monster, although he now assured me that his term was "purely analytical." An Italian post-Communist talked of needing Europe to "balance" the power of the United States—"balance" being the polite word. These resentments and longings were initially strengthened by the arrival of President George W. Bush, seen by many in Europe as a unilateralist Texan cowboy.

Indeed, there has been much criticism of the United States during the war, and many Europeans argue that September 11 shows the need for a more sophisticated, multilateral approach to a complex, often nasty world. But it is more difficult to define yourself primarily against America at a time when America and Europe both seem to be under attack, as part of one Western, Christian or post-Christian, materialist, decadent civilization.

In that attack, Osama bin Laden thrusts upon Europe the prospect of another Other, at once very new and the oldest of them all. For "Europe" was originally defined as a conscious entity in the conflict with the Islamic world. The first political usage of the term comes in the eighth and ninth centuries, as the descendants of the Prophet—the "infidels," in Christian parlance—are thrusting, by force of arms linked to a faith that we would now call fanatical, into the underbelly of Europe. "Europe" begins its continuous history as a political concept in the fourteenth and fifteenth centuries, first as synonym for, then as successor to, the Crusaders' notion of Christendom—and once again, its Other is plainly the Arab-Islamic world.[4]

There is a real temptation to revive that ancient European bogey. While I was traveling around the continent, one European leader spectacularly succumbed to the temptation. The Italian prime minister, Silvio Berlusconi, told Italian journalists that we should have confidence in the superiority of our culture. "The West," he said, "given the superiority of its values, is bound to occidentalize and conquer new people. It has done it with the Communist world and part of the Islamic world, but unfortunately a part of the Islamic world is 1,400 years behind."[5] The sentiment would have been applauded by the

---

4. This is explored in several splendid works of historical scholarship, including Denis Hay's *Europe: The Emergence of an Idea* (Edinburgh University Press, 1957) and Bronislaw Geremek's *The Common Roots of Europe* (Polity Press, 1996).

5. Quoted in a report by Steven Erlanger, *International Herald Tribune*, September 27, 2001. The original Italian quotations, as noted down by the *Corriere della Sera* correspondent present at the briefing, can be found at www.corriere.it/Primo_Piano/Esteri/09_Settembre/26 /berlusconi.shtml.

Knights Templar and Pope Pius II. In a volcanic essay, the veteran Italian journalist Oriana Fallaci added, "We might as well admit it. Our churches and cathedrals are more beautiful than their mosques." And she described Arab immigration to Italy as "a secret invasion."[6] Is it an accident that these two voices come from Rome, the center of Western Christendom?

However, this is not just about Western Christendom. President Vladimir Putin's remarkable strategic response to September 11, immediately and strongly positioning Russia with Europe and the West, is justified ideologically by the claim—deep-rooted though not undisputed in the history of Russian self-identification—that the world of Eastern Christendom, of Orthodoxy, stands on the front line against Islamic and "Asiatic" barbarism (typified for Putin by Chechen and Afghan "terrorists"). Samuel Huntington has advanced the notion that a dividing line of clashing civilizations runs through Eastern Europe, between "Western Civilization," including both the Europe of Western Christendom and North America, and "Orthodox Civilization," including Russia. Putin replies that the true line runs between a West that includes all of post-Christendom and a threatening East exemplified by Islamic Central Asia. The voice of "the third Rome" (Russia) reinforces those from the second Rome. And Berlusconi actually made his now notorious remarks after a meeting with Vladimir Putin.

Most European leaders and intellectuals of course reject this polemical (re)construction of our identity. Even if some claim of cultural superiority were justified—and the record of European barbarism in the twentieth century should make us humble in that regard—it would be madness for Europe to embrace this rhetoric. The entire West is already at risk of alienating Muslims throughout

---

6. Quoted in a report by Melinda Henneberger, *International Herald Tribune*, October 31, 2001. Fallaci's article was in *Corriere della Sera*, September 29, 2001.

the world in what George W. Bush once ill-advisedly called our "crusade." This would be particularly dangerous for Europe, which sits just a few miles north and west of a diverse, frustrated, and in large parts impoverished Islamic and Arab world, in what Europeans used to call the *Near* East, in North Africa, the Caucasus, and Central Asia. Above all, it would be suicidal for a continent in which perhaps as many as twenty million Muslims already live.

As I write these lines, I am sitting in North Oxford. The newsagent from whom I bought today's newspapers is Muslim. The local pharmacist is Muslim. The young woman working at the cleaners is Muslim. They are all courteous, friendly, highly competent people, speaking perfect English, and, so far as I can see, at once accepting of and fully accepted in British society. Until September 11 it would not have occurred to me to describe them as "Muslims," any more than I would describe the local post office manager or hardware dealer as "Christians." Yet now we hear on the radio the voices of British Muslims saying that Islam, not Britain, is their homeland, and they are going to fight for the Taliban. They represent a tiny, no, an infinitesimal, minority of British Muslims, but they are the ones that catch the headlines— and simple-minded people will start to get suspicious of all Muslims. I am told by friends in a position to know that even wholly peaceful, liberal-minded, and moderate British Muslims have felt a certain crisis of identity, even before September 11. It is now all the more important that we help them feel at home.

Although London and a few other English cities have their share of Islamic radicals, Britain is still relatively fortunate in the civic integration of Islamic minorities. The Turkish communities in Germany, for example, are less well integrated. A senior German politician told me that Germany has more extremist teachers of Islam than Turkey does. In a working-class quarter of Madrid, I spoke to a twenty-three-year-old illegal immigrant from Morocco called Yacine. Yacine came to Spain hidden under a bus. He does not have the papers to get a job, so he lives by stealing. "I live," he said, "like a wolf." Did he think the Western response to September 11 was directed against Islam? "Yes, it's an attack on Islam." Many of his relatives in Morocco, he added, "think the Jews will have a part in the attack—and so do I."

Muslims in Europe will not be reassured simply by President Bush or Tony Blair pronouncing, as fresh-baked Koranic scholars, that Osama bin Laden's message is a perversion of Islam. As the French writer Olivier Roy has argued, we need a much deeper reflection on what it means to talk of European Muslims or "European Islam." The very notion challenges those deep assumptions about Europe as post-Christendom that one often glimpses beneath the elevated rhetoric of European unification.[7]

We must therefore hope that this latest new-old Other is immediately put back in its box, and the lid firmly closed—although many Muslims will already suspect that Berlusconi was merely saying what Europeans really think. Meanwhile, the Russian Other is largely gone, especially if Putin continues his pro-Western course. The American Other remains a candidate, but one that looks rather out of place in the post–September 11 world. In the end, it will never fit the bill, for Europe and America are not, in fact, two separate civilizations, but one, albeit containing a wide spectrum of social, economic, and political models, ranging from the American right to the French left. And there is no other Other in sight.

Thus the task for those who believe, as I do, in a project called "Europe" is to build a strong, positive European identity, one that binds people emotionally to a set of institutions, without the help of a

7. Some may say that the EU's decision to admit Turkey contradicts that, and it is a significant step. But Turkey's candidacy was hotly disputed on just these cultural lines, Turkey is being treated differently from other candidates, and anyway, Turkey is being encouraged precisely so it should *not* become an Islamic state.

clear and present Other. The current war clarifies that task, but also complicates it. For the time being, I must conclude that this is yet another defining moment at which Europe declines to be defined.

—November 14, 2001

PANKAJ MISHRA

The Afghan Tragedy

1.

IN AFGHANISTAN IN 1996 the Taliban inherited a profoundly damaged country; and five years later, the tasks of reconstruction and healing were more urgent, even before the US bombing began. The Taliban government's budget for the last year of their regime amounted to $82 million—and the meagerness of this sum for a country geographically bigger than France only tells part of the story. More than half of the income was expected to come from the semi-extortionate toll taxes imposed by their Mujahideen predecessors and continued by the Taliban; and more than half of those revenues were swallowed by the contingency fund to support the wars against the Tajiks in northern Afghanistan, formerly headed by Ahmed Shah Massoud, and against the Shia Hazaras in the central highlands. The outlay for development was only $343,000, while the ministry that looked after the *madrasas*, religious schools, received $14 million, which in turn was five times more than the allocation for the Ministry of Health.[1]

In a country seething with endemic disease, and with the second-highest infant mortality rate in the world, these priorities look nothing

---

1. All statistics are taken from the Pakistani newspaper *Dawn*, June 4, 2001. They do not include revenues from the opium trade.

but skewed. The outlay for the powerful Ministry for the Promotion of Virtue and Prevention of Vice—which punished those whose beards were not the prescribed eight centimeters long, and those who did not observe prayers and fasts, and worked hard to ensure that male minds remained free of the sinful thoughts incited by the presence of unveiled women—was three times as much as that for development. For Mullah Omar and his advisers from the rural clergy, it was enough to be pious and virtuous, and a healthy Islamic society would be created by itself. And the punishment for those who strayed from virtue was draconian: adulterers were stoned to death, women were known to have the tips of their thumbs cut off for wearing nail polish. Not surprisingly, such cloud-cuckoo-land ideas—partly the result of their limited *madrasa* educations—and their brutal consequences made the Taliban increasingly unpopular among even the Pashtuns in the countryside who, oppressed by the Mujahideen, had initially welcomed them as liberators.

In the derelict Pashtun village I visited east of Kabul last spring, five months before the attacks on the World Trade Center and the Pentagon, in an area heavily bombed and mined by the Soviet military, people talked, as they did elsewhere, of the irrelevance—indeed the nonexistence—of the Taliban government and the good deeds of the white men from the foreign NGOs and the UN, who were active all through the last two decades of war, supplying seeds, food, and health care, and who—like the aid workers arrested for allegedly preaching Christianity—worked in constant danger of being kidnapped and beaten up by the Taliban.

There were three Afghans sitting on the floor of the bare, low-roofed room, all of them in their late forties, variously disabled during the anti-Communist jihad, and prematurely aged, even the dim light from the lantern seeming harsh on their sunburned wrinkled faces and wiry gray beards. The village now had only some disabled and elderly-seeming men like these. The soldiers in black turbans

I had seen hurtling around the dirt roads in the back of Toyota pick-ups came regularly to look for fit young men. Those young men who had escaped the draft had fled to Pakistan, where many of their relatives already lived in the much worse conditions of the refugee camps.

The conversation inside the room was of the quality of seeds, the lack of fodder and drinking water for the livestock, and the refugees from the war in the north, who, turned away at the border with Pakistan, were now draining away the already meager supply of food and water in the province. The three-year-long drought had created, along with the continuing civil war, more than half a million internal refugees. It wasn't as severe here as in central and northern parts of Afghanistan; but most of the land was still uncultivated. The harvest from last year's seeds had been poor; it had been just enough to feed a few families. The news had come of white men—most probably volunteers of the World Food Program—distributing new seeds in a nearby town. The news was good; but there remained the complicated negotiation about how to divide the harvest from the seeds; there remained the long journey to the town, on foot and on trucks, past many checkpoints where the bribes—corruption, despite the draconian Islamic punishments, flourishing as usual—could be very steep.

Outside, in the courtyard, where tufts of grass grew wild in the cracks of the mud walls, an emaciated cow slumped on the ground; and somewhere inside the rooms around it I could sense the presence of women, could hear occasionally the rustle of thick cloth and the clink of pots and pans. Later one of them hurried across the courtyard to throw some leftovers of the dry bread served to us to the cow: a brisk, silent figure in the dusk, whose shapeless heavy chadori, with the narrow mesh across her eyes, seemed in that brief moment like the habit of a viciously persecuted medieval sisterhood.

But it was the outsider's vision: according to Nancy Hatch Dupree, a distinguished writer on Afghan issues, the chadori has usually been worn by village women as a status symbol—a sign of their husband's education or employment—and was more common in the towns and cities. Under the Taliban you could still glimpse women without it in the villages, where everyday life has been traditionally autonomous of what goes on in the cities. As Dupree saw it, women in rural Afghanistan, where 90 percent of the country's approximately 20 million people still live, were less vulnerable to the Taliban's arbitrary brutality. Dupree mentions instances of women being beaten and killed outside Kabul, but on the whole they weren't as much affected by the restrictions and controversies arising out of the Taliban's harsh gender and other policies as women in the cities. Of the minuscule 3 percent of school-age Afghan females who went to school during Communist rule, the majority came from the urban areas. It is the women in the cities, encouraged into education and employment by Zahir Shah, the Communists, and, most recently, the UN agencies, who suffered most.[2]

The rural–urban divide has always complicated the process of change in Afghanistan, as it has in many underdeveloped countries. So have the heavy-handed ways in which change has often been imposed upon the countryside from above, by the country's tiny, Westernized, and mostly non-Pashtun, Persian-speaking urban elite in Kabul. The rural elite of religious and tribal leaders has tended to respond to their efforts at modernization by going back even further into time. In 1929, conservative mullahs bullied women back into thicker chadoris and sacked museums and libraries after overthrowing the liberal-minded King Amanullah, who had abolished the veil, opened coed schools, and ordered Afghans in Kabul to wear Western clothes. Not until 1959 did women appear without the chadori on the streets of Kabul, and this continued for over thirty-five

2. See Nancy Hatch Dupree, "Afghan Women Under the Taliban," in *Fundamentalism Reborn? Afghanistan and the Taliban*, edited by William Maley (NYU Press, 1998). For a detailed historical and anthropological account, see Louis Dupree, *Afghanistan* (Princeton University Press, 1980).

years, until they faced the cruelest restrictions yet on their freedom of movement and dress.

The Afghan Communists had encouraged women in Kabul to wear skirts and employed them in the government. This was part of their plan to modernize Afghanistan. New textbooks sent out to the villages carried an image of three men in European suits leading a traditionally dressed crowd to a glorious future. Volunteer teachers in the literacy campaign forced old men and girls to attend classes while at the same time, and often in the same villages, the Communists were arresting and massacring tens of thousands of young Muslim men.

Much of the chaos and violence suffered in Afghan villages during the Communist era was engineered by a Westernized elite at the head of an active government in Kabul—a city which, with its Persian-speaking population and apparently liberated women, was already alien to most Pashtuns. This may partly explain why the sons of Pashtun peasants and nomads who made up the Taliban imposed their harshest laws upon the women of Kabul soon after driving out the moderate Islamist Tajik commander Ahmed Shah Massoud from this most Westernized of Afghan cities in 1996 and forcing him to the north. (Some 35 to 45 percent of the population is Pashtun. The majority is made up of Tajiks, Uzbeks, Hazaras, and others.) Suddenly, in yet another Afghan regression, women found themselves sentenced to the chadori and confined to their homes. They could neither educate themselves nor work—Dupree estimates that the prohibitions directly affected anywhere between 40,000 to 150,000 working women and about 100,000 girls at school. Women had to be accompanied by male relatives outside their homes, where the possibility of public humiliation—usually beatings with sticks but also harsher punishments—by the religious police was ever-present.[3]

---

3. In 1996, the Taliban's radio announced that 225 women in Kabul had been beaten in a single day for violating the dress code. Soon afterward, Mullah Omar warned that Taliban officials

The Taliban claimed they were shielding women from the sexual predation they had suffered in the days of the Mujahideen warlords. A Taliban official, who had studied at a *madrasa* in Pakistan, told me that he couldn't trust his men with unveiled women; and in any case Mullah Omar, whose original mission had allegedly been to protect women from rapists and bandits, had to preserve at all costs the Taliban's reputation as uncorrupted men who had brought peace and security and "true Islam" to Kabul.

The Taliban official wouldn't be drawn into a discussion of what "true Islam" was or could be. But then what he really seemed to be articulating was the deep and longstanding fear and resentment of Western lifestyles, particularly the independence of women, among Pashtun men in the countryside—the modern ways that the Communists had brutally imposed upon Afghanistan, and that Kabul, with the presence of foreign aid workers there, represented. Mullah Omar expressed his contempt by staying away altogether from what remained the official capital of Afghanistan and living in Kandahar. For the rural men who dominated the Taliban, the women in Kabul and other Afghan cities, the relatively modern Shia and Persian-speaking minorities, the Communists of the past, and the foreign aid workers of today were part of the same large, undifferentiated threat to the Pashtun dictatorship that they, with some help from the *sharia*, or Islamic law, wished to maintain.[4]

These complex social and economic resentments help to explain why the Taliban, while ruthless with the Shias and NGO workers, did

responsible for such public punishments of women would be treated as "great sinners." But these kinds of punishments continued to occur in Kabul. Dupree attributes them to both corruption and an excess of Islamic zeal among the Taliban's rank and file.

4. The politicization of the poor, unrepresented masses in such Muslim countries as Algeria, Turkey, and Iran has also led to a cultural regression especially with respect to women, and, in some cases, to the irony of secular ruling elites trying to maintain with brute military force the rights of women.

not curtail the religious practices of the five thousand or so mostly poor Hindus and Sikhs in Afghanistan, even though the latter were briefly required—to avoid harassment from the religious police, the Taliban claim—to carry yellow identification badges at all times. They also help to explain the many incidents such as the one in which the religious police, who were answerable only to Mullah Omar in Kandahar, closed down an Italian-funded hospital in mid-May after they caught women workers dining with the male staff. In June, the UN closed down a food program for 300,000 people in Kabul because the Taliban refused to let Afghan women work for it.

There were fewer such problems in the rural areas, where women, confined to looking after their families, appeared part of the pre-modern moral order Mullah Omar apparently wished to recreate. You sensed that there was paradoxically a slightly greater freedom available to the women you saw traveling in the same buses as men, if in segregated rows, than to the women in Kabul, where the lines were clearly drawn.[5]

UNESCO had supported the Communist literacy campaign which was opposed by many Muslims; and during the anti-Communist jihad in the Eighties many UN agencies and other NGOs carried on, among other development projects, the tasks of women's education and empowerment in Communist-controlled Kabul. When the UN agencies argued that the Taliban had to allow Afghan women to work—particularly as nurses and doctors, since under the Taliban women could not be treated by men—the hard-line leaders of the Taliban interpreted such insistence as further proof of the UN's complicity with the various forms of Western imperialism—cultural, social, military—that they imagined were arrayed against them. The

---

5. The NGO workers I spoke to attested to a relatively lax atmosphere in the countryside. See also Chapter 11, "Hostages," in Michael Griffin, *Reaping the Whirlwind: The Taliban Movement in Afghanistan* (London: Pluto, 2001).

consequences for keeping women confined to their homes included cases of severe depression and suicide.[6]

This is where some earlier exposure to the outside world might have helped—one can't overestimate the value, in these circumstances, of the small educated Afghan middle class that twenty years of war dispersed across the world. But the Pashtun village mullahs who formed the central leadership of the Taliban knew little else besides the Koran. This is why the Taliban, unlike such radical Islamist groups as the Muslim Brotherhood of Egypt and Pakistan's Jamiat-i-Islami, offered no coherent ideology or doctrine—as distinct from the fatwas that emanated randomly from Kandahar against women, idolatry, kite-flying, football, music, dancing, squeaky shoes, and American hair styles.

Their aggressive puritanism—which includes a distrust of Shia Muslims, hundreds of whom were massacred by Taliban soldiers in the last five years—is far from the twentieth-century modernist ideologies of Islam that influenced an earlier generation of Afghan Islamists: Professor Burhanuddin Rabbani, the president of Afghanistan for two years in the early 1990s, was a graduate of the al-Azhar university in Cairo, while Mullah Omar doesn't have the basic educational qualifications you need to call yourself a mullah.

The harsh arbitrariness of the mullahs in Kandahar and the religious police went under the name of "true Islam," but it sought for the most part to reconfigure the old Pashtun dominance over Afghanistan's ethnic minorities—a new alignment of power that imposed Pashtun tribal ways over nearly all of Afghanistan and made unassailable the Pashtun religious elites in the villages that for the last century were continuously threatened and undermined by the modernizing rulers of Afghanistan in Kabul.

---

6. More than two thirds of the female respondents in a survey conducted in Afghanistan in 1998 said they had contemplated suicide. See *Women's Health and Human Rights in Afghanistan: A Report by Physicians for Human Rights*, www.phrusa.org.

The obstinacy and destructiveness of the Taliban are part of the history of Afghanistan's calamitous encounter with the modern world. Afghanistan missed the nineteenth century, which was a period of new beginnings for many old societies in the region. No country was less equipped to deal with the twentieth-century ideologies of communism, anticommunism, and radical Islam. No country was less prepared for the assortment of strategists and adventurers, people alien to and uncomprehending of Afghanistan, who managed to enlist the country's already great inner turmoil—the tragic violence and disorder of a near-primitive society modernizing too fast—into the wider conflict of the cold war; who managed to introduce more effective means of destruction and left behind a ruin more extensive than any the Afghans had known in their war-weary history.

In retrospect the Taliban may seem as much a consequence of a brutalized society as the warlords they had once supplanted, and who as I write are seeking to replace them. The undereducated young men and former Mujahideen and village mullahs who made up what we know as the Taliban never seemed to be offering any coherent idea of the state or society during the last five years of drift and arbitrary cruelty. Still, their vengeful attitude toward women and ethnic minorities alone couldn't have caused their international isolation. What initially helped to further isolate the Taliban was their refusal to extradite Osama bin Laden to the United States, where he was wanted for, among many other crimes, the bombing of American embassies in Kenya and Tanzania in 1998 and the attack on the World Trade Center in 1993.

2.

During the anti-Communist jihad about 35,000 to 40,000 Muslim volunteers from the Middle East, North Africa, and Southeast Asia traveled to Pakistan and Afghanistan. Thousands of them were given military training at camps set up by Pakistani intelligence, the Inter-Services Intelligence (ISI), with CIA and Saudi money, in Pakistan and Afghanistan. These volunteers, from whom have emerged the majority of the world's Muslim militants in the last decade, were part of a joint Saudi-Pakistani-American plan to organize a global jihad against the Soviet Union. Saudi Arabia, which was the first Islamic fundamentalist state in the world, was the prime sponsor of this jihad. Private and official donors in Saudi Arabia had long been bankrolling new *madrasas* in Pakistan, where an extreme Saudi version of Islam, Wahhabism, was preached.[7] The Saudis now matched dollar for dollar the American assistance to the jihad.

Osama bin Laden was one of the men assigned by Prince Turki al-Faisal, head of Saudi intelligence until this year, to help mobilize the foreign volunteers. Bin Laden's family owned one of the largest construction companies in Saudi Arabia, which was entrusted with the renovation of the holy Islamic sites at Mecca and Medina. The head of the family established two fellowships in Islamic studies at Harvard University in the early Nineties. Among the recent high-profile guests to the family's headquarters in Jiddah were former President George H. W. Bush and James Baker.

Bin Laden's early years don't much hint at his later interests. His Syrian mother wore Chanel suits without a burqa; his playmates were sons of Saudi princes. A recently excavated photograph shows him in Sweden at the age of fourteen, wearing bellbottoms and leaning against a Cadillac. Apparently he frequently got into fights over women in Beirut's tony clubs.[8] The profile matches that of the many rich Muslims and Hindus in the Indian subcontinent who turn to an austere

---

7. See S. V. R. Nasr, "The Rise of Sunni Militancy in Pakistan," *Modern Asian Studies*, Issue 34, 1, pp. 1329–1380 (Cambridge University Press, 2000).

8. See Mary Ann Weaver, "The Real bin Laden," *The New Yorker*, January 24, 2000.

form of religion after a listlessly decadent early youth. Such transfor-
mations often take place in countries where secular ideologies like
nationalism, socialism, and liberal capitalism are seen to have failed,
and where a shared faith appears to offer the only sense of political
and cultural community. It is not clear when and how bin Laden's
conversion happened but the Soviet invasion of a Muslim country
certainly seems to have given him a sense of purpose.

Contrary to the legend bin Laden encouraged about himself, he
did not throw himself into jihad immediately after the Soviet invasion
in 1979, the year he took his engineering degree, and he was not
much around on the Afghan battlefields. At first he traveled across
Saudi Arabia and other Gulf countries where he raised funds for the
Mujahideen in Afghanistan. When in 1984 he traveled to Peshawar,
the Pakistani city closest to the border with Afghanistan, and a front-
line city for the CIA-backed jihad, he brought his own construction
equipment into Afghanistan and built roads and hospitals and tunnels for the Mujahideen.

Ahmed Rashid, a respected Pakistani journalist, writes in his book
Taliban of bin Laden's intellectual insecurity and need for mentors.[9] In
Pakistan, he became a follower of Abdullah Azzam, a charismatic Palestinian Islamist who first set up the worldwide network of Muslim
militants that bin Laden is so often credited with having directed.
Azzam, who in the early Seventies had broken with the PLO on the
grounds that it was not Islamic enough, had first met bin Laden at the
King Abdul Aziz University in Jiddah, Saudi Arabia, where Azzam was a
teacher and bin Laden a student of civil engineering. Azzam had moved
to Pakistan soon after the Soviet invasion of Afghanistan and set up
Makhtab al-Khidmat, or Services Center, in Peshawar. The organization received money flowing in from Saudi Arabia and channeled

---

9. *Taliban: Militant Islam, Oil and Fundamentalism in Central Asia* (Yale University Press,
2000).

it toward Muslim volunteers and their families. During the 1980s, Azzam made twenty-six fund-raising trips to the United States; his organization had offices in Detroit and Brooklyn, and his activities were encouraged by the Reagan administration.[10]

By 1989, the year the Russians withdrew from Afghanistan, Azzam, as a founding member of Hamas, had already turned his attention to the Occupied Territories, where the first intifada had erupted the year before. In 1989, a few months after the Soviet withdrawal from Afghanistan, Azzam and his two sons were assassinated in Pakistan by a car bomb. No one knows who killed him—Peshawar in those days was a city of intelligence agencies and a whole lot of unexplained murders —although the locals I spoke to earlier this year mentioned Mossad and the CIA among the possible suspects.

After Azzam's death, bin Laden took over Makhtab al-Khidmat and set up an organization called al-Qaeda, or the Base, which continued Azzam's work: receiving money from private and government donors in the Gulf, helping volunteers for the jihad and their families, and coordinating their activities in Afghanistan, where they had bases and military camps constructed by the ISI with CIA and Saudi money. A lot of the Muslim extremists arrested around the world confessed to learning how to use explosives and light arms at these camps, which remained open after the Soviet Union had withdrawn from Afghanistan. In 1989 or 1990, bin Laden went back to his family business in Saudi Arabia, disappointed, he told journalists later, by the infighting among the Mujahideen. This may be one of his fictions, since the infighting did not start in earnest until well after 1990.

His political vision until this time seems to have been limited to

---

10. See "Making a Symbol of Terror," *Newsweek*, March 1, 1999. The blind Egyptian cleric Sheikh Omar Abdul Rahman, who was later convicted for the bombing in 1993 of the World Trade Center, was assisted by the CIA in his recruiting trips to the US in the Eighties. See "The Road to September 11," *Newsweek*, October 1, 2001.

expelling the infidel Russians from Afghanistan. In Saudi Arabia, which in the early Nineties was experiencing unemployment and political unrest after the end of the oil boom, bin Laden found new causes and mentors. He came under the influence of two militant clerics who were part of the fast-growing Islamist opposition to what was widely perceived—even in the US State Department annual reports—as a corrupt, incompetent, and brutal Saudi regime. He was already critical of the Saudi royal family when, as it turned out, another cause presented itself to him. In August 1990, Saddam Hussein invaded Kuwait. Bin Laden immediately offered to raise an army of Arab volunteers—the kind he had been part of in Afghanistan—for the defense of Saudi Arabia. Much to his shock, the Saudi royal family ignored him and invited half a million American troops into Saudi Arabia.

This was the beginning of a new phase in bin Laden's career. According to Ahmed Rashid, he claimed to be outraged by the proximity of American soldiers, some of them women in un-Islamic dress, to the holiest sites of Islam. To him, it was no less offensive than the presence of Russian infidels in Afghanistan. That thousands of American troops stayed in Saudi Arabia after the Gulf War ended in 1991 offended bin Laden more. He began to openly denounce the Saudi royal family, and eventually was declared persona non grata after he accused the Saudi interior minister of being a "traitor to Islam." In 1991 or 1992 bin Laden moved to Sudan, where an Islamist regime had come to power in the early Nineties and which had become a sanctuary for Muslim militants from Tunisia, Algeria, Iran, Palestine, and Egypt.

In Sudan bin Laden established himself as a businessman but also began to gather around himself some of the Muslim militants, also known as "Arab Afghans," he had met during the jihad in Afghanistan. Among them were refugees from Hosni Mubarak's crackdown on radical Islamists in Egypt, such as Ayman al-Zawahiri, who allegedly ranked second to bin Laden in al-Qaeda, and other Muslims who were enraged by America's military humiliation of Iraq, the continuing presence of American troops in Saudi Arabia, and the pro-American attitudes of the Arab ruling elites. They either worked in his businesses or allied themselves with the militant groups in various Muslim countries bin Laden is believed to have funded. The difficulty of separating business from political interests partly accounts for the persisting uncertainty about what al-Qaeda is, or was.

The Saudi royal family stripped bin Laden of his citizenship in 1994 and American and Saudi pressure on the Sudanese government led to bin Laden's departure from Sudan in May 1996. He flew with his four wives, children, and supporters to Jalalabad, the Afghan city closest to Pakistan, and sought refuge there with an Afghan Mujahideen commander he knew from the days of the anti-Soviet jihad. In July 1996, bin Laden gave an interview to Robert Fisk of *The Independent*, and demanded the withdrawal of American, French, and British troops stationed in Saudi Arabia—a demand that remained at the top of his agenda.

It was in Jalalabad, a month later, that bin Laden first met up with the Taliban, who were then in the middle of the blitzkrieg that would bring almost the whole of Afghanistan under their control by the end of the year. Rahimullah Yusufzai, a Pakistani journalist who interviewed bin Laden in 1998 and is probably the most reliable source of information about him, told me in Pakistan earlier this year that the leaders of the Taliban at first suspected bin Laden, on no clear basis, of supporting Massoud, the Tajik commander of the Northern Alliance, who still held Kabul at that point. The Taliban were won over probably by bin Laden's wealth, estimated to be between $200 and $300 million, which, Ahmed Rashid claims, bankrolled the Taliban's conquest of Kabul later that year. According to Yusufzai, the Taliban asked bin Laden to move to the southern city of Kandahar, where the reclusive Mullah Mohammad Omar was based. It is here that bin Laden was to spend the next five years in between spells at different hideouts across Afghanistan. During this time, bin Laden is believed to have provided the Taliban with financial and military support and, according to some unconfirmed reports, managed their money from the drug trade. The Taliban also allowed bin Laden to run the military camps in Afghanistan where thousands of Muslims from all over the world were trained.

In February 1998, bin Laden issued a manifesto for what he called "The International Islamic Front for Jihad against Jews and Crusaders," in which he denounced the United States for "occupying the lands of Islam in the holiest of places, the Arabian Peninsula, plundering its riches, dictating to its rulers, humiliating its people, and terrorizing its neighbors." He also spoke of the US bombing and economic blockade of Iraq and accused the US of turning Saudi Arabia, Iraq, Egypt, and Sudan into "paper statelets" in order to "guarantee Israel's survival." The manifesto went on to declare that

> to kill the Americans and their allies—civilians and military—is an individual duty for every Muslim who can do it in any country in which it is possible to do it, in order to liberate the al-Aqsa Mosque and the holy mosque [Mecca] from their grip, and in order for their armies to move out of all the lands of Islam, defeated and unable to threaten any Muslim.

In May 1998, bin Laden invited Pakistani journalists to Afghanistan and repeated this fatwa. Mullah Omar was reportedly furious with bin Laden for organizing the press conference without his permission, and told bin Laden that there could only be one ruler in Afghanistan. A few months later, bin Laden made a point of his loyalty to Omar in an interview with al-Jazeera, the TV station based in Qatar, praising the Taliban for attempting to establish an Islamic state in Afghanistan. He also said that the Taliban did not permit him to operate against any other state and that his "inability to move out of

Afghanistan" meant that he could only be an "instigator" in the jihad against America and Israel. However, the Muslims he had inspired were, he said, "largely active"; they were of "diverse nationalities" and had a "large margin of movement."

On August 7, 1998, a few months after bin Laden's fatwa, the US embassies in Kenya and Tanzania were bombed, killing 226 people. In November 1998, a Manhattan federal court issued an indictment containing 238 charges of terrorism against bin Laden: it held him responsible, among many other crimes, for the 1993 bombing of the World Trade Center, an assassination plot against President Clinton in 1994, and funding Islamist groups in New Jersey. It also identified bin Laden as a prime suspect in the bomb attack on American soldiers in Dhahran, Saudi Arabia, in 1996. In 1999, the United Nations Security Council passed a resolution condemning bin Laden for sponsoring international terrorism and imposed sanctions on the Taliban.

The trial held early in 2001 in New York of the four men accused of involvement in the bombing of US embassies in East Africa offered the fullest public account of al-Qaeda. One of the defendants, Wadih el-Hage, a US citizen, had fought in the anti-Communist jihad in Afghanistan and then had become bin Laden's private secretary in Sudan; he was not charged with the bombings but with participating in the global conspiracy that prosecutors said bin Laden had mounted against American lives and property. Two other defendants, a Saudi and a Tanzanian, who carried out the bombings, had trained in Afghanistan in the Nineties. The government's chief witness was Jamal Ahmed al-Fadl, a Sudanese citizen, who defected from al-Qaeda in 1996 after taking commissions worth $110,000 from a business owned by bin Laden, and who claimed to have been informed about bin Laden's attempt to acquire nuclear and chemical weapons. The portrait he provided of al-Qaeda made it seem unlike such tightly knit militant organizations as the Italian Red Brigades or the Palestinian Black September and more like a large clearinghouse which provided money, training, and logistical support to radical Islamist groups in Algeria, Yemen, Egypt, the Philippines, Russia (Chechnya), and many other countries.

Al-Fadl's testimony showed that the links between radical Islamists in the Middle East and Southeast Asia and bin Laden had been made during the anti-Communist jihad in Afghanistan. Many of these "Arab Afghans" were political dissidents who were escaping from their home countries. Most of them were from Egypt, of which Mohammad Atta, one of the September 11 hijackers, was a citizen, and where there had been a steady growth of radical Islamists in the late Eighties and early Nineties. Many of these Egyptian Islamists, such as bin Laden's deputy, Dr. Zawahiri, who some analysts believe took control of many of bin Laden's activities in al-Qaeda,[11] moved to safer places in Afghanistan, Sudan, or even the West, where they could plan attacks against President Mubarak and his closest ally, the United States. Sheikh Omar Abdul Rahman, who entered the US in 1990 with the CIA's assistance, had already established by 1993 an American network of sympathizers and donors for Egypt's radical Islamic groups—just before the time when the first of the hijackers of September 11, 2001, enrolled in a flight school.[12]

Similarly, in Algeria, the military's brutal suppression of FIS, the Islamist political party that swept the elections in December 1991, created extremist organizations like the Armed Islamic Group (GIA), one of whose sponsors is believed to be bin Laden, and whose members

---

11. See "The Hunt for Public Enemy No. 2," *The Guardian*, September 24, 2001.

12. In early 1996, when bin Laden was just becoming better known to US intelligence, the journalist Mary Ann Weaver met a Western diplomat in Pakistan who told her that many veterans of the Afghan jihad had established "an informal network of small, loosely organized underground cells, with support centers scattered around the world: in the United States, the Persian Gulf countries, Germany, Switzerland, Scandinavia, Sudan, Pakistan, and Afghanistan." See "Blowback," *The Atlantic Monthly*, May 1996.

in December 1994 hijacked an Air France plane with a view to crashing it into the Eiffel Tower but failed because of their lack of piloting skills.[13]

3.

The pronouncements of bin Laden, who has been the most visible of these militants, and certainly has the keenest instinct for publicity, served for some time as what Ahmed Rashid in *Taliban* calls a "simple, all-purpose explanation for unexplained terrorist attacks." According to Rashid, Washington was "not prepared to admit" that the Afghan jihad against the Communists before 1989 had, with the support of the CIA, "spawned dozens of fundamentalist movements across the Muslim world which were led by militants who had grievances, not so much against the Americans [as against] their own corrupt, incompetent regimes." But of the terrorism of radical Muslims in Algeria, Egypt, and elsewhere, Rashid writes,

> Bin Laden knew many of the perpetrators of these violent acts across the Muslim world, because they had lived and fought together in Afghanistan. His organization, focused around supporting veterans of the Afghan war and their families, maintained contacts with them. He may well have funded some of their operations, but he was unlikely to know what they were all up to or what their domestic agendas were.

---

13. Ramzi Ahmad Yousef, who is currently serving a long sentence in Colorado for the bombing of the World Trade Center in 1993, and whose true identity is still unknown, wanted to fill up a plane with explosives and crash it into the CIA headquarters in Virginia or an American nuclear facility. See "The Road to September 11," *Newsweek*, October 1, 2001.

In the last two years, bin Laden and al-Qaeda have also been linked by American authorities to the suicide attack on the USS *Cole* in Yemen; to Jordanians of Palestinian descent who were planning to attack Christian sites in Jordan during the millennium celebrations; and to an Algerian called Ahmed Ressam who was arrested at the US–Canadian border while carrying explosives in his car. Ressam was convicted earlier this year; facing a sentence of more than a hundred years in prison, he began to cooperate with the authorities and confessed to having trained in Afghanistan. He will be an important witness in the forthcoming trial of Zacarias Moussaoui, a French citizen of Moroccan descent who is the first to be indicted among the hundreds of men arrested in connection with September 11.

A clear picture of these Muslim extremists in different countries, who had, in bin Laden's own words, a "large margin of movement," and the precise nature of bin Laden's affiliations with them is only beginning to emerge. These extremists are commonly described by government officials and the media as al-Qaeda operatives; but it is not certain whether all of them have the kind of intimacy with and loyalty to bin Laden that, according to testimonies offered during the embassy bombings trial, are required for membership in al-Qaeda. For instance, there are not only Arabs among the foreign fighters in Afghanistan described as al-Qaeda forces but also Pakistanis sponsored and sent to Afghanistan by religious groups in Pakistan, about eight thousand of whom are currently missing in action. A lot of them are students from Pakistani *madrasas*, where many leaders of the Taliban were also educated.

According to *The New York Times*, Jean-Louis Bruguière, France's chief antiterrorism judge, acting on information "from one of Osama bin Laden's most important operatives in Europe," arrested plotters preparing to bomb the US embassy in Paris. His office also uncovered a "cell of al-Qaeda active in Europe and Canada" and pressed a French court to convict seventeen cell members for plotting terrorist attacks. Nevertheless he suspects that "neither the demise of the Taliban nor the capture of Osama bin Laden would diminish the terrorist threat" since many of the new extremists "do not need orders from Osama bin Laden."[14]

Bin Laden became the official prime suspect soon after September 11. Although the Bush administration backed out of its promise of publishing a white paper on the evidence against him, the British government produced, on October 4, three days before the beginning of the military campaign in Afghanistan, a detailed outline of the case against bin Laden, setting out his political views, modus operandi, and links with previous terrorist attacks.

The pages in the dossier about bin Laden's background and methods followed closely the US government's indictment against bin Laden and al-Qaeda in the embassy bombings trial; the dossier officially included the allegation that al-Qaeda participated in the killings of American soldiers in Somalia in 1993. While not citing specific sources, the last pages present the evidence related to September 11:

- In the run-up to 11 September, Bin Laden was mounting a concerted propaganda campaign amongst like-minded groups of people—including videos and documentation—justifying attacks on Jewish and American targets; and claiming that those who died in the course of them were carrying out God's work.

- We have learned, subsequent to 11 September, that Bin Laden himself asserted shortly before 11 September that he was preparing a major attack on America.

- In August and early September close associates of Bin Laden

---

14. "A Powerful Combatant in France's War on Terror," *The New York Times*, November 24, 2001.

were warned to return to Afghanistan from other parts of the world by 10 September.

• Immediately prior to 11 September some known associates of Bin Laden were naming the date for action as on or around 11 September.

• Since 11 September we have learned that one of Bin Laden's closest and most senior associates was responsible for the detailed planning of the attacks.

• There is evidence of a very specific nature relating to the guilt of Bin Laden and his associates that is too sensitive to release.[15]

But it is the video recording discovered in Afghanistan and released by the US government on December 12, and which shows bin Laden boasting about the success of September 11 before a legless former Arab Afghan fighter from Saudi Arabia and other supporters, that contains the most convincing evidence so far of his involvement. It is likely to have a much greater impact not only on the West but also on Muslim public opinion than anything so far made public. In this amateur recording, which was apparently made in Kandahar on November 9, bin Laden claimed considerable foreknowledge of the plot. On the tape he said that "we calculated in advance the number of casualties who would be killed, based on the position of the tower"; he named Mohammad Atta of "the Egyptian family" as having been "in charge," and said that among the hijackers "those who were trained to fly didn't know the others," and that "we did not reveal the operation to them until they boarded the plane."

---

15. An updated version of this document, published by the British government on November 14, 2001, can be found in the appendix to this volume, pp. 353–372.

He said that he had turned on his radio on the evening of September 11 because "we had notification since the previous Thursday that the event would take place that day." He claimed to have told his "overjoyed" supporters to "be patient" after the first plane hit the World Trade Center. He said he was "more optimistic than the others..., thinking that the fire from the gas would collapse the area where the plane hit and all the floors above it. That is all we hoped for."

The fact that the videotape was acquired and released for public viewing by the US government led many Muslims who distrust Western governments to automatically doubt its authenticity. But the tape should eventually help to further undermine bin Laden's status in much of the Muslim world, and give greater credibility to the military action in Afghanistan, which bin Laden in a recent video statement depicted as a "ferocious crusade campaign against Islam," a view disturbingly close to the one held by many people outside the West, even those unsympathetic to bin Laden, who see the American intervention in Afghanistan as an overbearing display of imperial power, part of a long tradition of punitive Western expeditions in Asia and Africa. This view has been reinforced by incidents such as the one near Mazar-e-Sharif, where hundreds of Taliban soldiers held captive in a fort were killed by Northern Alliance forces and US air strikes during an attempted uprising. British and US governments refused to hold an inquiry despite strongly worded questions about the suspected use of disproportionate force from Amnesty International, Human Rights Watch, and the UN commissioner for human rights. In other incidents, which the Pentagon initially claimed did not occur, more than a hundred civilians were killed by air strikes directed at the Tora Bora mountain caves where bin Laden was believed to be hiding.

4.

A large question for the future is how successful the strategy of splitting the Taliban will turn out to be. This strategy was promoted by, among others, Abdul Haq, the former Mujahideen commander who was captured and executed by the Taliban inside Afghanistan earlier this fall. With most of the Taliban leadership having survived the American bombing of Afghanistan, the strategy remains relevant, and has been taken up by Hamid Karzai, the US-backed Pashtun tribal leader from the south, who is now the prime minister in the UN-brokered new interim government of Afghanistan. It always had a good chance: for all their much-hyped fighting skills and religious fanaticism, the Taliban conquered most of Afghanistan through bribes paid to tribal chiefs and Mujahideen warlords. In fact, much of the Taliban's military capacity rested upon conscription and bluster, and destroying it through an infinitely superior firepower, or forcing the Taliban's hard-core fighters to retreat to the hills or to Pakistan, may prove much easier than meeting the challenge of social and political engineering that is thrown up by the formal collapse of the Taliban regime.

The students from the Afghan and Pakistani *madrasas*, and the Pashtun religious and tribal elites that organized themselves as the Taliban seven years ago, snatched power from the warlords, disarmed the population, and imposed a central authority upon much of Afghanistan for the first time in two decades, are not likely to go away. Pragmatism, rather than the desire for martyrdom, is likely to dictate the present attitudes of many of these Pashtuns, for whom the severe quasi-Islamic ideology of the Taliban has been primarily the means to power, and can be, in altered circumstances, as easy to trim as their beards. Certainly, American military might and the sudden empowering of anti-Taliban factions, Pashtun and non-Pashtun, alone don't explain the relatively swift crumbling of the Taliban–al-Qaeda forces in Afghanistan and the defections of middle-ranking Taliban commanders amid desperate appeals by Mullah Omar to "stand and fight."

What is becoming clearer is that the fanatical world view—the longing for a global jihad against America—was not very widely or profoundly shared among even the Pashtuns who had benefited most from the Taliban's rule over Afghanistan—and many of whom were subsequently relieved and happy when the Taliban lost power. What seemed from afar a monolithic alliance was mostly built upon the much narrower and fragile base of bin Laden's largesse and his personal friendship with and intellectual influence upon the hard-line leaders of the Taliban in Kandahar.

But to underestimate the power and influence of the rural Pashtun elites, to whom Mullah Omar and his advisers belong, just because the Taliban military appears to be in retreat, or to exclude Taliban members from any power-sharing arrangement in Afghanistan would likely turn out to be a mistake. Hamid Karzai appears to recognize this in calling for a general amnesty for Afghans—from which he, under American pressure, later exempted Mullah Omar—and reaching out to former leaders of the Taliban and tribal chiefs in the south as part of the UN-sponsored drive to create a broad-based government in Afghanistan. As a representative of the dominant Pashtun community that has always produced, apart from two short-lived exceptions, the ruling class of Afghanistan, Karzai's own credentials for coalition-building seem unusually broad-based, and further attest to the fluid nature of political identities in Afghanistan.

In the 1980s, Karzai, whose father headed the Pashtun tribe of the Popalzais in the south, acquired a degree in political science from the university in Simla, India, and helped channel aid from the CIA and the ISI to the Mujahideen fighting in the anti-Communist jihad. For two years from 1992, he was the deputy foreign minister in the short-lived post-Communist government of Mujahideen leaders in Kabul. Like many Pashtuns, he welcomed the Taliban as they went about imposing Pashtun rule over Afghanistan. He and his brothers run a chain of Afghan restaurants in Chicago, San Francisco, Boston, and Baltimore; his familiarity with America led the Taliban government in 1997 to name him as their representative to the United States before Mullah Omar canceled the appointment on the grounds that Karzai did not have a Taliban-style beard. Two years later, his father was assassinated, allegedly on the orders of the Taliban.

Karzai, who has lived in exile in the Pakistani city of Quetta since 1994, renewed apparently longstanding links with the US government when he entered Afghanistan in October, at about the same time as Abdul Haq, in order to provoke an anti-Taliban rebellion in the south, during which attempt he once had to be—although Karzai denies this—rescued by American Special Forces. He has also apparently maintained friendly contact with officials in the Pakistani government, which, made anxious by the anti-Pakistan positions of most of the Northern Alliance leaders, is somewhat reassured by the presence of a Pashtun leader in Kabul.

But in Kabul Karzai faces a tough challenge. During the early Nineties, when Karzai was deputy foreign minister in the coalition government of Mujahideen leaders, real power in Kabul rested with Ahmed Shah Massoud, the late Tajik leader and then defense minister, while Pashtuns and other ethnic group leaders occupied largely ceremonial posts. Then, as now, the city was militarily controlled by the Tajiks, a fact resented by the Hazaras, the Pashtuns, and the Uzbeks, and which eventually led to the four-year-long civil war that left 50,000 people dead in Kabul. The Tajiks at present hold the important portfolios of defense, interior, and foreign affairs in the interim government, and have demanded that the UN multinational forces to be based in and around Kabul be limited to five thousand soldiers. Karzai's position vis-à-vis these well-placed Tajiks in Kabul will depend on how much support he gathers for himself in the Pashtun-dominated south, which has been overrun by a host of Mujahideen commanders-turned-warlords.

These warlords emerged as a separate, altogether new elite in Afghanistan during the anti-Communist jihad, when traditional elites in the villages were dispersed by war, and loyalties often formed locally around the men who managed to get the largest amounts of guns and cash from the CIA and Saudi Arabia. One of these warlords, who later controlled Afghanistan's predatory economy of road tolls, smuggling, and opium cultivation, is Gul Agha Shirzai, who was the much-feared governor of Kandahar until his expulsion by the Taliban in 1994. Agha fought with American assistance against the Taliban in the recent battle for the city and was nominated to his old post by Karzai after a tense stand-off with a rival pro-Taliban mullah that almost erupted into a violent battle. It is hard to predict that the temptation of receiving foreign patronage—the billions of dollars that Western nations have promised to pour into Afghanistan if the conditions of a stable, broad-based government are met—would turn such war profiteers into moderate politicians, and how large a role the Northern Alliance, itself largely led by warlords, would allow them in the complicated process of governing Afghanistan. Some of them may well be content to reestablish the mini-empires of smuggling and opium and road tolls that the Taliban had broken up, and that in recent days are reported to be coming back.

As I write, Abdul Rashid Dostum, the notoriously ruthless leader of the Uzbek militia that controls the northern area around Mazar-e-Sharif, is hinting at going his own way and boycotting the interim government. Karim Khalili, who leads the Hazara Hizb-e-Wahadat party in the central highlands, is also reportedly dissatisfied with his role in the new arrangements in Kabul. However, both Dostum and Khalili are relatively secure in their own bases, unlike the Pashtun warlords in the south, some of whom have few or no affinities with the village mullahs and tribal chieftains who formed the social base of the Taliban in the countryside, and have even less support among the younger generation of Pashtuns in Pakistan which supported the

Taliban. Subdued at present, the Pashtuns of the Taliban are likely to reemerge as strong players in the future, whatever new ideological banners they organize themselves under.

Much of what these and other supplanted Pashtuns do next will of course depend on the authority acquired by Karzai and his allies, and how they are treated in the country they have grown accustomed to ruling—the country which from their perspective is once again beholden to a foreign power, and in large part controlled by local warlords or the shaky coalition of the Tajik, Shia Hazara, and Uzbek leaders, all of whom the Pashtuns of the Taliban see themselves as having comprehensively defeated in the past. For their part the non-Pashtun ethnic groups, who make up some 60 percent of the population, will resist any return to Pashtun domination.

In any case, humanitarian aid to Afghanistan seems a more urgent priority than political reconfiguration. The UN agencies have been warning of a human catastrophe: according to a statement by UNICEF in December, "Children are especially at risk. Almost 20 percent of the vulnerable population are children under the age of five. For them, hunger, illness, and cold conditions can easily lead to death. More than 100,000 Afghan children could perish in the next six months under the worst case scenario." Up to 1.5 million more Afghans are expected to join the five million refugees in countries neighboring Afghanistan, particularly Pakistan, where the refugee camps are already full and seething with disease and disaffection.

Compared to the billions of dollars spent on the anti-Communist jihad, humanitarian aid to Afghanistan in the last five years has been meager: from 1996 to 1998 the UN received an average of $58 million from donor nations for its aid programs, less than half of what it asked for. Last year, even as news of famines and epidemics kept pouring in from Afghanistan, the fund-raisers got less than half of the $221 million they hoped to collect: the aid worked out to $5 per Afghan, in contrast to the $48 per capita allocation in Angola.

The bombing of Afghanistan that began in early October initially disrupted the supply of aid to Afghanistan from agencies based in Pakistan and Iran, leaving up to six million Afghans who were being fed by the World Food Project exposed to starvation. On December 31, the World Food Project claimed to have averted the possibility of famine by trucking record quantities of food into Afghanistan. But few of the hundreds of NGO staff members who, working invisibly in remote, dangerous areas, and braving the hostility of the Taliban, had helped the Afghans to cope with their devastated country have been available to distribute food and medicine. Things were expected to get better after the defeat of the Taliban, but the gratifying scenes of new social freedoms being experienced by Afghans in the cities have managed to obscure the bad news from the countryside, especially the northern provinces, large parts of which have been rendered inaccessible to aid agencies by lawlessness and banditry—conditions unlikely to be improved much by the arrival of UN multinational forces in Kabul. It is not clear whether the transitional government will have forces that will protect delivery of aid.

A report from Oxfam last year reported families in the remote western province of Badghis saying that "they would not leave their villages because they felt they had nowhere to go and, even if they thought there was an escape they felt they had no way of getting there." When asked by the Oxfam representative what they planned to do, they said that "they expected to die." Even a superhuman effort at humanitarian aid may not forestall this grim future for many Afghans as winter sets in and the hunt for bin Laden and Mullah Omar and the remaining al-Qaeda leaders goes on in the terrifying blankness of Afghanistan, among the derelict villages, the dried-up canals and wells, the rotting dead animals, and the barren fields and orchards which—still treacherous with tiny invisible mines, many of them dropped from Russian helicopters long ago—had been awaiting, until September 11, seeds and water.

—*December 31, 2001*

THREATS

RICHARD L. GARWIN

The Many Threats of Terror

AS NO COMMISSION report could ever do, the terrorist acts of September 11, 2001, have galvanized the United States. More than six thousand people died in New York—one of every thousand workers in the city.[1] Taking over a commercial aircraft to use it as a piloted cruise missile evidently exploited a terrible vulnerability of modern society. No commercial pilot could be induced by threats to do this, but the imagination of public officials did not encompass those willing and even wishing to die to kill hundreds or thousands of others.

This instrument of kilo-terrorism is fragile; it can be defeated by not much more than a sturdy locked cockpit. The terrorist planners knew this and went to the trouble, and risked the vulnerability, of planning at least four such hijackings within minutes of one another—too little time to spread the word effectively throughout the aviation system.

My purpose here is to discuss threats and not primarily solutions, although the two are interlinked. If hijacking a passenger aircraft will no longer work, motivated terrorists will doubtless choose something else. I have heard from at least six of my colleagues proposals, for example, to modify the aircraft flight control system so that the pilots can irrevocably switch control to the ground. Or to program the

---

1. As of year's end 2001, the official figure has declined to about 3,000.

aircraft to automatically land at the nearest suitable airport. Such remedies are unnecessary and distracting. It is enough to lock a strengthened cockpit door and to make all understand that it would not be
opened even if hijackers kill the passengers and cabin crew. Clearly,
once the aircraft radar transponder is switched to emergency or hijack
mode, it should not be possible to switch it back until the aircraft has
landed. There is a case to be made for improved 1990s-era crash-proof
recorders that will capture video and audio from the cabin as well as
the cockpit.

Both smaller and bigger terror weapons exist, and their use may be
expected. But even if we have seen the end of hijacked passenger jets as
cruise missiles, that is not the end of their equivalent—the use of rented
or stolen cargo jets as piloted cruise missiles. Opportunities range from
large fleets such as those of UPS or Federal Express to the hundreds of
707s and even 747s available for lease at airports in the United States
and elsewhere. More skill but less violence would be involved in stealing such an aircraft. It might be used against buildings or against operating nuclear reactors, which are not designed to withstand the impact
of a jumbo jet at high speed. It is relatively simple to have an auto-
matic radar that shuts down a nuclear reactor if a high-speed aircraft
is detected within a few seconds of collision; but even in that condition
a reactor might suffer a core meltdown because of interference with
the emergency core cooling system and other engineered safeguards.

Thomas Friedman in his *New York Times* column of September 25
characterizes the new type of terrorist as evil, educated, and suicidal.
Of course, the terrorists don't characterize themselves as "evil" or
even "suicidal." A brief anecdote. After a few years of being involved
in building and testing nuclear weapons (from 1950 on, at Los
Alamos), I began to work on North American air defense, and in the
mid-1950s joined several panels of the President's Science Advisory
Committee (PSAC)—among them the Strategic Military Panel. This
panel met two days each month until the demise of PSAC in 1973.

I had already spent a month in Korea and Japan during the Korean War. I never understood why it was a source of comfort for some US strategists that the Soviet Union had not mastered in-flight aerial re-fueling of bombers; most people seemed to feel more secure in the knowledge that Soviet bombers armed with nuclear weapons would not have fuel to return home after a nuclear attack on the United States. I argued that I, for one, would be quite willing to participate in a one-way retaliatory nuclear strike on the Soviet Union, and I regard myself as rational—not suicidal.

Just as I struggled for years in Washington to bring cruise missiles into the US force rather than unmanned bombers (because of the rel-ative simplicity and increased payload of the one-way mission), so have committed terrorists found a way to exchange commitment for complexity. It is a powerful tool. During the 1960s I recall discussions with experts on terrorism in the PSAC and intelligence community who judged at the time that terrorists did not really want to kill peo-ple but to gain sympathy for their cause. Hence, it was said, they wanted to show their power to explode bombs at places and times of their choice, with a propensity to warn so as to reduce the damage.

Now that almost three times as many Americans have been killed in one day as died at Pearl Harbor, and twice as many as died in the entire history of the "troubles" in Northern Ireland, and without a demand being made, that old judgment must be definitively retired. And it doesn't take years of preparation for a person to gain access to an aircraft and to detonate a few-pound bomb disguised as a book or a computer, thus killing a few hundred people and further disrupting the modern economy.

It is doubtful that the terrorists had confidence that the World Trade Center towers would collapse—which they did, not from the impact but from the softening of the steel from the intense fire fed by the aircraft fuel. In fact, the amount of fuel in the form of paper in filing cabinets on a given floor is comparable with that delivered by the plane, but it is more difficult to ignite and easier to put out. It is entirely feasible to build into tall buildings features that would be adequate for fighting such fires and furthermore to equip buildings with means for rapidly bringing firefighters to any floor. This latter might be done on a World Trade Center–like structure by having a number of pulleys of twenty-ton capacity projecting from the roof, with a lead line down near ground level. Firefighters could snag the line and with a ground-based winch pull up a heavy cable which, in turn, could be used to carry platforms, hoses, and pumps to the floors involved. But it would be preferable to have dispersed foam nozzles in a hardened sprinkler system.

Terrorists have other means of turning the strength and assets of American society against itself. These include targeted attacks on chemical plants, but even more important, on shipments of industrial chemicals such as chlorine, which are transported in tank cars or trucks. The terrorist driver might apply for a job with the intent of fitting the tank truck with detonators and exploding it in a community; or such a truck might be ambushed and the material dispersed by a rocket-propelled grenade. While the use of nerve gas or other material would give a far higher number of casualties per ton of material, the vast amounts of dangerous chemicals that move in commerce make this a significant problem.

Some failures to protect particular vulnerable points would cause tremendous damage and inconvenience to modern society—at the major bridges and tunnels, for instance. Not only destruction but radiological contamination of tunnels could be very disturbing, even if it killed few people.

Detonating thousands of tons of ammonium nitrate loaded on a ship in a harbor would have the impact of a small nuclear explosion. Three hundred tons (0.3 kilotons) of ammonium nitrate apparently exploded in France on September 24, killing twenty-nine people and injuring more than 2,500.

Terrorist acts are possible that would be less significant in damage but highly significant in causing terror and weakening perceptions of American strength. Attacks on spectators in a sports stadium seem a particular hazard, especially in the case of events shown on TV. Such an attack could combine explosives and chemical agents; it could even be made by diving a small aircraft loaded with fuel into the stands. The attractiveness of such tactics to terrorists might be reduced by a several-second delay in TV transmission, so that there would be no broadcast, even if thousands of people were killed and several times that number injured.

Concerning nuclear and biological terrorism, the largest amount of damage would be caused either by a nuclear explosion in a city or by a biological warfare attack. It is abundantly clear that the same nineteen terrorists who hijacked the aircraft and destroyed buildings and thousands of lives in what seemed an instant would not have hesitated to detonate a nuclear explosive if they had acquired one. A first-generation (10-kiloton) nuclear explosive would kill at least 100,000 people in a typical urban environment. The theft and detonation of one of the 500-kiloton strategic weapons would probably kill a million people in an instant and flatten 100 square kilometers of buildings. Fifty-five years of development of technology and spread of knowledge make it relatively simple to build a 20-kiloton nuclear weapon if sufficient highly enriched uranium were available, of which there is a thousand-ton surplus in Russia. Much excess plutonium that was developed for making weapons is available as well, although it is somewhat more difficult to use. We must give the security of such materials the attention it deserves.

As for biological warfare, many tons of anthrax may still exist in Russia. Infection can be prevented by prior vaccination; but it is extremely durable as a spore and kills 30 percent or more of the people who have been infected, if there is no adequate prolonged treatment with antibiotics. Even more potentially dangerous are biological warfare agents that are contagious, by contrast with those, such as anthrax, that are simply infectious. High among the contagious agents is smallpox. Although legitimate stocks of smallpox have existed only in two places—in the US and in Russia—it is not precluded that other stocks may have survived the smallpox eradication campaign.

Even though some of these threats are ill-defined and it may be hard to prevent their being carried out, some nonspecific solutions are eminently practical. None will give 100 percent protection, but 99 percent protection could be the difference between a million deaths and ten thousand deaths. In a war, that is a great difference. To the 99 percent, it is the difference between life and death. And some of the solutions can be implemented by individual families, corporations, or localities.

The first and most practical defense against biological warfare attack is to maintain "positive" pressure of filtered air within buildings. It takes a very small capital expenditure and a very small expenditure in power to provide a positive pressure so that normal winds will not infiltrate a building, and the anthrax spores or other microbes will be kept out. To do this the air intake to a normal building— whether an office building, an apartment building, or a private house —should be provided with a small blower that delivers air through a High Efficiency Particulate Air filter (HEPA) at a rate that exceeds the leakage of air in or out of the building. Such "makeup" air will then produce excess pressure in the building so that air flows out through any cracks or apertures, blocking any inflow of unfiltered air. If no form of air intake exists, a window or a portion of a window can be removed to make one. It is interesting to note that any normal building, no matter how tightly closed, will have the same exposure to a biological warfare agent as it would if the windows were wide open— it takes longer for the agent to enter, but it stays there a much longer time. Positive-pressure filtered air largely eliminates this problem.

Other approaches that should be implemented contribute not only to the reduction of threats but to lowering the cost of reducing the threats. Such measures would include sealing at the point of departure trucks, ships, or cargo containers, so that auto parts entering Detroit from Canada, if they were inspected at the factory, would not have to be inspected individually. Electronic manifests and bills of lading could be required in advance, and shipments that comply with these efficiency- and security-based rules would incur less delay and less cost than those shipped the old way.

Similarly, people willing to carry biometric-based identification (a thumbprint plus photo, for instance) could be given "EZ-Pass" treatment. These people would have had a suitable interview and would have provided data to be kept in an electronically accessible file. Those without the EZ-Pass would be delayed longer in driving their trucks into a city or in boarding aircraft.

Thus far, I have discussed a few of the threats that might be expected from terrorists; some of these are greatly increased by the willingness to die for the cause. On the assumption that there are dozens or even hundreds of similar agents already in place, it is unlikely that their motivation can be annulled; hence the critical importance of ensuring that such attempts in the near term will not succeed. Here are some near-term measures:

• To prevent a hijacked passenger aircraft being used as a manned cruise missile, strengthen and lock the cockpit door. Assign air marshals to many flights. Ensure that the radar transponder, once switched to emergency mode by a pilot who is being attacked, cannot be switched back.

• To counter the use of rented or stolen large aircraft, ensure that each aircraft landing gear is blocked by heavy concrete barriers or other means that would sound an alarm and disable the gear if moved without authorization.

• Foreign aircraft entering US air space must be subject to the same standards as US aircraft.

• To counter biological warfare, individuals, firms, government, and other organizations should consider installing a unit to provide positive-pressure HEPA-filtered makeup air to their buildings. For most establishments, these units should not be used to guard against biological warfare agents liberated within the building but against those from outside. Because of the far smaller hazard from chemical warfare or industrial chemical attack, HEPA filters should filter only particles from the air. These are typically not individual virus particles, but bacteria or viruses that are attached to some inert material in the range of diameters from about one to five microns.

• To facilitate travel and access to sensitive areas, a first-generation biometric identification pass should be made available. Those who have had an adequate interview and have information on file could rapidly be provided with a picture ID augmented by a thumbprint. This would be analogous to the EZ-Pass now widely used at tolls.

• To facilitate the movement of cargo, more use should be made of sealing at the departure point containers, ships, aircraft, or trucks, so that inspection would occur there with adequate time and space, rather than on the fly at bridges or other choke points. Electronic manifests could be sent ahead and would also accompany the vehicle. Lower customs charges for inspection and accelerated processing would be given to those vehicles and containers packed so as to facilitate high-energy x-ray or neutron scanning. Such vehicles would be processed more rapidly and at a lower cost than those without such helpful features.

There are many more potential terrorists than there are terrorists. In moving against terrorist organizations and states and others supporting terrorism, we need hardly fear that those who are implacable enemies of society will become more deeply implacable. But it would be easy enough to swell the ranks of terrorists with those who up to now have been largely passive. Accordingly, if the United States were, for example, to undertake military action against the Taliban, it should be accompanied by an effective and sincerely concerned program to relieve the plight of the people of Afghanistan.

In taking action against terrorists and their co-conspirators, it would be useful to recall that in the United States conspiracy to commit a crime is in itself an offense. While aiding and abetting the actual crime has the same penalties as the crime itself, conspiracy has a lesser penalty. But one can be imprisoned for conspiracy even if the crime is never committed. Such doctrines could be drawn on to lay the basis for the legitimacy of US action in protecting against and responding to terrorism.

I have neither tried nor succeeded in providing here a complete evaluation of terrorist threats to modern society—let alone a reasoned evaluation of the effectiveness and cost of countermeasures. For instance, cyberterrorism is a serious potential problem, and individual hackers have already caused billions of dollars' worth of damage. It is clear, however, that acting as individuals and as a society as a whole, we will need to make considerable investments in reducing our vulnerability. If we do this wisely and make use of market incentives wherever possible, the cost in efficiency and diversion of resources should be tolerable.

—*October 2, 2001*

EPILOGUE

Since my article was published in early October, several people have died from inhalation anthrax, and others have become ill with the cutaneous form of the disease.

Some of the illness arises from anthrax spores that emerge from envelopes being handled in post offices—especially by automated equipment. An envelope normally has some air in it. If one bends or compresses the envelope, the air comes out—either through apertures or perhaps through the paper; and anthrax spores are small enough to penetrate a standard envelope. An envelope containing a couple of grams of anthrax spores can contaminate an entire post office. Many spores are deposited on other envelopes and taken to their destinations, transferring their spores to other envelopes on the way.

The health hazard involved is not easy to estimate. It is a misconception that there is a threshold dose of anthrax consisting of thousands of spores. I believe it is more accurate to say that a single inhaled anthrax spore has about one chance in 8,000 of initiating the infection. The limited number of experiments done decades ago with monkeys to determine the infectiousness of anthrax spores did not distinguish between the two cases. It is much more likely, in principle, that the spores act individually, so that as long as one or more spores are present, there is no "threshold" below which one is safe from infection. In addition, some people will be more susceptible to infection than others.

If there were a threshold of 8,000 spores, then simply diluting the contamination would reduce the overall hazard. An envelope that had picked up 10,000 spores from a neighboring envelope might cause infection; but on the assumption of a threshold of 8,000 spores, and if the envelope transferred half of its spores to several others, no one would become ill. By contrast, if the single-spore hypothesis were valid, the number of people infected would only increase with greater dilution.

Thus if a million spores were delivered to one person, that person would very likely contract inhalation anthrax. If the million spores were divided among 100 people (whether a single-spore or an 8,000-spore dose was valid) there would be about 100 cases. But if the million spores were delivered to ten million people, so that each person received no more than one spore, there would be still, according to the single-spore hypothesis, about 120 cases of anthrax.

This may be the explanation for the death of a sixty-one-year-old hospital worker in New York, who had no occupational contact with anthrax, and little contact with the post office. And the same might be said for a ninety-four-year-old woman in Connecticut who died from inhalation anthrax in November.

The source of these contaminated letters is of great interest. I believe that if al-Qaeda were responsible for the letters, there would be not three or four but perhaps 10,000 mailed within a few days of one another. That this was not the case argues strongly against al-Qaeda as a source. A small number of letters has disrupted mail service and caused widespread fear, but these presumed goals of a terrorist organization could have been accomplished much more effectively with 10,000 letters than with a few. And al-Qaeda's other proclaimed goal of killing would also have been achieved. Instead, we now have been put on guard by a brief encounter with anthrax.

What can be done to minimize infection from spores still in existence from these few letters, and in the future? Transparent, flexible plastic curtains could be hung over mail-handling machines, so that the machines are accessible as needed from the sides at waist level for maintenance and the transfer of mail. The interior of the enclosure, in which the machines are located, should have a slightly lower pressure than the rest of the room. The pressure would be maintained by a blower that continuously draws air from the semi-enclosed region between the hanging plastic and the barriers that might extend to the floor, and returns the air to the room through a High Efficiency Particulate Air filter (HEPA). (See illustration on page 248.)

This is analogous to the fume hoods in chemistry labs, with which we have much experience, except that for the fume hoods a blower expels the noxious fumes that might be generated within the hood directly to the outside. In the case of anthrax spores or other biological warfare agents, HEPA filters, which typically collect 99.97 percent of particles that are 0.3 microns in size or larger, would reduce the likelihood of infection by a very large factor—probably 1,000 or more.

As I wrote in my original article, both homes and office buildings can benefit from the installations of small blowers that deliver air through a HEPA filter at a rate that exceeds the leakage of air in and out of a building, and thus prevents biological warfare agents from leaking in from outside. Maintaining such pressure is a simple matter in a home or in an office suite with its own heating, ventilation, and air conditioning. Where it is not implemented, some benefit can still be obtained from devices that circulate HEPA-filtered air and will thus reduce the concentration of biological warfare agents in a room. The effectiveness of such circulators is limited by the amounts of air

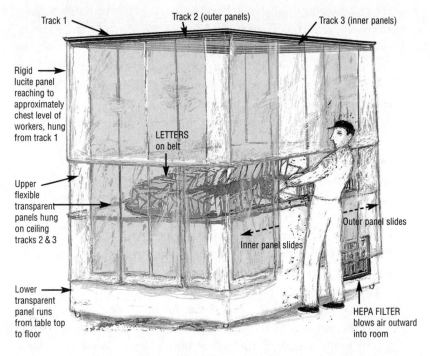

Postal workers may be substantially protected from contamination caused by the squeezing and jostling of letters containing anthrax in postal machinery. The sketch shows a machine largely enclosed by curtain panels which can be slid back and forth along tracks to give access to the mail. A blower within the enclosure exhausts air into the workroom through a HEPA (High Efficiency Particulate Air) filter and ensures that air moving through any gaps or apertures in the curtains will flow into the enclosure and that bacteria such as anthrax will be removed from the air as it is being returned to the room. If tests show that spores are discharged at certain locations in the machinery that processes mail, only those particular places need to be partially enclosed and equipped with directed, filtered airflow. (Illustration by Judy Glasser.)

infiltrating the building; the result might be to reduce the concentration of the agent only by a factor of ten rather than the hundredfold or thousandfold reduction that can be achieved when positive pressure is employed to prevent infiltration of unfiltered air.

Of course, anthrax is not the only biological warfare agent that should cause concern. In a 1970 report of the World Health Organization, "Health Aspects of Chemical and Biological Weapons," we find an estimate that the release of fifty kilograms of anthrax along a two-kilometer line upwind of a population center of 500,000 would kill 95,000 people and incapacitate 125,000; with the release of fifty kilograms of Q fever germs, only 150 would die, while 125,000 would be incapacitated.

As for smallpox, I believe that every practical measure must be taken to ensure that we have enough vaccine for the entire country (and ultimately the world). For this, not only is new production desirable but also other means for increasing the current US stock of some 15 million doses. Efforts are under way, for example, to demonstrate the effectiveness of vaccination with one fifth or one tenth of the usual concentration of vaccine virus. Furthermore, during the smallpox eradication campaign, extensive experience demonstrated that less vaccine is required with the bifurcated needle than with a simple needle. The bifurcated needle holds a drop of vaccine between two tines, and thus one gets about four times as many doses from a vial of vaccine as one does by using a single needle to make the superficial skin punctures called scarification. The bifurcated needles cost four dollars per thousand, and should be produced in quantity so that enough are available. They can be sterilized and reused but, at this price, new production would be desirable. (By the end of November 2001, the US government had contracted for 155 million normal doses of smallpox vaccine and bifurcated needles were being produced in large quantities.)

Other lethal biological warfare materials are not germs at all, but toxins produced from bacteria, such as botulinum toxin. In the US there are several hundred cases each year of illness from botulinus bacteria growing in food and secreting the toxin. The lethal dose orally is about seventy micrograms, whereas by inhalation it is on the order of one microgram.

The United States had an enormous offensive biological weapons program before 1969. It explored and produced materials to be used in offensive war both against humans and crops. In particular, the United States incorporated anthrax and several other biological warfare agents in weapons. Executive orders in 1969 and 1970, under President Richard M. Nixon, banned offensive biological warfare research and were soon followed by the 1972 Biological Weapons Convention.

Unfortunately, the Soviet Union and Iraq (and several other nations) did not cease their biological warfare activities once they signed the Biological Weapons Convention. In particular, after the 1991 war in the Persian Gulf, the UN inspection team in Iraq discovered, and Iraq admitted, that Iraq had adapted botulinum toxin, anthrax, and aflatoxin for military use. As noted, toxins are bacterial products—produced by living material, but not in themselves alive.

According to the UN, Iraq had produced nineteen tons of concentrated botulinum toxin and loaded about ten tons of it into missiles and bombs. Thirteen 600-kilometer-range missiles were loaded with botulinum toxin; ten with aflatoxin; and two with anthrax spores.[2]

Although a single anthrax spore weighs about one trillionth of a gram, the 8,000 or so spores needed to provide death by inhalation with high reliability weigh about 0.01 microgram—considerably more effective than botulinum toxin. And botulinum toxin degrades rapidly in air. Despite its small size, it is likely to be readily filtered by HEPA filters or by a mask appropriate to protect against other biological warfare agents, since it is difficult to disseminate in particles below 0.2 microns in size.

---

2. S. S. Arnon et al., for the Working Group on Civilian Biodefense, "Botulinum Toxin as a Biological Weapon," *JAMA*, Vol. 285, No. 8 (February 28, 2001).

Such agents, whether in the form of bacteria or toxins, are a credible threat. We should provide positive-pressure filtration to protect against them. Meanwhile, we should make it more difficult to put biological warfare agents into the air intakes of buildings, which in many cases are accessible from ground level. The nations of the world should pursue the initiatives calling for control of biological materials advanced by Under Secretary of State John R. Bolton in Geneva, on November 19, 2001. Among these initiatives is one relating to Article IV of the Biological Weapons Convention, according to which:

> "National Implementation": to go from the suggestion to the mandatory commitment that each nation criminalize and set penalties for individual behavior in violation of that nation's adherence to the BWC.

The United States, in turn, should support the use of challenge inspections under the Biological Weapons Convention. It should refine, not kill, the protocol which has long been under negotiation.

NUCLEAR MEGATERRORISM

Osama bin Laden has declared that acquiring nuclear weapons is a "religious duty." And the Justice Department indictment for the bombing of the US embassies in Kenya and Tanzania in 1998 includes the ominous statement, "At various times from at least as early as 1993, Osama Bin Laden and others, known and unknown, made efforts to obtain the components of nuclear weapons."

To make a nuclear weapon requires highly enriched uranium, or weapon-grade plutonium, or plutonium metal obtained from commercial reprocessing of fuel from power reactors. In Russia there are more than 1,000 tons of highly enriched uranium; in fact, the

United States has already acquired more than 130 tons of such uranium from Russia and diluted it—in the process called "blending down"—in order to make power-reactor fuel. The US also has a contractual agreement by which Russia will deliver to the US another 370 tons of enriched uranium by 2014—enough to make about 6,000 Hiroshima-type bombs. The US has agreed to pay $12 billion for the uranium, primarily to compensate Russia for its costs of enrichment in originally increasing the U-235 content from 0.7 percent in natural uranium to 90 percent or thereabouts for weapon uranium. (In fact the US will pay only for the enrichment costs required to achieve a U-235 content of 4.4 percent.)

In contrast, blending down is cheap. It would only take some tens of millions of dollars for Russia to blend down the material from the range in which it is usable in weapons to the point where it would have a U-235 content of 19.9 percent. The result would be low-enrichment uranium, which is not usable in bombs. Such preliminary blending down would ensure that any such material stolen or diverted could not be directly used in nuclear explosives. It is urgent that this dilution of Russia's weapon-grade uranium soon take place; and there is no reason why Russia would not be willing to perform this work if the Russian government were given financial incentives.

In addition, Russia probably has enough excess weapon-grade plutonium to make 10,000 nuclear weapons of the type that destroyed Nagasaki. And enough plutonium has been separated from the spent fuel from French, Japanese, and German power reactors to make more than 10,000 plutonium weapons.

It is also urgent for us to understand that making a nuclear weapon from so-called civil plutonium—which has been produced in the course of making electrical power, rather than in a plutonium production reactor—is not much more difficult in degree and very similar in nature to making a weapon with weapon-grade plutonium.

In January 2001, the Bush administration was advised by the report of a bipartisan task force, co-chaired by former Senate Majority Leader Howard Baker and former White House Counsel Lloyd Cutler, that

> The most urgent un-met national security threat to the United States today is the danger that weapons of mass destruction or weapons-usable material in Russia could be stolen, sold to terrorists or hostile nation states, and used against American troops abroad or citizens at home.

The United States has been spending some $700 million a year on Cooperative Threat Reduction; but the task force advised increasing that expenditure to between $3 and $4 billion per year.

Unfortunately, rather than meet the needs for improved security, and instead of following up on the campaign commitment by President Bush to solve this urgent problem, the Bush administration cut its budget request for such reduction by about $100 million. Appearing November 18, 2001, on NBC's *Meet the Press*, National Security Advisor Condoleezza Rice denied that the funding had been cut. But she was mistaken.[3] The administration proposed to reduce the scale not only of efforts to secure nuclear materials but also of efforts to provide security for nuclear weapons in Russia. Fortunately, the final appropriations bill passed at year-end 2001 adds $120 million and contains virtually all the funds proponents had sought for improving security of Russian nuclear materials. Furthermore, Secretary of Energy Spencer Abraham appears now to appreciate the importance of this program, and President Bush himself seems engaged.

A terror nuclear weapon need not be a weapon designed to fit on a ballistic missile or be carried by an aircraft and dropped toward its

---

3. See the analysis by the Russian-American Nuclear Security Advisory Council (RANSAC) at http://www.ransac.org.

target. The weapon can be stored in an airplane, the hold of a ship, or in a shipping container or truck. Since we do not know with any confidence that material for making nuclear weapons, or even entire weapons, has not been diverted to al-Qaeda, heightened vigilance is necessary in order to prevent what could be the loss of an entire city, in comparison with the three thousand lives tragically lost in New York on September 11.

RADIOACTIVE CONTAMINATION AS A TERROR WEAPON

A separate danger could arise not from the direct effects of a nuclear explosion but from the spread of radioactive contamination, for example by attaching radioactive materials to an ordinary explosive and thus producing a "dirty bomb." The US and other countries have experience with radioactive contamination (which is described in my recent book[4]). In Brazil in 1987, a source of radioactive cesium for radiotherapy was dismantled by junk dealers. The townspeople were attracted by the glowing cesium and used it to paint luminous patterns on their skin. Heavy internal exposures resulted when people's hands were contaminated with cesium and then used for eating. Fifty-four persons were hospitalized and four died. Some four thousand tons of soil had to be removed in the cleanup.

In 1966, US aircraft collided above the Mediterranean coast of Spain. Two nuclear weapons struck the ground at high speed and their explosives detonated, but without a nuclear explosion. According to a 1993 UN report, 2.26 square kilometers of uncultivated farmland and urban land were contaminated. There were no casualties.

---

4. Richard L. Garwin and Georges Charpak, *Megawatts and Megatons: A Turning Point in the Nuclear Age?* (Knopf, 2001). See Chapter 12, "Current Nuclear Threats to Security" including nuclear explosives, nuclear contamination, and BW threats.

In fact, according to the most conservative estimates by the International Committee for Radiation Protection, there is a 4 percent chance of a single lethal cancer among people living on the contaminated land exposed during the accident.

In my book I describe the estimated consequences of a hypothetical explosion of a kilogram of plutonium in Munich, Germany. The average population density of Munich is about 4,300 people per square kilometer. The study estimated that twelve cancers would occur per milligram of inhaled plutonium. Under the pessimistic assumption that very still air would cause the radioactive cloud to hover over the city for twelve hours, about 120 deaths from cancer would eventually be anticipated. (This would be in addition to the 400,000 people in the city who would likely die of cancer from natural causes.)

The 103 US nuclear power reactors are refueled every year or eighteen months, and the "spent fuel elements," each about fifteen feet long, are stored vertically for years in a deep pool adjacent to the reactor building. Conventional explosives detonated in the pool might be thought to rupture the wall. Loss of the water would prevent proper cooling of the fuel; that most recently removed from the reactor might melt and release radioactive materials created during the four years the fuel had remained in the reactor. Such risks would be countered by preventing the placement of explosives in the pool, and by provision for expedient cooling (water sprayed by a fire-engine pump) to make up for the thirty gallons of water per minute evaporated by the hot nuclear fuel.

Although there are vast amounts of radioactive material available in pools of spent fuel near reactors, transporting such radioactive material and dispersing it by means of an explosion would be difficult; and even if such a venture succeeded it would not be very hazardous. Radioactive materials are very readily detected, and local authorities should be equipped with radiation detection devices. If such an incident took place, the area should be quarantined and decontaminated by being washed down. Residual contamination might prevent people from living or lingering in the area. In 1983 the Sandia National Laboratory in Livermore, California, published the results of a hypothetical explosive attack on a shipping cask containing spent nuclear fuel. The US Nuclear Regulatory Commission then indicated that for the most densely populated area studied (up to 200,000 persons per square mile) at evening rush hour on a business day, there would be no immediate fatalities and fewer than three fatalities from latent cancer. This would result from a hole that was some six inches in diameter; but the radioactive fuel released as aerosol—fine particles wafted in the air—would be only three grams. As with the hypothetical example for Munich, more harmful consequences could be achieved by using conventional explosives in a sports stadium.

We can hope that the recent attacks will create the sense of urgency that has been lacking both in public policy toward weapons of terror and in public awareness of them. They have too long been dismissed as unreal, with the result that entirely practical means of prevention have been neglected.

—*December 22, 2001*

MATTHEW MESELSON

Bioterror: What Can Be Done?

VIRTUALLY EVERY MAJOR technology has been exploited not only for peaceful purposes but also for hostile ones. Must this also happen with biotechnology, which is rapidly becoming a dominant technology of our age? This is a question that comes to mind when reading *Germs: Biological Weapons and America's Secret War*, a clear and informative account of biological weapons here and abroad by the *New York Times* reporters Judith Miller, Steven Engelberg, and William Broad.[1]

Germs begins by describing the deliberate contamination in 1984 of salad bars in the small town of The Dalles, Oregon, with *Salmonella typhimurium*, a common bacterium that attacks the stomach lining and causes cramps and diarrhea. The bacteria were spread by members of a religious cult, who were apparently testing a plan to gain control of local government by keeping other citizens from voting in a coming election. Although they caused no deaths, their criminal actions caused sickness in some 750 people and illustrated a community's vulnerability to even a relatively minor biological attack. A year passed before federal and state investigators established that the outbreak was not natural, and they were able to do so only because the cult leader himself called for a government investigation. The

---

1. Simon and Schuster, 2001.

leader's personal secretary and the cult's medical care supervisor were sentenced to the maximum prison penalty of twenty years; they served less than four years and then left the country. Federal law enacted in 1994 raised the maximum penalty for such nonlethal biocrimes to life.

Americans have now experienced a far more sinister form of biological attack: eighteen confirmed cases of inhalation and cutaneous anthrax with five people dead and the person or persons responsible still at large. Yet the scale of the recent anthrax attacks was minuscule in comparison with the scale of preparations for continent-wide biological warfare conducted by major countries—notably the United States before President Richard Nixon categorically renounced biological weapons in 1969, and the Soviet Union, which even expanded its program after it was made illegal by the Biological Weapons Convention in 1975.

The advent of industrial-scale microbiology and therefore of industrial-scale biological weaponry was made possible by the proof of the germ theory of disease and the development of methods for growing pure bacterial cultures in the nineteenth century. These are accomplishments for which Robert Koch and Louis Pasteur are celebrated and which underpin the studies of tuberculosis for which Koch was awarded the 1905 Nobel Prize in medicine. It was Koch who in 1876 described with great clarity the life cycle of the bacterium *Bacillus anthracis* and completed the proof that it causes the disease that is known in German as *Milzbrand* (fiery spleen), in French as *charbon* (because of the blackened scab it makes on the skin), in Russian as *Sibirskaya yazva* (Siberian ulcer), and in English as anthrax (from the Greek for coal).

Anthrax is primarily an affliction of grazing animals. When multiplying in an infected animal, the bacteria are rod-shaped. But anthrax bacteria from the dead or dying animal, upon exposure to oxygen, form within themselves a tough-shelled ovoid spore that can remain dormant and infectious in the environment for years. The disease took a heavy toll among herds in Europe, Asia, and Australia until the introduction of effective veterinary vaccines, the first one developed by Pasteur and then a safer and more effective vaccine developed in the 1930s by Max Sterne, a South African veterinary microbiologist. Sporadic natural outbreaks continue to occur throughout the world and have caused animal deaths and nonfatal human cutaneous cases in Minnesota, the Dakotas, and Texas this year.

The disease in human beings takes three principal forms, depending on what part of the body the spores enter and therefore on how the body responds. Most common and most easily curable with penicillin and other antibiotics is the cutaneous form, observed among people who come into contact with contaminated hides, hair, or bone meal or who butcher infected animals. The gastrointestinal form, contracted by eating contaminated meat, is not uncommon in some poor countries and has not been much studied. Highly fatal in some outbreaks, it is less so in others. The inhalation form, mainly associated with occupational exposure to contaminated hides or animal hair, is usually fatal unless treated with antibiotics before or immediately after symptoms develop. It is this form of anthrax that has attracted the attention of those who seek to make biological weapons and those concerned to defend against them. Anthrax spores can be dispersed by bombs, aircraft spray tanks, or missiles as an aerosol sufficiently fine to remain suspended in the air and, if inhaled, to reach the depths of the lungs. Such weapons may be capable of rivaling nuclear ones in their power to kill people over large areas.

Crude anthrax bombs were produced by Unit 731 of the Japanese Imperial Army, which attacked villages in Manchuria with anthrax, plague, and typhoid during the Sino-Japanese war in the 1930s and 1940s. Under its creator and leader, General Shiro Ishii, the unit conducted vivisection and other lethal experiments on humans. After the Japanese surrender, he and several of his associates were granted immunity from war crimes trials by American officials in exchange for data from the Japanese biological weapons program.

The US biological weapons program, as the authors of *Germs* write, began in 1942, first directed by George W. Merck, then president of the chemical and pharmaceutical company founded by his father. Research, development, and pilot-scale production of biological weapons were conducted at Camp (subsequently Fort) Detrick, in Maryland. By the end of the war it had some 250 buildings and employed approximately 3,500 people, engaged in both offensive and defensive work. Large-scale production of anthrax spores and of botulinal toxin was planned to take place in a plant at Vigo, Indiana, near Terre Haute, built in 1944. The plant was equipped with twelve 20,000-gallon fermentors for culturing bacteria and with production lines for filling bombs. Its production capacity was estimated to be 1,000,000 to 1,500,000 British-designed four-pound anthrax bombs per month, requiring some 320 to 480 tons of a concentrated liquid suspension of anthrax spores. As noted in Brian Balmer's deeply researched examination of British biological warfare policymaking,[2] Winston Churchill, in placing an initial order with the US for 500,000 anthrax bombs in March 1944, wrote that it should be regarded only as a first installment. Although the Vigo plant was ready to begin weapons production by the summer of 1945, the war ended without its having done so.

In 1947, the Indiana plant was demilitarized and leased and subsequently sold to Charles Pfizer and Company for the production of animal feed and veterinary antibiotics. It was replaced by a more modern biological weapons production facility constructed at Pine Bluff Arsenal, in Arkansas, which began production late in 1954 and operated until 1969.

A sizable effort of the 1950s, discussed in *Germs*, was the development, testing, and production of anthrax bombs for possible attack on

---

2. *Britain and Biological Warfare* (Palgrave, 2001).

Soviet cities. The weapons to be used were cluster bombs holding 536 biological bomblets, each containing a liquid suspension of anthrax spores and an explosive charge fused to detonate upon impact with the ground, thereby producing an infectious aerosol to be inhaled by persons downwind. In order to determine the area effectively covered by the aerosol from a single bomblet and therefore the number of bombs required, 173 releases of noninfectious aerosols were secretly conducted in Minneapolis, St. Louis, and Winnipeg—cities chosen to have the approximate range of conditions of urban and industrial development, climate, and topography that would be encountered in the major cities of the USSR.

A problem with this project, which had the code name St. Jo, was uncertainty about the average number of inhaled spores needed to give a high probability of killing. Experiments at Fort Detrick involving 1,236 monkeys indicated that the ID50, the dose that would infect half the monkeys inhaling it, was 4,100 spores. Other experiments, carried out under different conditions, gave monkey ID50 values ranging from 2,500 to 45,000 spores. The army estimated that the ID50 for people might be between 8,000 and 10,000 spores, with lower doses expected to cause a correspondingly lower percentage of infections. But even leaving aside the variability of results with monkeys, one could not know for sure if data derived from experiments with monkeys were at all applicable to people.

Inability to establish reliable munitions requirements and the possibility of creating long-lasting contamination eventually led the US Air Force to abandon plans to use anthrax as a lethal biological agent. It was replaced by *Francisella tularensis*, the bacterium that causes tularemia, a disease that inflames the lymph nodes and causes lesions in many organs of the body and can be fatal. Inhalation tularemia can be dependably cured by prompt administration of antibiotics, and this made it possible to measure its infectiousness in human volunteers—Seventh-Day Adventist conscientious objectors in the 1950s and 1960s. Inhalation of approximately twenty-five bacteria was found to be sufficient to give a 50 percent chance of infection. Untreated, the death rate of inhalation tularemia was thought to be up to 60 percent, depending on the strain employed.

Other agents were introduced into the US biological arsenal, including the bacteria of brucellosis and Q-fever and the virus of Venezuelan equine encephalomyelitis—all three of them incapacitating but much less often lethal than anthrax or tularemia—as well as fungi for the destruction of wheat and rice crops. The US arsenal also contained improved biological bombs for high-altitude delivery by strategic bombers and spray tanks for dissemination of biological agents by low-flying aircraft. These developments culminated in a major series of field tests of biological weapons using various animals as targets and conducted at sea in the South Pacific in 1968.

Germs tells the little-known story of Pentagon plans to attack Cuba with biological weapons in the event of a US invasion of the island during the 1962 missile crisis. The plans called for using incapacitating agents that were considered to be of relatively low lethality, and were expected to kill about one percent of those made ill. The authors quote a former Fort Detrick scientific director as believing that the use of such agents would have saved American lives. Others at the Pentagon thought it could have had the opposite effect. According to their hypothesis, not described in *Germs*, the defenders, feeling too ill to retreat, would have stayed in their foxholes and fortifications, using up all their ammunition before being overrun. The American attackers would therefore have been exposed to more fire than if germs had not been used, with correspondingly more loss of life. Whatever the result might have been, the use of biological weapons, even if expected mainly to incapacitate rather than kill, could, by breaking the prevailing international norm against germ warfare, have exposed Americans to far greater dangers later on.

Soon after becoming president in 1969, Richard Nixon ordered a comprehensive review of US biological and chemical weapons programs and policies, the first full study of the biological warfare program in more than fifteen years. Each relevant department and agency was instructed to evaluate several matters: the threat of biological weapons to the US and ways of meeting it; the utility of the weapons to the US; and issues raised by the possible distinction between weapons intended to be lethal and those meant only to incapacitate.

Six months later, on November 25, 1969, with the full support of the Departments of Defense and State, the President issued National Security Decision Memorandum 35, declaring that the United States would renounce all methods of biological warfare and that US biological programs would be confined to research and development for defensive purposes. In doing so he said that "mankind already carries in its hands too many of the seeds of its own destruction." Three months later, after further interagency review, he similarly renounced the use of toxins (poisonous substances from living organisms), whether produced biologically or by chemical synthesis.

The US biological and toxin weapons stockpiles were destroyed and the facilities for developing and producing them were ordered dismantled or converted to peaceful uses. US biological stocks at the time were not very extensive, amounting to some 10,000 gallons of liquid incapacitating agents (the pathogens of Q fever and Venezuelan equine encephalomyelitis), half a ton of dried lethal agents (anthrax and tularemia), some eighty tons of anti-wheat and anti-rice fungi, and about 100,000 munitions filled with various agents and simulated agents. Pine Bluff maintained a large standby production capacity for bacterial and viral antipersonnel agents, and a factory in Colorado was capable of supplying anti-crop fungi; there had, therefore, been no need to maintain large stocks.

President Nixon also announced that, after nearly fifty years of US recalcitrance, he would seek Senate agreement to US ratification of the 1925 Geneva Protocol prohibiting the use in war of "asphyxiating, poisonous or other gases, and of all analogous liquids, materials or devices" and of "bacteriological means of warfare." Following the example of several other states, however, the US reserved the right of retaliation in kind and maintained active stocks of chemical weapons until the total ban, even on possessing such weapons, imposed by the Chemical Weapons Convention of 1993 took effect. Finally, Nixon announced support for a treaty proposed by the United Kingdom prohibiting the development, production, and possession of biological weapons, leading to the Biological Weapons Convention (BWC) of 1972.

These initiatives went far beyond the mere cancellation of a program. The US had categorically renounced the option to have biological and toxin weapons, whether intended to be lethal or only incapacitating. What was the underlying logic? First, it had become evident from the results of the US and British biological weapons programs that biological weapons, although subject to substantial operational uncertainties, could kill people, livestock, and crops over large areas. Second, US officials realized that the American biological weapons program was pioneering and legitimizing a technology that, once brought into existence, could be duplicated by others with relative ease, enabling a large number of states to acquire the ability to threaten or carry out destruction on a scale that could otherwise be matched by only a few major powers. The US offensive program therefore risked creating additional threats to the nation with no compensating benefit and would undermine prospects for combating the proliferation of biological weapons. If the US offensive biological program had continued to the present day, legitimating the weapons and advancing the technology for making them, how much greater would the threat now be and how much less would be the prospect of containing or averting it?

While the United States renounced biological weapons and abided by the Biological Weapons Convention, the Soviet Union secretly continued and intensified its preparations to be able to employ biological weapons on a vast scale. An example described at length in *Germs* was the standby facility built in the early 1980s for the production of anthrax bombs at Stepnogorsk, in what is now the independent republic of Kazakhstan. Subsequently dismantled in cooperation with Kazakhstan under the US Defense Department's Cooperative Threat Reduction Program, it was equipped with ten 20,000-liter fermentors, apparatus for large-scale drying and milling of the spores to a fine powder, machines for putting it into bombs, and underground facilities for storage of filled munitions.

The first director of the Stepnogorsk facility, Kanatjan Alibekov, defected to the US in 1992 at the age of forty-two and simplified his name to Ken Alibek. In his account of the Soviet biological weapons program,[3] he describes the atmosphere of fear in which it flourished. Incorrectly believing that the US renunciation was a hoax and citing "the biggest American arms buildup our generation had seen," he found it easy to believe that the West would seize upon the Soviets' moment of weakness to destroy them. The Stepnogorsk facility conducted dozens of developmental and test runs with anthrax so as to be ready to start full production should Moscow declare a "special period" for doing so. Moscow never did, and Stepnogorsk never produced a stockpile of weapons. Still, the purpose of the facility was to start production on short notice if it was ordered to do so. Other facilities at other locations were also established to produce infectious agents for war, not only the pathogens of noncontagious diseases such as anthrax and tularemia but also highly contagious ones, plague and smallpox. Alibek writes in his book that in the 1970s the Soviet military command ordered the creation of a smallpox stockpile of twenty tons. In its 1992 declaration to the member states of the Biological Weapons Convention, the Russian Federation stated that the Soviet Union built facilities for large-scale production of biological weapons but that no stockpiles were ever created.

---

3. Ken Alibek, with Stephen Handelman, *Biohazard* (Random House, 1999).

Soviet field-testing of biological weapons was conducted on Vozrozhdeniye Island in the Aral Sea. In a 1998 interview published in *The Moscow Times*, General Valentin Yevstigneev, then the senior biological officer in the Russian defense ministry, is quoted as saying that activities at the test site in the 1970s and 1980s were "in direct violation of the anti-biological treaty."

To this day, the Russian Federation has done little to convince other nations that the offensive core of the Soviet biological weapons program has been dismantled. Despite the opening to international scientific collaboration of several of the largest research and development centers of the old program, such as the bacteriological research establishment at Obolensk and the virus research center at Novosibirsk, the former Soviet research and production facilities at Ekaterinburg, Sergiyev Posad, and Kirov, now belonging to the Russian Ministry of Defense, remain entirely closed to foreigners. The discussions of the US and the UK with Russia during the 1990s achieved agreement on the principle of reciprocal visits to each other's military biological facilities as a means of resolving ambiguities, but they eventually ended in failure.

Nor has the Russian military seriously addressed remaining questions about the outbreak of inhalation anthrax in 1979 that killed at least sixty-four people in the Siberian city of Sverdlovsk (now restored to its former name of Ekaterinburg), despite the indisputable evidence described by Jeanne Guillemin in her authoritative book *Anthrax: The Investigation of a Deadly Outbreak*[4] that the spores emanated from the Sverdlovsk military biological facility. Resolving these and other questions and establishing conditions that will allow the two nations to cooperate on an equal footing in fostering global compliance with the Biological Weapons Convention will require that biological weapons be given high priority in the dialogue between the

---

4. University of California Press, 1999.

US and Russia. Making common cause against terrorism, including bioterrorism, may provide the needed motivation.

One of the troubling implications of the anthrax bioterrorism since September 11 is that, even if the person or persons responsible for it desist or are caught, it may attract imitators. On the other hand, very few other lethal agents are as widely accessible and as stable in the environment as anthrax spores, and better means of prevention and better therapy for inhalation anthrax are on the way. But there are thirty different bacteria, viruses, and fungi on the NATO list of biological weapons threats and there are additional agents on other lists. With sufficient effort, many of these could probably be modified so as to evade existing vaccines and antibiotics. It therefore seems reasonable also to consider more widely inclusive protections, not only those specific to a particular agent. A neglected yet simple measure that could offer considerable protection against any major aerosol attack and would also contribute to the reduction of respiratory disease caused by air pollution is filtration of the air that enters and circulates within large buildings.[5] The most generic measures of all, however, are those that help to prevent and deter biological warfare and bioterrorism in the first place. Important among them is the Biological Weapons Convention.

The BWC serves the essential function of setting an international norm to guide the actions of states who see it in their interest to comply with the treaty, to dissuade states that may be tempted to violate it, and to facilitate joint international action against those found to be in violation. The convention obliges its members

> never in any circumstance to develop, produce, stockpile or otherwise acquire or retain:

---

5. See the comments on such filters by Richard Garwin in his article "The Many Threats of Terror," pp. 235–256, and his reply to a letter from Stanley Crouch in *The New York Review*, November 29, 2001.

(1) Microbial or other biological agents or toxins, whatever their origin or method of production, of types and in quantities that have no justification for prophylactic, protective or other peaceful purposes;

(2) Weapons, equipment or means of delivery designed to use such agents or toxins for hostile purposes or in armed conflict.

A reasonable question can be raised about which biodefense activities are compatible with the spirit and the letter of the Biological Weapons Convention, and what information about legitimate activities should be kept secret. In their book and in their subsequent reporting, the authors of *Germs* reveal the existence today of three secret US biodefense activities: the partial recreation of a Soviet biological bomblet; the construction of a simulated biological weapons facility; and an attempt to recreate a strain of anthrax against which the standard Russian vaccine was reported by Russian scientists to be ineffective in laboratory animals.

The defensive value of these activities, each sponsored by a different government agency, is difficult to assess without more detailed information. Nevertheless, general information about the location, nature, and rationale of legitimate biodefense work ought to be available to Congress and the public. When the same information comes to light only as a leak to the press, this increases the risk of fueling arguments for provocative or prohibited biological weapons activities by governments elsewhere. What appears to be lacking here is any high-level oversight group authorized to keep watch on the entire range of secret defensive projects and qualified to judge the legitimacy, utility, and risks of each.

With some 144 states party to it, membership in the BWC is now almost universal. The most important holdouts are in the Middle East. Egypt signed the treaty but has not ratified it. Syria and Israel, both thought by the US to have offensive biological programs, have not even signed. Iraq, required to join the convention under the terms of the Gulf War cease-fire agreement, is thought to have resumed its BW program after UN monitors left in 1998.

The Chemical Weapons Convention, with headquarters in The Hague, requires declarations from its member states of past and current activities and has some two hundred full-time inspectors trained to conduct both routine and short-notice inspections. By contrast, the BWC has no standing organization, no legally binding requirement for declarations, and no provision for investigations. Seeking to remedy this situation, in 1994 the member states of the BWC mandated the development of a protocol to strengthen the convention, including measures for verification. Last summer, with negotiating positions seeming to converge, the chairman of the group, Ambassador Tibor Tóth of Hungary, produced a consolidated text intended to gain general acceptance.

At that point, the Bush administration withdrew, rejecting the entire approach on grounds that it would do little to increase US confidence in compliance by others and would threaten disclosure of US biodefense and pharmaceutical company secrets. The government seems not to have appreciated that the potential value of such a protocol is not so much to increase US confidence as to decrease the confidence of any government weighing the pros and cons of noncompliance that their activity could long be kept hidden from other nations and shielded from sanctions.

One must wonder if the administration adequately appreciated the disadvantages of its action. Having rejected the current protocol approach after participating in it for seven years, how will we regain sufficient political credibility to win meaningful support for any new proposals we may advance? Without a mutually agreed verification arrangement, how will we find an international forum to undertake action to clarify present and future ambiguities in Russia and elsewhere? Without an internationally supported protocol, and short of peremptory acts of war, how will we deal with facilities believed to be engaged in prohibited activities? And without the provisions of a protocol, how can we persuade others of the fact that we ourselves are not developing biological weapons, a perception that would be directly contrary to the US interest in preventing proliferation? The existence of US criminal law against biological warfare activities, applicable to private acts but not to acts of state, is not a sufficient answer.

Even with an agreed international mechanism empowered to investigate suspected violations and resolve ambiguities, backed up by national means of gathering information, there is a need for a system of internationally approved sanctions to reinforce the norm and help deter violations. The prohibitions embodied in the Biological Weapons Convention and the Chemical Weapons Convention are directed primarily to the actions of states, not persons. Yet any production or use of biological weapons must be the result of decisions and actions of individuals, whether they are government officials, commercial suppliers, weapons experts, or terrorists. So why not make the production and use of biological and chemical weapons a crime under international law? Treaties defining international crimes are based on the concept that certain crimes are particularly dangerous or abhorrent to all and that all states therefore have the right and the responsibility to combat them.

Such international criminal law would oblige each state that is a party to the treaty: (1) to establish jurisdiction with respect to the specified crimes extending to all persons in its territory, regardless of the place where the offense is committed or the nationality of the offender; (2) to investigate, upon receiving information that a person alleged to have committed an offense may be present in its territory; and (3) to prosecute or extradite any such alleged offender if the state is satisfied that the facts so warrant. The same obligations are included in international conventions now in force for the suppression of aircraft hijacking and sabotage (1970 and 1971), crimes against internationally protected persons (1973), hostage-taking (1979), theft of nuclear materials (1980), torture (1984), and crimes against maritime navigation (1988). It was on the basis of the Torture Convention that Britain asserted jurisdiction in the case of Spain's request for extradition of former Chilean president Augusto Pinochet.

If such a convention were adopted and widely adhered to, this would create a new system of constraint against biological and chemical weapons. It would do so by applying international criminal law to hold individual offenders responsible and punishable should they be found in the territory of any state that supports the convention. Such people would be regarded as *hostes humani generis*, enemies of all humanity. The norm against biological and chemical weapons would be strengthened, deterrence of potential offenders would be enhanced, and international cooperation in suppressing the prohibited activities would be facilitated.

What about the question we began with? Will biotechnology, with its great potential for human betterment, also, like earlier technologies, come to be extensively exploited for hostile purposes? That such an outcome is inevitable is assumed in "The Coming Explosion of Silent Weapons" by Commander Steven Rose,[6] an arresting article that won awards from the US Joint Chiefs of Staff and the Naval War College:

> The outlook for biological weapons is grimly interesting. Weaponeers have only just begun to explore the potential of the biotechnological revolution. It is sobering to realize that far more development lies ahead than behind.

If this prediction is correct, biotechnology could profoundly alter not only the nature of weaponry but also the environment within

---

6. *Naval War College Review*, Summer 1989.

which it is employed. As our ability to modify life processes continues its rapid advance, we will not only be able to devise additional ways to destroy life but will also become able to manipulate it—including the fundamental biological processes of cognition, development, reproduction, and inheritance. In these possibilities could lie unprecedented opportunities for violence, coercion, repression, or subjugation. Thinking about the distant future has not heretofore been necessary in the history of our species. Averting or at least containing the hostile use of biotechnology may be an exception.

—*November 15, 2001*

EPILOGUE

The prospects for strengthening constraints against biological weapons any time soon appear to have faded during the few weeks since my article was written. Last summer, the United States withdrew from negotiations to develop a verification protocol to strengthen the 1972 Biological Weapons Convention; but it was expected that the Bush administration would present new proposals at the convention's Fifth Review Conference, held in Geneva between November 19 and December 7. However, at the conference the US mainly put forward old proposals that individual states adopt voluntary measures, without the force of international law.

The chances that the US proposals, or any others, would be endorsed by the conference were torpedoed on the last day, when the US delegation proposed to terminate permanently the mandate agreed upon in 1994 for the US and the other BWC member states to negotiate a protocol for verifying compliance with the convention. It was well known that most of the delegations opposed terminating the mandate. Since the Review Conference ordinarily operates by consensus, the US proposal was, in effect, a poison pill that forced the conference to immediately adjourn. Its draft final declaration, subsequently described by the conference chairman as "95 percent ready," was never issued. With no final declaration and therefore no international endorsement of any of the US government's proposals, it is hard to see what the administration was seeking to accomplish. It appears that the administration itself may have been internally divided, even over its own proposals put forward earlier during the Review Conference.

The Bush administration has made it clear that it is opposed to multilateral verification measures; it fears that carrying out such measures might reveal US biodefense activities it hopes to keep secret. Yet the administration is deeply worried about the menace of biological weapons. In promising much but so far only causing this year's BWC Review Conference to fail, the US has dismayed governments that share the same worry. The White House thus seems to have no integrated long-term strategy to prevent the barriers against biological weapons from becoming eroded.

What can be done? Controls over acquiring dangerous pathogens were established in the US several years ago and additional controls could be introduced, both here and abroad. Controls can make access to microbial agents of disease more difficult for terrorists who have no state support and who lack the necessary expertise to make use of them. But many pathogens that could be used as weapons occur naturally in many parts of the world and could be obtained from nature by determined and competent terrorists as well as by any number of states. Some civilian biodefense measures are worth taking but are unlikely to provide reliable protection against an enemy that can choose the agent, the target, and the timing of an attack. Nor have such biodefense measures much direct value in preventing the development and production of biological weapons, or in sustaining the international standards of behavior that have largely kept such weapons from being used until now—standards that are in danger of being eroded. For all these reasons, any effective policy for constraining those who would acquire or use biological weapons must address their intentions.

Fortunately, most states and most military organizations have, for both practical and moral reasons, rejected the use of disease as a weapon. That leaves those who might nevertheless be tempted to acquire biological weapons, for one reason or another, and those who may have already decided to do so. We need to influence the intentions of such people, whether they are terrorists, government officials, or others. A wide spectrum of measures may be appropriate, including efforts to ameliorate the deep fears and antagonisms that may lead people to acquire biological weapons. More directly, much can be done to discourage and deter persons and states from violating the Biological Weapons Convention. Like genocide and torture, manufacture and use of biological and chemical weapons should be a crime under international law. A new international treaty is needed by which anyone who orders or knowingly renders substantial aid in producing or using biological or chemical weapons will risk indictment and prosecution or extradition, should that person be found in a state that subscribes to such a treaty. Some states are privately giving favorable consideration to the idea and some, notably Switzerland, have publicly said they are doing so. Although some officials in the US government favor international criminalization, others do not and the idea seems to have been shelved for now. If no action is taken, a major opportunity will have been lost.

—*January 7, 2002*

INTELLIGENCE

DANIEL BENJAMIN AND STEVEN SIMON

A Failure of Intelligence?

TO UNDERSTAND WHY Americans did not recognize the true threat posed by the terrorists of al-Qaeda before September 11, consider the following exchanges. They are quoted from the transcripts of the testimony of Jamal Ahmed al-Fadl, the prosecution's first witness in the trial for the bombings of two American embassies in East Africa on August 7, 1998. Al-Fadl was questioned about chemical weapons that were allegedly made in Khartoum, the capital of Sudan.

> Q. Are you familiar with a section in Khartoum called Hilat Koko?
> A. Yes.
> Q. Did you ever travel to the section of Khartoum called Hilat Koko with any member of al Qaeda?
> A. Yes, I did.
> Q. Who did you go with?
> A. I remember one time I went with Abu Rida al Suri, and one time I went with Abu Hajer al Iraqi.
> Q. Anyone else?
> A. And one time I went with—
> Q. We will go through that name. M-U-Q-A-D-E-M. Is that a name or a title?

A. No, a title. He got one eagle and one star.

Q. Does that mean he is an officer?

A. Yes, he is in the army.

Q. In which army?

A. Sudanese army.

Q. His name?

A. Yes. Abdul Baset Hamza.

Q. Tell us about the time you went to Hilat Koko with Abu Hajer al Iraqi, what you discussed.

A. I learn that in this building they try to make chemical weapons with regular weapons.

Q. Can you explain what you mean by chemical weapons with regular weapons.

A. I remember another guy, he explain more to me about this.

Q. Who was that?

A. Amin Abdel Marouf.

Q. What did Amin Abdel Marouf explain to you?

A. He say the war between the government and the Sudan and the rebels in south Lebanon, it's like 30 years, and always the rebels during the rain time, they took the Sudanese army to north, and he say if we use weapons like that, it easy for us to win.

Q. Was there a war going on in the south of Sudan?

A. Yes.

Q. That was between who and whom?

A. Between Islamic National Front, they run the government, and John Garang group.

Q. Returning to your conversation with Abu Hajer al Iraqi, did he discuss with you who it was that was trying to make the chemical weapons in the area there of Hilat Koko?

A. *He tell me the al Qaeda group try to help Islamic National Front to do these weapons, to make these weapons.* [italics added]

...

Q. There came a time you talked about when you went to Hilat Koko in Khartoum, remember that time?

A. Yes.

Q. And you went there with Salim, didn't you?

A. Yes.

Q. And when you went there, you were going to a place where they were making chemical weapons, right?

A. Yes, that's what I told—they told me.

Q. And that's what you believed?

A. Yes.

Q. Do you know what chemical weapons are used for?

A. No.

Q. Do you know that they're used to kill people?

A. They say they use it with regular weapons, that's what I hear.

Q. What?

A. They use it with regular weapons.

Q. With regular weapons?

A. Yes.

Q. What did they mean when they said they use it with regular weapons?

A. I really I have no idea about what they mean.

Q. Okay. So I'm asking you, do you know that chemical weapons are used to kill people?

A. Yes, that's what I hear from them.

Q. You know that, for example, they use gas to kill people, right?

A. Yes.

Q. And whoever is in the area where that gas goes runs the risk of being killed?

A. Yes.

Q. And when you went there with Mr. Salim—by the way, what year was that?

A. Maybe during '93.

Q. During?

A. '93 or early '94.

Q. When you went there with Mr. Salim, did you say to him, this is a terrible thing, let's not get involved in chemical weapons production?

A. No, I didn't tell him that.

Q. Did you say, I refuse to get involved in chemical weapons production, I quit al Qaeda?

A. No.

Q. Just went about your business, right?

A. Yes.

A native of Sudan, al-Fadl had lived in Saudi Arabia and the United States before leaving for Pakistan in the late 1980s to join the Mujahideen in Afghanistan and fight against the forces of the Soviet Union. By his own testimony, he became a member of Osama bin Laden's al-Qaeda organization sometime in 1989–1990 in the Afghan city of Khowst and was one of the first to join it. At the end of 1990, bin Laden and the organization, including al-Fadl, moved to Sudan, attracted by its proximity to the Arab world and the group's developing relations with the National Islamic Front (NIF) government that had come to power there. Again by his own account, al-Fadl fled Sudan in 1996 after bin Laden discovered that he had been pocketing commissions on the sales of goods imported by one of the Saudi's businesses. He approached a number of countries with information about bin Laden and Sudan, and eventually walked into an American embassy—the location has not been disclosed—and announced that he had information about impending terrorist attacks.

His initial debriefings, conducted by officials who were not identified at the trial but were presumably intelligence officers, lasted three weeks. He was later interviewed as well by FBI and Justice Department officials. Eventually, he was brought to the United States, entered a plea agreement with the Justice Department for his terrorist activities, and was put in the Witness Protection Program. Al-Fadl's appearance beginning on the second day of the trial in New York marked the high point of interest in the proceedings. Reports about it appeared in *The New York Times*, *The Washington Post*, the *Los Angeles Times*, the major television networks, and many of America's other leading news-gathering agencies.[1]

According to Sudanese exiles, including some who had served in the government, Hilat Koko, the neighborhood described by al-Fadl, is in the northern part of Khartoum, where the country's National Security Agency maintains a large compound. Abu Hajer al-Iraqi is an alias used by Mamdouh Mahmud Salim, a top lieutenant of bin Laden's who was arrested in Germany in 1998 while apparently seeking to procure components for weapons of mass destruction. From information that emerged at the embassy bombings trial and from his indictment, it appears that Salim had several responsibilities in al-Qaeda, ranging from lecturing recruits on the doctrinal basis for killing civilians in jihad to managing the group's finances and unconventional weapons program. Germany extradited Salim to the US, and he was charged with several crimes in the same indictment as the embassy bombers, though his case was separated from the first group of conspirators who were tried this year. On September 11, 2001, Salim was six days away from the beginning of a separate trial in

---

1. Al-Fadl provided prosecutors with so much detailed information that they asked him, at the beginning of the trial, to provide jurors with a general account of bin Laden's organization as it developed over six years. During the trial, some of the details he provided were contradicted by succeeding witnesses. In view of the high degree of "compartmentalization" practiced by al-Qaeda, and the large number of people in its network, this is not surprising.

federal court in lower Manhattan, not far from the World Trade Center. That case did not relate to the terrorism charges but subsequent ones lodged after Salim, in an escape attempt, allegedly put out the eye of a prison guard using a sharpened comb.

Al-Fadl's testimony provides partial, but nonetheless striking, corroboration of the Clinton administration's 1998 claim that al-Qaeda was involved in producing chemical weapons in Khartoum. Evidence of that activity included a soil sample that showed the presence of the chemical o-ethyl methylphosphonothioic acid, or EMPTA, which is produced near the completion of the process to synthesize the nerve agent VX. The Central Intelligence Agency concluded in an assessment that there was no other reason, including an accident, for this "precursor" to be present in the quantity demonstrated in this particular soil sample, except in connection with the production of VX. This information, together with intelligence showing that the bin Laden network had set in motion other terrorist conspiracies against the US, led President Clinton to authorize a cruise missile attack against Khartoum on August 20, 1998, thirteen days after the bombing of US embassies in Nairobi and Dar es Salaam.

The target of that attack was not the Hilat Koko compound but the al-Shifa chemical plant, located a few miles away and the site where the CIA's soil sample was collected. Al-Fadl's testimony thus raises the possibility that the United States struck the wrong target when it hit al-Shifa—something that some Sudanese opponents of the National Islamic Front regime argued after the 1998 missile attack. While acknowledging that they were not privy to all NIF weapons activities, they were, they said, suspicious of other plants as well. But the high level of EMPTA in the soil sample at al-Shifa cannot be disregarded. EMPTA could have been synthesized at one of the two sites and then transferred to the other for storage or for completing the chemical process for producing VX and incorporating it in weapons. In view of al-Fadl's testimony and the chemical analysis of the soil sample, the most plausible explanation is that both plants were involved and thus appropriate targets.

The most astonishing aspect of al-Fadl's testimony about Hilat Koko is the reaction it elicited: none. In the news stories that followed al-Fadl's testimony, much attention was paid to his description of how al-Qaeda is organized, bin Laden's denunciations of America, and a murky effort by al-Qaeda to buy a cylinder of uranium for $1.5 million. (The cylinder, two to three feet long and with markings indicating South African origin, was being sold by a senior Sudanese military officer. Al-Qaeda sent al-Fadl to make contact with the officer and conduct a preliminary inspection of the material. His part in the transaction, however, ended before money changed hands, and he did not know whether the group actually bought the cylinder.) But no newspaper gave serious attention to the testimony about chemical weapons, which must have taken several minutes on each of two days—and the issue resurfaced in another cross-examination of al-Fadl later in the trial and in closing arguments.[2]

The omission is telling because it underscores how thoroughly journalists were by this time ignoring the issue of chemical weapons production in Khartoum, probably because the August 20 strike in Khartoum came to be regarded as the greatest foreign policy blunder of the Clinton presidency. Since the attacks on the World Trade

---

2. We have found only two passing mentions in the press of chemical weapons, the first during al-Fadl's testimony, the second after the cross-examination. Colum Lynch wrote in *The Washington Post* of February 8, 2001, "The testimony appeared to be aimed at supporting the government's contention that bin Laden's group—known as al Qaeda, Arabic for 'the Base'—planned terrorist acts and sought to acquire chemical and nuclear weapons in a crusade to drive American forces out of the Islamic world. But US weapons experts cautioned that there is no evidence that Sudan or al Qaeda has ever possessed nuclear materials." Benjamin Weiser, in *The New York Times* of February 21, 2001, reported that al-Fadl "testified that there was moving of weapons and explosives and attempts to buy uranium and to get chemical weapons."

Center and the Pentagon, reporters have returned to al-Fadl's testimony as though it were a sacred text on al-Qaeda, using it as the basis for numerous articles on the organization. Still, no one has mentioned the testimony about chemical weapons.

Apart from establishing that al-Qaeda seeks and may possess chemical weapons—it cannot be ruled out that they indeed have vx nerve gas produced in Khartoum—does this testimony matter? Yes, because it shows that both the evidence discovered at al-Shifa and the attacks themselves should have been taken far more seriously. The information collected by US intelligence strongly suggested that the terrorists were preparing for extensive killing and were seeking extremely destructive weapons to achieve that goal. Press coverage of that evidence was not merely skeptical but plainly dismissive. Congress was largely silent about the administration's case concerning chemical weapons at al-Shifa, and those members who were not exploited the doubts about the missile strike for partisan reasons.

To those within the US government, including the present writers, who served at the time on the National Security Council staff, the attacks on the embassies in Nairobi and Dar es Salaam on August 7, 1998, were a turning point. No previous terrorist operation had shown the kind of skill that was evident in the destruction, within ten minutes, of two embassy buildings hundreds of miles apart. The number of people killed was comparable to the most lethal attacks in the past— 241 were killed in the Beirut barracks in 1983—and the violence of the African bombings was unprecedented in being so indiscriminate. In addition to the 224 dead, many of whom were African Muslims, roughly five thousand people were injured. A general rule of terrorist operations has been to avoid harming those who might sympathize with the cause. These attacks dramatically departed from that rule.[3]

---

3. Several unsuccessful conspiracies in recent years showed a similar intent, including the first World Trade Center bombing, which failed to achieve its planners' goal of toppling one

After a terrorist attack, a torrent of intelligence typically arrives in Washington, as members of the group responsible contact one another to discuss their accomplishments and US intelligence officials step up their pressure on sources for information. After the August 7 bombings, al-Qaeda sent faxes declaring its responsibility for the attacks to media organizations in France, Qatar, and the United Arab Emirates. Searches of residences and businesses belonging to al-Qaeda members in London turned up claims of responsibility by "the Islamic Army for the liberation of the Holy Places," a fictitious group.[4] These clear indications of the involvement of bin Laden and his organization deepened the sense among government officials that the practice of terrorism had changed in important ways.

Bin Laden's involvement moved him instantly to the top of the list of terrorist threats to America. A subject of US concern for several years, bin Laden had funded terrorist training camps in Sudan and, through use of his considerable financial resources on behalf of Sudan's National Islamic Front, had obtained both government protection and support for his terrorist operations. That led Washington to press Khartoum to expel him, an effort that succeeded in 1996. But no responsibility for any terrorist attack had yet been definitively attributed to him. His fatwa of February 23, 1998, calling on "every Muslim who believes in God and wishes to be rewarded to comply with God's order to kill Americans and plunder their money wherever and whenever they find it," had drawn the attention of counterterrorism experts because of its distinctively religious tone and sweeping goals of driving the US out of the Arabian peninsula and its "armies

---

tower into the other, causing thousands of deaths. The East Africa bombings were the first to fulfill the ambitions of those behind them and show a willingness to use unconstrained violence.

4. "Responsibility for the Terrorist Atrocities in the United States, 11 September 2001," British government document. See the Appendix to this volume, pp. 353–372.

out of all the lands of Islam, defeated and unable to threaten any Muslim." The Nairobi and Dar es Salaam attacks showed bin Laden to be a man of his word.

In addition to the signs of bin Laden's responsibility in the intelligence after the bombings, the CIA found in the "take" credible information showing that other al-Qaeda conspiracies were nearing completion. (Later that August, Albanian secret police working with US intelligence broke up a plot to bomb the American embassy in Tirana. Concern about such an attack had been so strong that "some 200 Marines, 10 Navy Seals and a number of plainclothes security men"[5] evacuated most of the embassy compound. Other embassies around the world also were shut down for varying periods of time because of threat information.) The destruction in East Africa showed that underestimating bin Laden's ability or desire to carry out additional attacks would be a serious mistake. The White House decided that it was imperative to disrupt the terrorists' operations and preempt possible attack, including through military means.

Adding urgency to that effort were intelligence reports indicating that al-Qaeda terrorists were seeking to acquire weapons of mass destruction. Briefing reporters immediately after the attack on Khartoum, a senior intelligence official laid out the following points:

> First, we know that bin Laden has made financial contributions to the Sudanese military industrial complex. [Actually, the Sudanese Military Industrial Corporation.] That's a distinct entity of which we believe the Shifa pharmaceutical facility is part.
>
> We know with high confidence that Shifa produces a precursor that is unique to the production of VX.

---

5. John Kifner, "US Fury on 2 Continents: In Albania, Raids by US Agents and Tirana Police Reportedly Thwarted Attack on Embassy," *The New York Times*, August 21, 1998.

We know that bin Laden has been seeking to acquire chemical weapons for use in terrorist acts.

We know that bin Laden has had an intimate relationship with the Sudanese government which is a state sponsor of terrorism.

We know that bin Laden has worked with Sudan to test poisonous gasses and to finance simpler methods of manufacturing and dispensing gas, methods which would be less time consuming and expensive than prior Sudanese efforts.

Even though he left Sudan in 1996, we know that bin Laden's businesses acquire restricted, high priced items for the Sudanese military including arms, communications, and dual use components for chemical and biological weapons.

With regard to the question you raised to the Secretary, why did we do this today? Obviously we felt the information was compelling. We wanted to act quickly. We had compelling evidence, indeed we have ongoing evidence that bin Laden's infrastructure is continuing to plan terrorist acts targeted against American facilities and American citizens around the world.

Responding to a question, the official added, "We know he has had an interest in acquiring chemical weapons. We know that he himself has talked about thousands of deaths."[6]

Experts from the intelligence agencies and the Pentagon drew up a list of potential targets for a US military strike and made recommendations.

---

6. Compare James Risen and Stephen Engelberg, "Signs of Change in Terror Goals Went Unheeded," *The New York Times*, October 14, 2001. The authors refer to a plan in an al-Qaeda communication intercepted last year to carry out a "Hiroshima." Citing unnamed officials, they write:

Looking back through the prism of Sept. 11, officials now say that the intercepted message was a telling sign of a drastic shift in the ambitions and global reach of Al Qaeda during the last three years. Clearly, the officials agree, the United States failed

The final selections of terrorist training camps in Afghanistan and the al-Shifa plant were made by the "principals committee," as the national security cabinet is known, and forwarded to President Clinton. Within the small circle of officials who knew of the plans, some felt uneasy. A decision to attack another country is rarely made on the basis of clandestine intelligence, and the United States does not normally pursue a strategy of preempting threats militarily.[7] Yet the perception of imminent danger was sufficient to overcome these concerns. The principals committee recommended unanimously that al-Shifa be attacked, and Clinton approved the strike.

The decision to bomb the terrorist camps in Afghanistan seems, on the whole, to have been readily accepted by the American press and public, even though the Tomahawk missiles arrived shortly after the al-Qaeda leadership departed. The response to al-Shifa was entirely different. Reporters had heard the conclusions of government officials quoted above, conclusions based on sensitive intelligence, most of which was, at least initially, unavailable to the press. The intelligence agencies and the government generally were reluctant to expose valuable sources and methods that had informed the decision to attack the

---

to grasp the organization's transformation from an obscure group of Islamic extremists into the world's most dangerous terrorists.

The senior intelligence official's remark suggests that was not the case. For more on the issue of how government officials assessed the intentions of al-Qaeda, see Daniel Benjamin and Steven Simon, "The New Face of Terrorism," *The New York Times*, January 4, 2000, p. 19; as well as Simon and Benjamin, "America and the New Terrorism," *Survival* (Spring 2000), pp. 59–75; and "America and the New Terrorism, An Exchange," *Survival* (Summer 2000), pp. 156–172.

7. Military action against terrorism based on clandestine intelligence is not unprecedented. In 1993, the United States attacked an Iraqi intelligence headquarters building after a plot to assassinate former President Bush was uncovered. The lack of opposition to that operation suggests that if the target of the military action has a well-established reputation for committing crimes, an action convincingly based on intelligence will gain public approval.

plant. But confronted by contrary claims from the Sudanese government and from people who had some acquaintance with al-Shifa, the journalists declined to accept the statements of US intelligence officials.

Determined to build up public support for its actions, Clinton administration officials decided to reveal some of the intelligence. This did not win them any converts. Intelligence is always incomplete, typically composed of pieces that do not fit precisely together and are subject to competing interpretations. By disclosing the intelligence, the administration was asking journalists to make connections between pieces of evidence, to construct a picture that would account for all the disparate information. In response, reporters cast doubt on the validity of each piece of the information provided and thus on the administration's case for the attack on al-Shifa.

One of the first aspects of the attack to be criticized was the plant's alleged link to bin Laden. As the senior intelligence official who briefed reporters had noted, al-Shifa was part of a larger entity run by the Sudanese government, the Military Industrial Corporation, in which bin Laden himself had a financial interest. Al-Fadl confirmed in his testimony that bin Laden had during his time in Sudan built up a sizable group of businesses, including a bank, construction firm, agricultural and import-export companies, and a tannery. He had also developed close ties to the National Islamic Front government, even helping it target opponents for assassination. When no deed of ownership for al-Shifa with bin Laden's name on it was produced—hardly surprising—reporters complained that the bin Laden connection to Sudan had not been shown convincingly. This put the administration in a bind: to reveal its intelligence, whether from communications intercepts, informants, or other clandestine means, would destroy its ability to continue collecting intelligence, and it would expose American methods to others around the world. In a country in which bin Laden continued to have deep roots, officials strongly believed, it would have been irresponsible to reveal more.

The next line of attack regarded the famous soil sample. The CIA had been reluctant to publicize how it had established that materials associated with chemical weapons were present at al-Shifa. It knew that if it revealed the soil sample, it could endanger the operative who obtained it and make it impossible for him ever to collect such a sample again. Moreover, the Sudanese (and other chemical weapons producers around the world) would immediately increase security at chemical plants, further damaging the ability of the US to collect samples. Still, once the sample was openly discussed, no amount of explanation would suffice. Some observers argued that the sample's chain of custody was improper, implicitly rejecting the notion that intelligence operations typically are not and cannot be conducted according to the standards of judicial proof. A single operative with a bag of soil in Sudan would be hard-pressed to prove that there was no possibility it was tampered with while in his control.

Still others contended that analyzing the soil sample at only one laboratory was scientifically unacceptable and that the chemical found could hypothetically have been a derivative of pesticide production. But the CIA's analysis, about which reporters were told on August 24, 1998, showed that EMPTA had no commercial use anywhere in the world. This conclusion was never refuted, but it was also widely ignored.[8] The officials who spoke with reporters also noted that Iraqi weapons scientists had been linked to al-Shifa, and this Iraqi connection was independently underscored by UN weapons inspectors.[9] Again,

---

8. In his excellent book *Terrorism and US Foreign Policy* (Brookings Institution, 2001), Paul R. Pillar, former deputy chief of the Counterterrorist Center at the CIA, writes that "a sample of soil collected outside the [al-Shifa] plant—unlike samples collected at other suspicious sites in Sudan—contained a chemical that is a precursor to the nerve agent VX (there are other conceivable reasons for the chemical to exist, but none that was a plausible explanation for it to be present at this location in Sudan)."

9. According to David Kay, a former United Nations weapons inspector, traces of VX were found on SCUD missiles in Iraq following the Gulf War. He says Iraq may even have helped

this conclusion was never refuted but it was also widely ignored. (As more of the intelligence was revealed to reporters, the joke circulated among National Security Council staff members that the government was performing the dance of the seven veils but the press was administering death by a thousand cuts.)

Amid all these charges, senior officials, in explaining the decision to attack al-Shifa, made errors that hurt their own case. Although the CIA knew that al-Shifa produced pharmaceuticals, Cabinet officials and National Security Adviser Samuel R. Berger, who had been referring to it simply as a chemical plant, never got that information and were caught flatfooted when confronted with it.[10] The same officials also initially said that al-Shifa was involved in producing chemical weapons when the intelligence only demonstrated the presence of EMPTA, not actual manufacture of nerve-gas weapons. These misleading statements were taken as further confirmation of administration incompetence and even malfeasance.

---

build the al-Shifa plant in Sudan. "Sudan is not a state that you'd normally expect to understand by itself the intricacies of the production of VX," Kay said. "I think most people suspect there was Iraqi help in this." CNN, August 21, 1998. Iraq is also the only producer of VX that uses a method involving EMPTA.

10. Large amounts of medicine—both human and veterinary—appear to have been produced at al-Shifa. Most accounts of this production, however, remain incomplete or anecdotal. Relying on numerous press stories, Michael Barletta wrote in *The Nonproliferation Review* (Fall 1998), "Shifa was reportedly the largest of six pharmaceutical plants in Khartoum, employing over 300 workers and producing dozens of medicinal products. Twelve of these were for veterinary use, including an anti-parasitic that played an important role in sustaining Sudan's livestock production. Shifa's human medicines—including drugs for treating malaria, diabetes, hypertension, ulcers, rheumatism, gonorrhea, and tuberculosis—were widely available in Khartoum pharmacies. The factory supplied 50 to 60 percent of Sudan's pharmaceutical needs, as well as exporting products abroad" (Report: "Chemical Weapons in the Sudan," cns.miis.edu/pubs/npr/vol06/61/barlet61.pdf). It would have been wise for the US to offer to make up the shortfall in pharmaceutical production to Sudan caused by the destruction of al-Shifa. This, however, was not done.

It was not surprising that such errors reinforced skepticism among reporters, but administration officials, who were still concentrating on the destruction in East Africa, were taken aback by the press's refusal to accept the details of the government's case. As a result, the administration's conclusion that the nation was genuinely threatened, and that the nature of the threat justified measures such as the bombing, was ignored. Perhaps the most telling example of the coverage was provided by the *New York Times* headline on a September 21, 1998, story by Tim Weiner and James Risen: "Decision to Strike Factory in Sudan Based on Surmise Inferred from Evidence." They wrote,

> Senior officials now say their case for attacking the factory relied on inference as well as evidence that it produced chemical weapons for Mr. bin Laden's use. And a reconstruction of how the "small group" and the President picked the bombing targets, based on interviews with participants and others at high levels in the national security apparatus, offers new details of how an act of war was approved on the basis of shards of evidence gleaned from telephone intercepts, spies and scientific analysis.

In fact, the attack was based on more than "surmise"; and more than "shards" of evidence were involved. Inference was indeed used; but its adequacy—indeed, necessity—as a mode of reasoning was something that was never accepted by the press.

Further confusion arose over a lawsuit by Salah Idris, the officially listed owner of the al-Shifa plant, against the US Treasury, which froze his assets following the bombing. When the Treasury released the assets several months later, US officials said that the government was not prepared to reveal additional important intelligence in court. The officials argued that if they had revealed their full knowledge of the financial relationships between bin Laden, the Military Industrial Corporation, and al-Shifa, they would have destroyed their ability to gather intelligence again about these and similar matters. But their statements went virtually unreported, and the Treasury's action was taken as a concession that the US had hit the wrong target.

At the same time, discussion of al-Shifa became obsessively focused on one trumped-up issue, publicized by Seymour Hersh in an article in *The New Yorker* in which he attributed to others a point for which he had no proof: "Some reporters questioned whether the President had used military force to distract the nation's attention from the Lewinsky scandal."

Clinton's grand jury appearance occurred three days before the August 20 attack, and all considerations of American security were swept aside in the discussion, both on talk radio and network television, of whether al-Shifa was a case of "wag the dog." In Congress, Senator Arlen Specter, the Republican moderate from Pennsylvania, declared, "The president was considering doing something presidential to try to focus attention away from—from his own personal problems," a sentiment that was echoed by others. Hersh's article—largely a string of blind quotes—concluded with remarks about the President from an unnamed "State Department veteran": "Survival is his most important issue. It's always on his mind. If Clinton was not in all this trouble, he wouldn't have done it [authorized the Tomahawk raids]. He's too smart."

In the midst of such comments, hardly anyone asked what should have seemed obvious questions: Why would a president determined to "wag the dog" attack two targets when one would do? There are few more damaging events for any administration than a failed or unpopular military strike.[11] Why would officials risk an embarrassing failure

---

11. Writing before the attacks on the World Trade Center and the Pentagon, Pillar observed in *Terrorism and US Foreign Policy*, "U.S. intelligence performed the same role in August 1998 that it always performs in supporting military targeting: namely, providing everything known about a large number of sites that are associated with the adversary and that could be

if they weren't absolutely convinced of the necessity of the action? Would an entire national security team—including Republican Secretary of Defense William Cohen and career military officers—really collude in such a crass maneuver, one that cost a guard at al-Shifa his life? What was never debated was whether a national leader confronted with the information that Clinton received could afford not to act.

Perhaps, in retrospect, the administration should have tried other tactics to get reporters and the public to better understand the intelligence justifying the attack and to respect the need to keep part of it secret. After President Clinton gave an Oval Office address about the strikes on August 20, his advisers followed the well-established practice of passing the task of public explanation of the details to the Cabinet and senior White House officials. Some would argue that Clinton should have continued to argue strongly in defense of the attack on al-Shifa, revealing some of the evidence in forceful speeches. In view of the tenor of reporting on the issue, we can doubt whether this would have made a difference.

The dismissal of the al-Shifa attack as a blunder had serious consequences, including the failure of the public to comprehend the nature

---

reviewed by military planners and senior decisionmakers for possible selection as targets. The intelligence did not show what role, if any, al-Shifa may ever have played in any vx program (production, storage, occasional transshipment, or whatever), nor did it point to any specific plans by bin Laden to use chemicals in a future attack. The intelligence also did not deny that the plan was engaged in the legitimate production of pharmaceuticals (chemical weapons programs elsewhere, as in Iraq, have had such dual-use facilities).

"The issue was thus not one of bad intelligence but rather whether, based on the partial information and still unanswered questions about al-Shifa, hitting the plant was prudent in view of the costs of doing so. Those costs included the public relations battering that the United States suffered from the al-Shifa strike itself, as well as the broader blow that the episode inflicted on the perceived integrity of US intelligence and US counterterrorist efforts generally." Perhaps, after al-Fadl's testimony in February and the events of September 11, the calculus looks different.

of the al-Qaeda threat. That in turn meant there was no support for decisive measures in Afghanistan—including, possibly, the use of US ground forces—to hunt down the terrorists; and thus no national leader of either party publicly suggested such action. In the months ahead, there will be efforts in Congress and elsewhere to evaluate the failure of America's intelligence agencies in not detecting and acting against the conspiracy of September 11. As part of that examination, we should look back into the events of the 1990s and consider the shortcomings of both the government and those who reported on it.

These inquiries will be important for American efforts to counter terrorism in the years ahead, and, in particular, to inform the public about how intelligence is used by policymakers. After the East Africa attacks, the CIA, working with other intelligence services, disrupted a number of terrorist cells and foiled attacks. These operations occurred in countries whose leaders view al-Qaeda as a grave threat to their regimes but are justifiably fearful of disclosing their cooperation with the US. Such intelligence operations will continue to be an important means of preventing attacks against Americans, and we may again find it necessary to attack a terrorist site or strike a facility related to weapons of mass destruction. Unless the American press and public have a better understanding of the role of intelligence and the legitimate need to protect the sources and methods that make intelligence-gathering possible, the difficulties in defeating the new terrorism will be greatly multiplied.

KANAN MAKIYA AND HASSAN MNEIMNEH

Manual for a 'Raid'

1.

THREE HANDWRITTEN COPIES of a five-page Arabic document were found by the FBI after the September 11 attack: one in a car used by the hijackers and left outside Dulles International Airport, one in a piece of Mohammad Atta's luggage that, by accident, did not get on the plane from Logan Airport, one in the wreckage of the plane that crashed in Pennsylvania. Only a part of this document—pages two through five —is publicly available; it was posted on the FBI Web site on September 28, 2001.[1] In view of the number of copies found, it is reasonable to assume that there were other copies in the luggage of the other hijackers. If so, it is unlikely that many of the hijackers did not know the suicidal nature of their mission, as some commentators have argued. Since one of the three copies was found in Mohammad Atta's luggage, it also seems unlikely that the hijackers were trying, by leaving copies of the documents behind, to mislead the investigators who would retrace their steps after the event.[2]

---

1. See www.fbi.gov/pressrel/pressrel01/letter.htm. No translation is now available on the FBI Web site. Our own translation can be found in the appendix at the end of this article, pp. 319–327.

2. Powerful evidence that bin Laden was behind the September 11 attack, and is therefore the inspiration behind the document, was provided by the videotape released by the Department

We don't know who wrote this document. From everything in it, the author seems to have been an organizer of the attacks. But the text contains a valuable record of the ideas that the hijackers would have been expected to accept. One of its underlying assumptions is that all its intended readers were going to die. It seems clearly intended for the eyes of the hijackers and no one else, and reads as if it were written to stiffen their resolve. One would expect each person to have studied his copy very carefully beforehand, reading it over many times before the mission.

The document is in effect an exacting guide for achieving the unity of body and spirit necessary for success. It is not a training manual of procedures, applicable to different situations; most of the sentences seem tailored to the particulars of the September 11 operation. There are no technical instructions or operational instructions in the four pages, only a fairly obvious list of practical precautions:

> [Check] the suitcase, the clothes, the knife, your tools, your ticket,... your passport, all your papers. Inspect your weapon

---

of Defense on December 13. The tape and its transcript do not bear out earlier reports in the press that the hijackers "did not know they were on a suicide mission" (*The New York Times*, December 11). The crucial passage occurs in a conversation between bin Laden and a former fighter from Saudi Arabia, in which bin Laden says: "The brothers, who conducted the operation, all they knew was that they have a martyrdom operation and we asked each of them to go to America but they didn't know anything about the operation, not even one letter. But they were trained and we did not reveal the operation to them until they are there and just before they boarded the planes."

The handwritten document that we discuss in this article, which never mentions targets, supports bin Laden's claim that the hijackers did not know the intended targets of their mission. It also makes it clear that the intended readers of the document (that is, the members of the team of hijackers not identified in the document by name or number) knew that they were carrying out a "martyrdom operation," to quote bin Laden. In view of the culture of martyrdom promoted by al-Qaeda, it is most unlikely that people who were not united in their desire to die for bin Laden's cause would have been chosen for such a critical undertaking.

before you leave.... Tighten your clothes well as you wear them. This is the way of the righteous predecessors, may God's blessings be upon them. They tightened their clothes as they wore them prior to battle. And tighten your shoes well, and wear socks that hold in the shoes and do not come out of them.

In fact, it seems that an effort has been made to eliminate clues about the intended target should the document happen to fall into the wrong hands before the raid was carried out. No mention of the target is made throughout the document, and letters substitute for names or places. For example, "M" is used for *matar*, or airport, and "T" is used for *ta'irah*, or plane.

Page two begins abruptly, without the traditional *basmallah*, or invocation of God's name, and without any of the formulaic phrases which one would expect in a text permeated with references to the Koran and the Prophet. *The Washington Post* published a translation—evidently leaked by US officials—of two extracts from page one of the copy found in the luggage of Mohammad Atta, who is thought to have been the ringleader of the terrorist group. This page contains the *basmallah* and the sentence,

> Remember the battle of the Prophet ... against the infidels, as he went on building the Islamic state.

The fragment of Islam's history that is implicitly glorified in the document is the ten-year "state-building" period between 622, the year of the Prophet's flight from Mecca, and 632, the year of his death. Before 622 the Prophet had followers and a calling that was at odds with the existing order of pagan worship in Mecca; after 622, he was the leader of an emerging political community that was at first limited to the township of Medina and struggled to extend its scope throughout the peninsula. This period, stripped of all historical context, becomes the mythical environment in which the hijackers view their actions.

To consolidate his position the Prophet engaged in "raids," the Arabic for which is *ghazwah*. Raiding for loot, not territory or retaliation, occurred frequently among the impoverished nomads of pre-Islamic Arabia. During the short period of his reign as the head of the emerging Muslim state, the Prophet, in his actions and instructions, sought to redefine the character and purpose of the raids and to make the object the benefit of the community, not individual gain. Over the centuries the frequency of raids in the name of Islam rose and fell. They came to an end in the early twentieth century with the collapse of the Ottoman Empire and the rise of a strong central authority under the House of Saud. The reconstituted *ghazwah* directed at the World Trade Center and the Pentagon and other targets is intended to overturn that history and bring men back to the example of the Prophet. According to the text,

> Consider that this is a raid on a path. As the Prophet said: "A raid...on the path of God is better than this World and what is in it."

2.

The object of the document is apparent: to have the hijackers act as a firmly committed group. To this end, the unknown author outlines a series of rituals that are to be performed beginning with "the last night." This section contains fifteen items; the first item directs the readers to make a "mutual pledge to die and [a] renewal of intent" to carry out the mission. If there was a ceremony accompanying the rituals, we have no full account of it. The text specifies that a ritual washing should take place; that excess hair should be shaved from the body, and perfume applied to it. The night is to be spent in prayer, going over the details of the plan, reciting selected chapters of the Koran. The reader is urged to maintain a positive attitude and purify his heart:

> Forget and force yourself to forget that thing which is called World; the time for amusement is gone and the time of truth is upon us. We have wasted so much time in our life. Should we not use these hours to offer actions that make us closer [to God]?

The "second phase" starts the following morning with the journey to the airport. The document urges the reader to repeatedly remind himself of God. This takes the form of a series of conventional invocations calling for God's blessing. At each point in the journey a different invocation is to be made. The text of the invocation is taken for granted and is not specified in the document. A typical such invocation for boarding a vehicle—a taxi in this case—would be "Oh God, may you make my entry to this car a safe entry, and my exit from it a safe exit. May you make my journey an easy one, and may you grant me support and success in all my endeavors." The hijackers are reminded of other invocations they should keep on reciting silently in order to fortify their resolve at each stage of their journey. Once each invocation has been made, the hijacker is told to

> Smile and feel secure, God is with the believers, and the angels are guarding you without you feeling them.

The hijacker is assured that "all their [the enemy's] equipment, and all their gates, and all their technology do not do benefit or harm, except with the permission of God." He is told not to fear such things. Those who do are "the followers of Satan." They are "the admirers of Western civilization," who have become besotted in their love of it. Their forebears are the ones who feared Satan over God to begin with, and became his followers:

> Fear is indeed a great act of worship offered by the followers of God and by the believers only to the One God who rules over all things....

This idea evokes the spirit of some of the most powerful passages of the Koran relating to the Day of Judgment—often expressed in short, forceful sentences and in the present tense. Dreadful punishments were inflicted by God upon sinful cities that refused to listen to the warnings of their prophets in the past. These were signs of what was coming, and coming soon. There was no time to waste. "The Hour has drawn nigh," the Koran warns, "the moon is split."[3] Men should live, think, and act on the premise that further horrible catastrophes lay just ahead. True Believers are those who tremble when they call upon God; their very skin creeps at the reciting of the Koran.

Taqwa, the fear of God, remains at the core of the Islamic relation between the human and the Divine. The anticipation of impending doom it fosters is balanced, however, by the worldly emphasis of the subsequent phases of the Prophet's experience as the ruler of Medina. Later developments in Muslim civilization relegate the most extreme forms of "fear as worship" to ecstatic and mystical experience, an emphasis found particularly within the Sufi tradition. By contrast, for the author of this manual an overpowering fear of God must rule in the mind of the True Believer, a fear that so focuses the mind as to rid it of all mundane considerations arising from experience and observation, thus enabling the Believer to remain utterly concentrated on

---

3. Koran, 54:2.

his mission. In support of this the manual cites the Koranic verse, "Fear them not, but fear Me, if you are Believers."[4]

3.

The "third phase" cited by the text begins when the hijackers set foot on the plane. Again, the author reminds his accomplices of the importance of performing in their hearts the necessary ritualistic invocations and supplications upon boarding the plane and being seated:

> Keep busy with the repeated invocation of God.... When the [airplane] starts moving and heads toward [takeoff], recite the supplication of travel, because you are traveling to God, May you be blessed in this travel.

More invocations and supplications follow the takeoff, which is identified in the document as the beginning of "the hour of the encounter between the two camps":

> Clench your teeth, as did [your] predecessors, God rest their souls, before engaging in battle. Upon the confrontation, hit as would hit heroes who desire not to return to the World, and loudly proclaim the name of God, that is because the proclamation of the name of God instills terror in the heart of the nonbelievers.

This passage is typical of several others that shed light on how the hijackers see themselves. Outwardly they are boarding a Boeing 757 departing from Logan Airport, or from Newark or Dulles; but according to the text they are living on a battleground, participants in a

---

4. Koran, 3:175.

great dramatic performance that conjures up the seventh-century heroic deeds of the Companions of the Prophet. It is as if men like Ali ibn Talib, the cousin and son-in-law of the Prophet, are going to be on the plane with Mohammad Atta, Marwan al-Shehhi, Ziad Jarrah, and the others. (The text cites approvingly a story about Ali ibn Talib never acting on the battlefield "out of a desire for vengeance.") The killings that the hijackers are about to undertake are no longer real but part of a sacred drama. Nowhere is this more apparent than in the following chilling instructions about what to do should the hijackers encounter unexpected resistance, as we know happened on United Airlines Flight 93:

> If God grants any one of you a slaughter, you should perform it as an offering on behalf of your father and mother, for they are owed by you. Do not disagree amongst yourselves, but listen and obey.

Here we find an explanation of what it means to kill a passenger who is attempting to resist. The Arabic word used for "grant" is *manna*, as in the biblical manna; it connotes the idea of a bounty or an act of grace conferred by God upon a person who has not asked for it. The Arabic for "slaughter" is *dhabaha*. The author has pointedly chosen it over the more common *qatala*, which means, simply, to kill. The classical dictionaries tell us the primary meaning of *dhabaha* is to cleave, slit, or rip something open. This is the word used for slitting the two external jugular veins in the throat of an animal. It is quick, direct, and always physically intimate; one does not slaughter with a gun, or a bomb, from afar.

The intimacy associated with *dhabaha* explains the vulgar usages of the word in street or colloquial Arabic, which are designed to shock the listener, to impress upon him or her how strongly the speaker feels toward the object of *dhabh* (more often than not a personal enemy, a tyrant, or a criminal). But it seems clear that this vulgar usage is not why *dhabaha* was preferred over *qatala* by the author of the document. Dhabaha is also what Abraham was prepared to do to his son on God's instructions—until Isaac in Jewish and early Muslim tradition, or Isma'il, Ishmael, in later Muslim tradition was replaced with a sheep at the last minute.[5] Because of the context of the word as used in the Koran, the son is called the *dhabih*, or the one-to-be-sacrificed. When a Muslim sacrifices a sheep on pilgrimage today, he does so as an act of remembrance of this test of faith imposed by God. *Dhabaha* in the context of the hijackers' document is such a ritual act, one that is normally performed to make an offering to God. *Dhabh* in this sense is an act prescribed in great detail by Muslim religious law.

The thought expressed by the author of the document is that a civilian passenger attempting to resist his hijackers is a gift bestowed by God upon the man chosen to kill him. Moreover, the killer is obligated to be selfless about the bounty that has descended upon him unasked. He is expected to turn it into an offering on behalf of his parents, "for they are owed by you." Between God's generosity in providing an occasion for slaughter and the obligation of filial devotion (greatly stressed in the Koran) is the act of slitting a passenger's throat with a box-cutter. This extraordinary interpretation of the explicit and implicit intent of the Koran continues:

> If you slaughter, you should plunder those you slaughter, for that is one of the sanctioned customs of the Prophet, on the condition that you do not get occupied with the plunder so that you would leave what is more important, such as paying attention to the enemy, his treachery, and attacks. That is because such action is very harmful [to the mission].

---

5. Koran, 37:102.

The author here is exhorting his fellow hijackers to "plunder" any passenger they may have slaughtered, an instruction that needs interpretation since the hijackers would obviously have no use for physical plunder. (The one item of plunder that would have been immediately useful to them was the cell phones they failed to demand from passengers, thereby making it possible for the passengers on one of the flights to learn about the other hijacked planes, and attack their captors.) The so-called "sanctioned custom of the Prophet" being referred to is from the *hadith*, the accounts of what the Prophet said and did, or of things said and done in his presence (and to which he might have given tacit approval, depending on which classical scholarly opinion one was relying upon). Among the *hadith* are accounts of the Prophet arbitrating disputes among warriors over the personal booty of those who had fallen in battle. The pre-Islamic custom was that a dead warrior's weapons, for instance, belonged to the man who had killed him. The Prophet is reported to have accepted this practice. The author of the document chooses to understand the *hadith* stories not as indicating rules for following existing practice, but as prescribing a task that had been sanctioned by the Prophet and has become a general obligation. But then the writer qualifies himself; he reminds his comrades that although it is an obligation, it is not one that should be allowed to get in the way of what is "more important."

The scene that is being evoked and used to instruct the hijackers here recalls something that often happened in seventh-century Arabia: an attack, for instance, on the tribe of Quraysh (prior to their conversion to Islam) was not followed up by the Prophet's followers because everyone was too busy plundering the warriors who had fallen. The writer of the manual is telling his comrades that although the Prophet had sanctioned such pre-Islamic nomadic practices as "plundering," this approval has to be tempered by the prerequisite of unity in action and faith in a higher purpose. True selflessness, in other words, requires an acknowledgment of the flesh-and-blood self, in order to become estranged from it.

Slaughter and plunder are thus ritualistic motions, not purposeful actions. Indeed, these motions might even interfere with the proper execution of the plan. But their importance as major components of the unfolding of the sacred drama outweighs any possible negative consequence. In the introverted world of the hijackers, a world that has effectively collapsed to the inside of the plane, practical considerations that surely would have been part of the planning stage (such as maximizing the number of casualties by targeting heavily populated buildings) are by now secondary to the need to sustain the intense psychological state crucial for completing the mission:

> Afterward, implement the sanctioned custom of prisoners of war. Capture them and kill them as God said: "It does not fit a Prophet to have prisoners of war until he subdues the land. You seek the goods of this World, while God looks for the Hereafter. God is almighty, all-wise."

In the eyes of the hijackers, the passengers in the plane are to be seen as combatants; and therefore they become prisoners of war the moment control of the plane passes into the hijackers' hands. It is worth recalling here that all Americans were declared combatants by bin Laden in his fatwa of February 1998:

> We—with God's help—call on every Muslim who believes in God and wishes to be rewarded to comply with God's order to kill Americans and plunder their money whenever and wherever they find it. We also call on Muslims...to launch the raid on Satan's US troops and the devil's supporters allying with them, and to displace those who are behind them.

Of all the Islamist movements "of global reach," including several that call for jihad, only bin Laden's World Islamic Front has attempted to legitimize in Islamic terms the equation between citizens and combatants.

4.

We can ask how the command to "capture and kill" the passengers, all prisoners of war, is justified in the document. The Koranic verse cited by way of justification in the hijackers' text is *al-Anfal 67*. It occurs in a seventy-five-verse chapter of the Koran which concerns the rules of war, in particular those governing the division of the spoils of war among Muslims, many of whom had had their property in Mecca confiscated for joining the new religion. According to the three greatest classical commentators on the Koran (al-Qurtubi, al-Tabari, and ibn Kathir), the verse in question was written after the battle of Badr, an important engagement for early Islam in which a small Muslim force defeated a large army from Quraysh, the town of Muhammad's own tribe, which had forced him into exile in Medina. Badr was a swift and stunning victory that yielded Muhammad and his followers considerable power and booty, as well as many prisoners.

In its aftermath, Muhammad's two main lieutenants, the future caliphs Abu Bakr and 'Umar, disagreed about the fate of the prisoners. While Abu Bakr favored their release in return for payment of tribute, 'Umar called for their execution, arguing that otherwise the attention of fighters in future battles would be diverted to capturing prisoners for the sake of personal gain, instead of remaining concentrated on combat for the sake of God. While Muhammad is reported to have endorsed Abu Bakr's position, a later Koranic revelation vindicates 'Umar by echoing his concerns. *Al-Anfal 67* is understood in the tradition as a gentle but divine reprimand directed specifically to the Prophet stressing that the purpose of battle is to defeat the enemy, not to capture prisoners for potential tribute.

Other more generally applicable verses of the Koran, however, are not mentioned in the hijackers' manual. *Muhammad* 4, for instance, clearly provides for the release of prisoners of war, with or without tribute, and urges forgiveness. In all cases, the action of Muslim warriors is explicitly bound by the clear injunction of *al-Baqarah* 190: "Fight for the sake of God those who seek to kill you, and do not commit aggression. God does not favor those who aggress." Over the centuries, commentators, basing themselves on the Koran and the traditions of the Prophet, have defined "aggression" as it is referred to in *al-Baqarah* 190.

The result is an Islamic theory of warfare which, while it varied according to the historical circumstances of Islamic states, has nonetheless been carried on within the bounds of a consensus about the treatment of people in war. The statement issued on November 4, 2001, by the Islamic Research Council at al-Azhar in Cairo, the highest moral authority in Sunni Islam, restated this consensus, which is rejected by the hijackers' text. The Cairo statement said: "Islam provides clear rules and ethical norms that forbid the killing of noncombatants, as well as women, children, and the elderly, and also forbids the pursuit of the enemy in defeat, the execution of those who surrender, the infliction of harm on prisoners of war, and the destruction of property that is not being used in the hostilities."[6]

5.

You will be soon, with God's permission, with your heavenly brides in Heaven. Smile in the face of death oh young man. You are heading to the Paradise of Eternity.... Know that the

---

6. *Al-Hayat*, November 5, 2001.

Heavens have raised their most beautiful decoration for you, and that your heavenly brides are calling you, "Come oh follower of God," while wearing their most beautiful jewelry.

The four pages of the document contain many references such as these to the physical pleasure and beauty of the afterlife. Human existence here is seen as a mere link between a glorious past and an even more glorious future. Self-sacrificing extremists since time immemorial have resorted to one variation or another of this vision, and there is nothing particularly Islamic about it. But concrete descriptions of the next life frequently occur in the Koran; and the hijackers' document makes abundant use of images describing different stages of being in the next world. First mentioned is *al-na'im al-muqim*, a realm which tradition holds is the residence of martyrs. Next comes the more common *jannah*, or Paradise, which is distinctly personal and more intimate in character. Finally, at the end of the manual, and with reference to the climactic end of the mission, a third abode is mentioned, *al-firdaws al-a'la*, the "Highest Paradise." This is the ultimate extra-reality within which God himself resides:

When the moment of truth comes near, and zero hour is upon you, open your chest welcoming death on the path of God. Always remember to conclude with the prayer, if possible, starting it seconds before the target, or let your last words be: "There is none worthy of worship but God, Muhammad is the messenger of God." After that, God willing, the meeting is in the Highest Paradise, in the company of God.

What could be more glorious than to be "in the company of God"? The quality that makes this document so startling and dangerous, however, does not lie here. It lies in the novel notion of martyrdom that the hijackers are attempting to inject into the Muslim tradition.

The sense throughout is that the would-be martyr is engaged in his action solely to please God. There is no mention of any communal purpose behind his behavior. In all of the four pages available to us there is not a word or an implication about any wrongs that are being redressed through martyrdom, whether in Palestine or Iraq or in "the land of Muhammad," the phrase bin Laden used in the al-Jazeera video that was shown after September 11. All the traditional Islamic distinctions between death, suicide, and martyrdom—which Muslim thinkers have wrestled with over the centuries and continue to do so in Lebanon and Palestine today—apparently do not exist for the author. Martyrdom here is not something bestowed by God as a favor on the warrior for his selflessness and devotion to the community's defense. It is a status to be achieved by the individual warrior, and performed as though it were his own private act of worship.

But in the tradition that is being turned on its head with this idea, the status of martyrdom has always been subject to assessments of the communal benefit at stake. Even in the case of those who defend a Muslim community or Islamic state against aggression, Islamic jurisprudence holds that violence must be proportional and that, in repelling an aggressor, only the necessary amount of force should be used. (An influential discussion of the question of proportion is to be found in the works of the medieval scholar Ibn Taymiyyah, a major reference for the Islamist movements themselves.)

Throughout Islamic history there has been a balance between, on the one hand, the sanctity of human life and, on the other, martyrdom. Only rarely in Islamic history have religious authorities endorsed actions in the community's defense that would mean certain death for believers. Beyond this, to justify calling someone who kills civilians and noncombatants a "martyr" is an entirely modern innovation—a change driven by invasion, occupation, and political and social breakdown in Palestine, Lebanon, and Algeria. The idea that martyrdom is a pure act of worship, pleasing to God, irrespective of God's specific command, is a terrifying new kind of nihilism.

The uses and distortions of Muslim sources in the hijackers' document deserve careful consideration. If arbitrary constructions of seventh-century texts and events have inflamed the imagination of such men, we should ask whether the ideas in the document will become part of the tradition that they misrepresent. To take the shell of a traditional religious conception and strip it of all its content, and then refill it with radically new content which finds its legitimation in the word of God or the example of his prophets, is a deeply subversive form of political and ideological militancy.[7] To contend with such an ideology effectively it is not enough to go back to the original core of the tradition as we have tried to do here. Well before the September 11 attacks, many Muslim intellectuals realized that bold and imaginative thinking must come from within the Muslim tradition in order to present social and political ideas that Muslims will find workable and persuasive. The tragic events of the past months have shown all the more clearly how urgently such ideas are needed.

—*December 19, 2001*

---

7. On how this was done by BJP Hindu ideologues to denounce Islam following the destruction of the Babri mosque in Ayodhya, see the excellent essay by Neeladri Bhattacharya, "Myths, History and the Politics of Ramjanmabhumi," in *Anatomy of a Confrontation: Ayodhya and the Rise of Communal Politics in India*, edited by S. Gopal (Zed Books, 1993).

APPENDIX

What follows is a translation of the publicly available portion of the handwritten Arabic document that is discussed in the preceding article. Three copies of the document were found by the FBI after the September 11 attacks: one in a car used by the hijackers and left at Dulles International Airport, one in a piece of Mohammad Atta's luggage that, by accident, did not make it onto his plane from Logan Airport, and one in the wreckage of the plane that crashed in Pennsylvania. The translation was made from reproductions of pages two through five of the document, which were posted on the FBI Web site on September 28, 2001. The first page has never been released.

This is a line-by-line translation in which the rendering of the text is as close to the original as possible. Arabic punctuation has been replaced by standard English punctuation with appropriate additions. Honorifics for God and the Prophet have been omitted. Koranic verses have been translated in context.

One of the Companions said the Prophet commanded us to read it before the raid, so we read it and we were victorious and safe.

The last night:
1. Mutual pledge to die and renewal of intent.
    • Shaving of excess hair from the body and the application of perfume.
    • Ritual washing.
2. Thorough knowledge of the plan in all its facets, and the expectation of reaction or resistance from the enemy.
3. Recitation of Surat al-Tawbah and al-Anfal with attention to

their meanings, and what God has prepared for the believers, a high paradise for martyrs.

4. Reminding the self to listen and obey that night. You will face decisive situations which require listening and obeying 100%. You should therefore tame your self, make it understand, convince it, and incite it to action. God has said: "Obey God and his Messenger, and fall into no disputes, lest you lose heart and your power depart, and be patient, God is with those who persevere."

5. Staying awake through the night and pleading in prayer for victory, enablement, clear triumph, ease of matters, and discretion upon us.

6. Multiplication of invocation. You should know that the best invocation is the recitation of the Holy Koran, by the consensus of scholars, as far as I know. It suffices for us that it is the word of the Creator of the Heavens and the Earth, toward whom you are heading.

7. Purify your heart and cleanse it of imperfections. Forget and force yourself to forget that thing which is called World; the time for amusement is gone and the time of truth is upon us. We have wasted so much time in our life. Should we not use these hours to offer actions that make us closer [to God] and actions of obedience?

8. Keep a positive attitude. There are between you and your departure but a few moments to start the happy God-pleasing life with the prophets, saints, and martyrs, who are the best of companions. We ask God for his grace. Be optimistic. The Prophet was optimistic in all of his endeavors.

9. Be prepared if you face adversity: how to behave and how to be steadfast, and to regroup, knowing that what has hit you could not have missed you and what has missed you could not have hit you, this being an affliction from God to raise your status and atone for your misdeeds, and know it is but moments before the adversity dissipates, with God's permission. Blessed is he who has won the great reward

from God. God has said: "Did you think that you would enter Heaven without God knowing of those of you who fought hard in His cause and those who persevered?"

10. Remember God's words: "You did indeed wish for death before meeting it, and now you are seeing it while you face it," and remember how often, by God's will, has a small faction vanquished a large faction. And remember His words: "If God helps you, none can defeat you, and if He forsakes you, who is to help you without Him? In God should the trust of the believers be."

11. Remind your self and your brothers of the supplications, and consider what their meanings are (the morning and evening invocations, the invocation for the locality, the invocations for [illegible], the invocations for the confrontation of the enemy).

12. [illegible] (with the self, the suitcase, the clothes, the knife, your tools, your ticket, [illegible], your passport, all your papers).

13. Inspect your weapon before you leave, and well before you leave. "Sharpen your blade and relieve your sacrifice."

14. Tighten your clothes well as you wear them. This is the way of the righteous predecessors, may God's blessings be upon them. They tightened their clothes as they wore them prior to battle. And tighten your shoes well, and wear socks that hold in the shoes and do not come out of them. These are all prescriptions that we are commanded to follow. For God suffices us and is the best disposer of affairs.

15. Perform the morning prayer in group, and consider its rewards. Afterward, [perform] the invocations, and do not leave your apartment except in a state of ritual cleanliness. [...]* God's words: "Have you thought that we created you with no purpose?" (Surat al-Muminun)

---

* The ellipsis here refers to words that were missing from the version of the text that the FBI made public.

After that, the second phase:

While the taxicab is taking you to the [airport], recite repeatedly the invocations to God (the boarding invocation, the invocation of the town, the invocation of the place, the other invocations).

When you arrive and see the [airport], and get out of the taxicab, recite the invocation of the place. Wherever you go, recite the invocation of the place.

Smile and feel secure, God is with the believers, and the angels are guarding you without you feeling them.

Then recite the supplication: "God is stronger than all his creation" and say: "God, to you is their end and in you we seek refuge from their evil," and say: "God, place a bar in front of them and a bar behind them, and blind them so they cannot see." And say: "God suffices us and is the best disposer of affairs," recalling God's words: "Those who were told an army is gathering against you, fear them, but it only increased their faith and they said, 'God suffices us and is the best disposer of affairs.'"

After reciting, you will find events unfolding beyond your power, for God has promised those who recite this supplication:

1. To return with the grace of God.
2. Not to suffer any harm.
3. To follow God-pleasing deeds.

God said: "So they returned with the blessings of God and his grace, and did not suffer any harm. And they followed God-pleasing deeds. For God is of great grace."

For all their equipment, and all their gates, and all their technology do not do benefit or harm, except with the permission of God.

The believers do not fear them. Those who fear them are the followers of Satan, those who had feared Satan to begin with, and became his followers [illegible]. Fear is a great act of worship that can be offered only to God, and He is most worthy of it. God said, following the aforementioned verses, it is Satan who causes fear in his followers.

These are the admirers of Western civilization, who have drunk their love for it and their hallowing of it with the cool water, and were afraid for their weak feeble stomachs. "Fear them not, but fear Me, if you are believers." Fear is indeed a great act of worship offered by the followers of God and by the believers only to the One God who rules over all things, with the utmost certitude that God will annul the treachery of the nonbelievers. For God has said: "Verily God will weaken the treachery of the nonbelievers."

You also have to perform in your heart one of the highest invocations. It should not be noticeable that you are repeating: "None is worthy of worship but God." If you say it a thousand times, no one should be able to distinguish whether you were silent or you were invoking God. An indication of the greatness of this invocation is the Prophet's saying: "He who said, 'None is worthy of worship but God,' with belief in his heart will enter Heaven." Or as the Prophet said in the same meaning: "If the seven Heavens and the seven Worlds are placed on the pan of a scale, and 'None is worthy of worship but God' is placed on the other, the latter would outbalance the former." You can smile while reciting it, for it is a great invocation.

When meditating on it, one notices that none of its letters are dotted. This is another sign of its greatness, since dotted letters and words are inferior to others.

It is sufficient that it is the invocation of God's oneness that you have come to raise and to fight under its banner, as did the Prophet, and his companions, and as do their righteous followers until the day of judgment.

Also, do not show signs of confusion or tension. Be happy and cheerful, be relaxed and feel secure because you are engaged in an action that God loves and is satisfied by it. You will be soon, with God's permission, with your heavenly brides in Heaven.

Smile in the face of death oh young man
You are heading to the Paradise of Eternity

Wherever you go and whatever you do, you have to persist in invocation and supplication. For God is with his believing servants, protecting them, facilitating their tasks, granting them success, enabling them, providing them with victory, and everything.

The third phase:

When you board the [airplane], the moment you step foot in it, before entering it, proceed with the invocations, and consider that this is a raid on a path.

As the Prophet said: "A raid or an attack on the path of God is better than this World and what is in it." The Prophet might have said it differently.

When you step into the [airplane], and take your seat, recite the invocations and known supplications that we previously mentioned and keep busy with the repeated invocation of God. God said: "Oh believers, if you encounter an [enemy] faction, be steadfast and invoke God repeatedly, so you may be successful." When the [airplane] starts moving and heads toward [takeoff], recite the supplication of travel, because you are traveling to God, May you be blessed in this travel.

Then, you will find that the [airplane] will stop, then will take off. This is the hour of the encounter between the two camps. Recite supplications to God as He states in his Book: "God, provide us with patience, strengthen us, and make us victorious against the nonbelievers." God also said: "All that they said was: 'Lord, forgive us our misdeeds and transgressions, establish our feet firmly, and help us against the nonbelievers.'"

The Prophet said: "Oh God, You who are the source of Revelation, who cause the clouds to pass, who have defeated the factions, defeat [our enemies] and make us victorious. Defeat them and cause them to tremble." Recite supplications that you and all your brothers be granted victory, triumph, and the hitting of the target. Do not be afraid.

Ask God to grant you martyrdom while you are on the attack, not in retreat, with perseverance and awareness.

Each one of you should be prepared to fulfill his role in a God-pleasing manner. Clench your teeth, as did the predecessors, God rest their souls, before engaging in battle.

Upon the confrontation, hit as would hit heroes who desire not to return to the World, and loudly proclaim the name of God, that is because the proclamation of the name of God instills terror in the heart of the nonbelievers. God has said: "Smite them above the necks, and smite off all their fingertips."

Know that the Heavens have raised their most beautiful decoration for you, and that your heavenly brides are calling you, "Come oh follower of God," while wearing their most beautiful jewelry.

If God grants any one of you a slaughter, you should perform it as an offering on behalf of your father and mother, for they are owed by you. Do not disagree amongst yourselves, but listen and obey.

If you slaughter, you should plunder those you slaughter, for that is one of the sanctioned customs of the Prophet, on the condition that you do not get occupied with the plunder so you would leave what is more important, such as paying attention to the enemy, his treachery, and attacks. That is because such action is very harmful. If the situation arises, the interest of the action and the group should be placed ahead of [the plunder], that is because this action is an obligation to be fulfilled [by each member of the group], while the plunder is a sanctioned custom, and the obligation precedes the sanctioned custom.

Do not act out of a desire of vengeance for yourself. Let your action instead be for the sake of God. Ali ibn Abi Talib, may God be pleased with him, had a duel with one of the nonbelievers. The nonbeliever spit on him. Ali paused his sword, and did not strike him. Then he struck him.

At the end of the battle, the Companions asked him about his deed, and about why he had paused before striking the nonbeliever.

He said: "When he spit on me, I feared that if I were to strike him, it would be out of vengeance. So I held my sword." He might have said it differently.

When he became sure of his intention, he struck and killed him. This indicates that the human being can secure himself in a short while that all of his action is for the sake of God.

Afterward, implement the sanctioned custom of prisoners of war. Capture them and kill them as God said: "It does not fit a Prophet to have prisoners of war until he subdues the land. You seek the goods of this World, while God looks for the Hereafter. God is almighty, all-wise."

If everything goes as planned, each of you is to hold the shoulder of his brother from the apartment, in the [airport], the [plane], and the [cabin], reminding him that this action is for the sake of God. Do not confuse or confound your brothers, but announce the good news to them, make them feel secure, remind them [of the purpose], and encourage them. How delightful it would be for one to recite Koranic verses, such as God's saying:

"Let those who forsake this World for the Hereafter fight on the path of God...," and his saying: "Do not reckon dead those who fight on the path of God...," or other verses. You may also chant as the Predecessors used to chant in the midst of battle to comfort your brothers and instill tranquility and happiness in their hearts.

Do not forget to take some of the spoils, even if only a cup of water, to drink from it and offer it to your brothers to drink, if possible. When the moment of truth comes near, and zero hour is upon you, open your chest welcoming death on the path of God. Always remember to conclude with the prayer, if possible, starting it seconds before the target, or let your last words be: "There is none worthy of worship but God, Muhammad is the messenger of God."

After that, God willing, the meeting is in the Highest Paradise, in the company of God.

• When you see the crowds of nonbelievers, remember the factions [gathered against the Prophet]: they numbered about 10,000 thousand fighters, and remember how God made his believing servants victorious.

God said: "When the believers saw the factions, they said this is what God and his Messenger have promised us. God and his Messenger are truthful. It only increased their faith and submission."

May God bless Muhammad.

—translated by Hassan Mneimneh

THOMAS POWERS

The Trouble with the CIA

1.

AS THE SUN rose along the eastern seaboard of the United States on September 11, the Central Intelligence Agency was in a state of what might be called permanent medium alert to detect and prevent terrorist attacks on US citizens and property. For fifteen years the agency had entrusted this task to a Counter-Terrorism Center (CTC) at CIA headquarters in Langley, Virginia, where as many as two hundred intelligence officers gathered and analyzed information from a wide range of technical and a somewhat narrower range of human sources. For five years there had been a separate task force within the CTC dedicated specifically to the danger posed by Osama bin Laden, the Saudi-born Islamic extremist believed to have been responsible for successful attacks on US troops in Saudi Arabia, US embassies in East Africa, and the USS *Cole*, almost sunk by suicide bombers in Aden harbor only a year before.

The CIA was not alone in its efforts to prevent terrorist attacks. The United States has not been slack in voting funds for numerous interagency committees, offices, divisions, centers, and task forces with substantial budgets focused on the problem of terror, but none of these special-purpose entities has a clearer responsibility for "warnings and indications" than the Central Intelligence Agency, which was established in 1947 as a direct consequence of the failure to foresee the Japanese attack on the American naval base at Pearl Harbor. Terrorism is only one threat to American security tracked by the CIA, but the danger is not remote or abstract; the agency itself has suffered grievous losses from terrorist attacks, notably in 1983, when a suicide bomber in Beirut devastated the US embassy and killed sixty-three people, including all six members of the CIA station. Visiting at the time was a legendary CIA field officer with long experience in the Middle East, Robert Ames, whose death was confirmed by the wedding ring on a hand retrieved from the debris.

The dead chief of station was replaced by another longtime CIA officer, William Buckley, who was kidnapped by terrorists in March 1984 and beaten to death over the following year. Four years later another CIA officer from Beirut, Matt Gannon, was killed when a mid-air explosion destroyed Pan Am Flight 103 over Lockerbie, Scotland. Gannon's wife was also a CIA officer, Susan Twetten, daughter of the agency's chief of operations, Tom Twetten, now retired and a book dealer in rural Vermont. Other CIA officers have been murdered by terrorists, including two just outside the gates of the agency itself.

The CIA thus has a visceral as well as a theoretical understanding of what terrorism is all about. The director of central intelligence, George Tenet, has often briefed Congress during his four years at the head of the CIA on the dangers of terrorism, on the threat posed by weapons of mass destruction, and specifically on the worldwide network commanded by Osama bin Laden from his protected refuge in Afghanistan. Less than a year ago Tenet told the Senate Intelligence Committee that bin Laden posed the "most serious and immediate threat" to the United States, and more recently still, probably in August or early September, three foreign intelligence services separately informed the CIA that bin Laden had urged one of his four wives, who was visiting Syria at the time, to return home to Afghanistan immediately—a suggestive sign that something was in the wind.

Neither the United States government nor the CIA were snoozing at their desks as the sun rose along the eastern seaboard of the United States on September 11. Both fully understood the danger of terrorism generally and of Osama bin Laden specifically. Nevertheless, when Logan Airport in Boston, Dulles Airport outside Washington, D.C., and Newark Airport began boarding aircraft that morning, nineteen men dispatched by Osama bin Laden walked through security checkpoints as easily as they had entered and operated throughout the United States during the preceding months—encountering as little interference, and arousing as little alarm, as if the Federal Aviation Administration had never heard the word "hijacking" and the CIA had never heard the word "terrorist" or the name "Osama bin Laden." By mid-morning on September 11 there can have been few Americans who had not watched—probably over and over—the collapse of the twin towers of the World Trade Center. The reason for drawing heightened attention to this single greatest failure of American intelligence since Pearl Harbor is that no official steps have so far been taken to find out how it could have happened.

People who deal with terrorism professionally tend to think of it as doctors do diseases with no cure, or as police do crime—as an ill of the human condition to be addressed one case at a time. Paul Pillar, a former deputy director of the CIA's Counter-Terrorism Center, has thought about the subject long enough to have it in comfortable perspective as a problem to be managed, never solved. In a study for the Brookings Institution, published last April under the title of *Terrorism and US Foreign Policy*,[1] Pillar argues persuasively that overexcitement is the enemy of sound counterterror practice. On some things, inevitably, September 11 has proved Pillar plain wrong; he cites, for example, "a drastic reduction in skyjackings" as a "major success story" and credits "a comprehensive security system." But

---

1. Brookings Institution, 2001.

most of what Pillar says holds up well, even when his common-sense approach is now tinged with irony. Put simply, his approach to managing terrorism is to proceed calmly, avoid inflating the significance of any single enemy (he includes bin Laden by name), and remember that, with coalitions, small and few is better than big and many since "limits...are set by the states least willing to cooperate." Pillar has much else to say. There is, he writes, no substitute for the local influence and expertise of foreign police and intelligence services. Bringing legal cases against terrorists takes time and dries up intelligence sources. International sanctions and resolutions work slowly when they work at all. You can't ask foreign banks to track financial transactions without providing account numbers. Military retaliation rarely hits the target intended, and for every terrorist killed two more aspire to take his place.

In the weeks following September 11 it was often suggested that really vigorous efforts freed of hand-wringing restraint—assassination of terrorist leaders, use of torture in interrogation, shutting off terrorist funds to the last penny, telling allies to cooperate or else—would solve the problem with finality. Pillar's advice is to put no hope in drastic measures but remember the current facts of life. There are limits to power, America has become a lightning rod for hatred, we can't stop people from trying to hurt us, and sometimes they will succeed.

But sensible as this advice is, it is undercut by one aspect of the attacks on September 11—their magnitude. In the counterterrorism business there has been a growing concern over the last two decades, and especially since the collapse of the Soviet Union, about the threat posed by weapons of mass destruction—what Pillar calls "the much-ballyhooed danger of chemical, biological, radiological, or nuclear terrorism inflicting mass casualties," and referred to by professionals as CBRN. In Pillar's view such dangers are real but exaggerated; CBRN weapons are difficult to get and to deliver; talking about them only convinces terrorists "how much they frighten people." For Pillar the one quality essential to "sound counterterrorist policy" is perspective, and nothing undermines it more than lurid American fears of "catastrophic," "grand," or "super" terrorism—threats whose consequences are horrifying but whose probability is low.

This would still be a sound point if not for the magnitude of the attacks on the World Trade Center, which killed several thousand people, destroyed billions of dollars' worth of property, pushed the United States deeper into recession, plunged us into a foreign war, precipitated a political crisis throughout the Middle East, and shattered the confidence of Americans that they are safe in their own homes and offices. The cost in dollars will be immense, probably many times the $30 billion annual bill for all American intelligence efforts. The psychic cost of terror cannot be measured, but it ticks up every time someone catches his breath on a plane, thinks twice about getting on an elevator to the eightieth floor, wonders what is in a package, is reassured to know that the FBI can now bug lawyers talking with their clients, or decides to move the headquarters of a Fortune 500 company out of New York City. Pillar, in short, and everybody else in his line of work, is going to have to put "catastrophic," "grand," and "super" terrorism at the top of the list because the other guys have a demonstrated ability to think and operate on the grand scale, and their efforts to obtain nuclear weapons could one day succeed.

Much about Osama bin Laden and his organization remains obscure. The son of a Yemeni-born construction tycoon in Saudi Arabia, bin Laden was one of fifty-three children and the seventeenth son, who inherited on his father's death a fortune variously estimated as $50 million or as much as $300 million. The family dynamics among fifty siblings are difficult to imagine, but a hint to bin Laden's character can perhaps be found in the fact that he was his mother's only child, that she was the eleventh or perhaps the twelfth wife, and that his older brothers called him "the son of the slave." This bit of information comes from Simon Reeve, a British journalist who wrote an account of the first World Trade Center bomb attack in 1993 called *The New Jackals: Ramzi Yousef, Osama bin Laden and the Future of Terrorism.*[2]

After obtaining a degree in civil engineering—study that usually involves a course on "strength of materials"—bin Laden was recruited, apparently by the head of the Saudi intelligence service, Prince Turki al-Faisal, to support the Mujahideen in the war to drive the Russians out of Afghanistan. Swept away by that success, bin Laden broke with his homeland when it turned to the United States for protection after the invasion of Kuwait by Saddam Hussein, moved to Sudan, built an Islamic extremist network called al-Qaeda (Arabic for "the base"), and embarked on a campaign of terror.

Under pressure from the United States in 1996, Sudan offered to extradite him to Saudi Arabia. Fearing that bin Laden was too popular to admit back into the country, Riyadh turned down the offer—something they told the Americans only months later—and bin Laden was allowed instead to fly back to Afghanistan where old friends in the Pakistani Inter-Services Intelligence (ISI) from the anti-Soviet war put him in touch with the Taliban, a religious party strongly backed by Pakistan in the Afghan civil war.

A recent biography of bin Laden by the director of the Congressional Task Force on Terrorism and Unconventional Warfare, Yossef Bodansky, reports in great detail the outward facts of bin Laden's progress from a builder of hospitals and military barracks in Afghanistan to the world's most wanted terrorist. Included are the names of many obscure groups, the dates of meetings, reports of individuals getting on and off planes, financial transactions, the movement of arms—all that superstructure of corroborative information which intelligence services like the CIA build into case files. From bin

---

2. Northeastern University Press, 1999.

Laden's own writings and videotaped interviews we know that he wants the United States to pull its forces out of the Muslim world, he wants the UN to end the sanctions imposed on Iraq, and he is angered by the suffering of the Palestinians at the hands of the Israelis.

But Bodansky's thorough book, *Bin Laden: The Man Who Declared War on America*,[3] tells us little about bin Laden's character, the people who shaped his thinking, how he came to embrace terrorism and build links with extreme Islamicist groups throughout the world. What the CIA and other intelligence organizations somehow missed between bin Laden's return to Afghanistan in 1996 and the attacks of September 11 was the transformation of al-Qaeda from an angry group of "Afghan Arabs" into a disciplined organization with the ability to hijack four airliners at roughly the same moment and fly three of them into what the Pentagon calls "high value" targets. At the time of the simultaneous attacks on the US embassies in East Africa in August 1998, the CIA officer Milt Bearden told a reporter, "Two at once is not twice as hard. Two at once is a hundred times as hard." What does that make four at once?

The CIA's failure on September 11 inevitably raises the question of what it may be missing now. This is not primarily a question of targets and means but of goals and strategies. In the absence of a secret bin Laden position paper one can still try to make sense of the attack on the World Trade Center, and Howard Hart, a retired CIA officer who ran operations against the Soviets in the Afghan war, has recorded his take in an eight-page paper privately circulated among friends. Hart resigned from the agency in 1991 and has seen no classified information since. But drawing on twenty years of experience in the Middle East and South Asia, including operations targeted on terrorist groups, Hart believes that bin Laden is not driven by hatred but is instead pursuing an ambitious grand strategy. His ultimate goal,

---

3. Forum, 1999.

Hart believes, is "a 'reborn,' combative and vigorous Islam" in control of governments throughout the Arabic world.

Bin Laden's initial targets, in Hart's view, are the conservative, highly centralized, relatively weak regimes of Jordan, Saudi Arabia, Egypt, and the Gulf States, all of which drift uneasily between the allure of Western material culture and the resentments of the poor and devout, who have little access to wealth themselves and are called to reject the modern world by fiery mullahs. Next on bin Laden's list, in Hart's view, are the authoritarian, mainly secular regimes of Iraq, Syria, and Libya, whose populations have been cowed by their "savage and highly effective internal security services. . . ."

Bin Laden has no armies to achieve these great ends; his method is the ancient strategy of the weak, using terrorism to precipitate a political crisis which can be expected to drive a deepening wedge throughout the Islamic world between the godless allies of America and the champions of Allah. In Hart's view the furious American response to the September 11 attacks was part of bin Laden's plan; he and his al-Qaeda companions expected that the US reaction would drive angry Muslims into the streets. Violent measures to suppress them would escalate a growing crisis

> until police and security forces will no longer be willing to fire on their own people, and the targeted governments will collapse. In short, a repeat of events in Iran in 1978–79. Skeptics should remember that in January 1978 no one in Iran—the Shah, his military, foreign observers, even Khomeini supporters —believed the regime could be toppled by "Islamic extremists." One year later the Shah's regime had been destroyed.

Hart watched this happen in Iran, where he arrived in the spring of 1978 to keep tabs on the growing crisis, something the CIA had avoided for years for fear of offending the Shah. The situation he found is ably described by another retired official of the CIA's Directorate of Operations, William J. Daugherty, in the current issue of the *International Journal of Intelligence and Counterintelligence*, an indispensable scholarly journal devoted to intelligence history and policy. American policy was to support the Shah unconditionally, Daugherty writes, and following the forced exile of the Ayatollah Ruhollah Khomeini in 1965 it was taken for granted in Washington that the opposition had been crippled beyond recovery and the CIA made little effort to reach its own judgment until Hart's arrival.

Some of Hart's reports in the spring of 1978 were so pessimistic that the CIA's chief of station refused to send them on to Washington, where he knew they would arouse fury in the White House. For more than three months during the summer of 1978 the CIA labored to write up a special National Intelligence Estimate (NIE) of the strength of the Shah's government. But the estimators could never agree on what was increasingly obvious: the Ayatollah had won control of the streets and the royal palace was next. Eventually the CIA's director, Admiral Stansfield Turner, shelved the NIE because it was politically too divisive. The result: official shock when the Shah's government collapsed, and bitter enmity for the United States from the Islamic activists who seized power in Iran.

Hart makes no facile claim that things might have gone the other way if only the CIA had sent a few agents into the souks. Khomeini had divined something the CIA had missed—the deep hostility toward the Shah's regime of a devout Muslim population being pushed too rapidly into the modern world. But not even Khomeini could foresee how events would unfold, Hart claims. By late 1978 the CIA had penetrated Khomeini's inner circle, and knew that the Ayatollah's closest advisers were still preparing to settle for some kind of power-sharing compromise. Having seen the fall of one regime built on sand, Hart is convinced that bin Laden, following a strategy similar to Khomeini's in the 1970s, can do it again. Whatever happens in the current American effort to hunt him down, he says, bin Laden has now been transformed into a hero of the Arab world. If he lives his charisma will shine all the brighter; if he is imprisoned or killed, others in the al-Queda network will carry on in his name. "The governments of Saudi Arabia and the Gulf States are also built on sand," he says.

Hart's interpretation is not easily proved or disproved. Pakistan, once thought vulnerable to Islamic revolt, seems to have survived the present crisis without great difficulty. Most scholars think Saudi Arabia is equally secure—but that is what they thought about the Shah of Iran, too, before 1978, and the CIA at the time went on claiming his throne was not in danger almost until the day he left the country. If the war against terrorism is going to persist for years, as the secretary of defense has said, governments in control today may be in trouble tomorrow. Hart knows that official policy and a CIA anxious to please can make it hard to spot—and even harder to report—the moment things start to deteriorate. He watched it happen in Iran, and the CIA's failure on September 11 makes him worried it could happen again.

2.

Failure is not easily confessed by the CIA. "Though we did not stop the latest, terrible assaults," George Tenet said in a statement to the agency's estimated 16,000 employees on September 12, "you—the men and women of CIA and our intelligence community—have done much to combat terrorism in the past." Failure was not a word Tenet could bring himself to utter. His executive director, A. B. "Buzzy" Krongard, came closer—a little—when he told a meeting of Washington investors in mid-October that the CIA had been worrying too exclusively about atomic bombs and other weapons of mass destruction. "Over and over again, in public testimony and private briefings, we have warned of a major attack by bin Laden," he said. "We had the scope correct. We missed the means."

Like Tenet, most of the CIA people I have talked to in recent weeks have balked at the word "failure," struggling to say it without saying it. Their reading of the event, stripped to its essence, is that no intelligence service can be reasonably asked to predict every attack mounted by a terrorist group, and that the CIA's performance is more fairly measured by what has followed—identifying the likely suspects, mounting a major investigation, calling on friendly intelligence services for help in blocking further attacks, and playing a vigorous and conspicuous role in the US military campaign to overthrow the Taliban and capture Osama bin Laden in Afghanistan. The performance of the CIA, therefore, should be measured on what an intelligence service can do—respond quickly and accurately—and not on what it can't do, no matter how good it is. By any fair measure, therefore, the CIA did not fail.

Behind this defensiveness is a lively fear of the CIA's perennial nightmare—reorganization under the prod of Congress. Like all directors of central intelligence, Tenet has done some reorganizing himself; one of the first things his friend Buzzy Krongard did as executive director was to abolish the Directorate of Administration, thereby drawing under his immediate control the former DA's five separate offices for in-house management—finance, security, personnel, and the like—long famous for their independence.

The history of the CIA is a record of constantly changing offices and lines of authority, usually to reflect shifting priorities in the White House. What the agency fears is not new decision trees but radical surgery. Until he retired a year ago Senator Daniel Patrick Moynihan openly advocated doing away with the CIA entirely as an unwieldy relic of the cold war. Other would-be reformers have suggested splitting covert action from intelligence analysis, perhaps even going so far as to give covert action to the Pentagon and analysis to the State Department—despite the fact that neither wants it.

Former director John Deutch, who ran the agency for eighteen months under President Clinton, published an article in *Foreign Affairs* in 1998 arguing that the agency's Counter-Terrorism Center should be transferred to the FBI. "Senators and congressmen all think they know what intelligence is all about," I was told by Richard Helms, who ran the CIA for six years until President Nixon sent him to Iran in 1973. "Reorganization is their main delight, but I myself don't think they're going to achieve anything by it." Most longtime intelligence professionals believe, like Helms, that basic intelligence work remains the same, however much the flow charts and diagrams are changed. President Bush appears to agree. Earlier this year he asked for a comprehensive intelligence review, still unwritten on September 11. But in the days following the attacks Bush made a point of being photographed in earnest discussion with his chief advisers—Vice President Dick Cheney, National Security Adviser Condoleezza Rice, and George Tenet. The message appeared to be clear: the President is sticking with the agency and the director he has got.

But there is a group of intelligence dissidents in Washington who think this would be a historic mistake. They argue that the CIA's failure to grasp the scope of al-Qaeda's plans reveals deep structural problems within the agency that go far beyond ordinary questions of funding and who reports to whom, and that no attempt to identify weaknesses or correct problems can go forward while George Tenet remains in charge. The criticisms come not from think tanks or bureaucratic rivals of the CIA like the FBI, but from a vocal group of former intelligence officers—mostly young, mostly field officers from the Directorate of Operations (DO), mostly well-respected and destined for solid careers until they chose to leave—who believe that the CIA is in steep decline. The most vocal of these critics is Robert Baer, a twenty-year veteran of numerous assignments in Central Asia and the Middle East whose last major job for the agency was an attempt to organize Iraqi opposition to Saddam Hussein in the early 1990s— shuttling between a desk in Langley and contacts on the ground in Jordan, Turkey, and even northern Iraq.

That assignment came to an abrupt end in March 1995 when Baer, once seen as a rising star of the DO, suddenly found himself "the subject of an accusatory process." An agent of the FBI told him he was under investigation for the crime of plotting the assassination of Saddam Hussein. The investigation was ordered by President Clinton's national security adviser, Anthony Lake, who would be nominated to run the agency two years later. The Baer investigation was only one of many reasons that the intelligence organizations resisted Lake, forcing him to withdraw his name in 1997, and clearing the way for George Tenet.

Eventually, the case against Baer was dismissed with the help of the Washington lawyer Jeffrey Smith, who served as the agency's general counsel under John Deutch. But for Baer the episode was decisive. "When your own outfit is trying to put you in jail," he told me, "it's time to go."

Baer's was one of many resignations in recent years; the dissidents' portrait of the agency which follows comes from him, from Howard Hart, from another veteran DO operator and former chief of station in Amman, Jordan, named David Manners, and from others who preferred not to be identified. They have differing career histories and views but on some things they agree. The Clinton years, in their view, saw a crippling erosion of the agency's position in Washington. Its leadership is now timid and its staff demoralized. Top officials, they say, worry more about the vigilantes of political correctness than the hard work of collecting intelligence in the field. The shock of discovering Aldrich Ames in 1994 was followed by a period of destructive self-criticism.

"That was the beginning of the 'Shia' era in the agency," said Manners. He was referring to the branch of Islam, centered in Iran, which stresses the unworthiness and sinfulness of man. "We all had to demonstrate our penance," Manners told me. "Focus groups were organized, we 'reengineered' the relationship of the Directorate of Operations and the Directorate of Intelligence." This meant dropping the bureaucratic wall between the analysts and the covert operators and introducing "uniform career standards." Henceforth a year in some country where it was dangerous to drink the water would get you no farther up the ladder than a year pushing paper in Langley. When John Deutch came in he appointed as chief of operations an analyst, David Cohen, who had never supervised an agent or even asked the chief of a foreign intelligence service to share information from his files. This was the era of "process action teams" which studied managerial questions like what sort of paperwork to use for agent handling. A committee of a dozen, split between case officers and analysts, might spend half a day wrestling with such questions twice a week for a year or more. "Navel gazing," Manners calls it.

In the reengineered CIA it was possible for Deborah Morris to be appointed the DO's deputy chief for the Near East. "Her husband was thrown out of Russia in 1994," said one of the dissidents, referring to James L. Morris, the Moscow station chief expelled during the Ames affair. "She worked her way up in Langley. I don't think she's ever been in the Near East. She's never run an agent, she doesn't know what the Khyber Pass looks like, but she's supposed to be directing operations —telling the operators if some pitch [i.e., plan] is a good idea."

The dissidents argue that "uniform career standards" did nothing to improve intelligence analysis but hurt field operations badly. Many DO veterans resigned and others lost heart when they saw what happened to Richard Holm, the Paris station chief who was yanked back after an attempt to recruit French officials went awry in 1995. US Ambassador Pamela Harriman fumed that whatever Holm was after, "it isn't worth the embarrassment to me." The word went forth from Langley—no more flaps, which meant don't stick your neck out, which meant safe operations or none at all. When Deutch arrived, Holm left, a harsh back of the hand for one of the agency's legendary operators. To fill the gap came a new emphasis on "reports"—the number of separate pieces of paper forwarded to Langley, whatever their quality. "What use is a Cray supercomputer at the Counter-Terrorism Center," Baer asks, "if you've got nothing to put into it?"

With the end of the cold war the agency cut back on recruiting agents, closed down many stations including most of those in Africa, and even quit accepting defectors from the old KGB in 1992—several years before the CIA uncovered Aldrich Ames and another DO spy, Harold Nicholson, less celebrated but almost as damaging—he was known around the DO as "Ranger Jim." At the same time the DO dismantled all the Counterespionage Groups, staffed mainly by "little old ladies" who knew the old cold war targets backward and forward but were no longer needed. Spies were a thing of the past; the new order of the day was to "manage intelligence relationships." In Morocco, the station chief told Baer he was crazy for trying to mount ambitious operations. "We were told to stand down," another dissident said. If you had checked the books you would have found just as many code names for secret agents, the dissidents say, but it was mainly window dressing—routine CIA informants puffed up in reports.

Along with the pullback in recruiting, the dissidents say, came a turn inward. Once operators had prided themselves on their grasp of local language and culture; now they stayed home watching American videos on TV. The CIA has long been wary of letting officers become too closely identified with any single country, language, or region; the British once called it "going native," the CIA calls it "falling in love." But the great operators in the past tended to speak languages like the natives, weren't afraid of the water, had a feel for the way national politics and culture were interconnected. That, at any rate, was what the dissidents had hoped to be when they joined the agency. Howard Hart, a graduate of the University of Arizona, was sent by the agency in 1966 to India, where he learned Urdu and Hindustani; later he added "passable German." Robert Baer learned French, German, Arabic, and even the Farsi dialect known as Dari when he was stationed in Dushanbe, the capital of Tajikistan. No Dari speakers served in Dushanbe after Baer left, and the agency has since closed the station down. "Do you know how many Pashto speakers the CIA has got?" he asks, citing the language of the principal ethnic group in Afghanistan, including most of the leadership of the Taliban. "The agency will tell you some imaginary number but I am telling you none. Do you know how many were sent to learn it after the embassy bombings? None."

With the mass resignations from the DO in recent years the match between station chief and country got ever more arbitrary; one recent chief in Beijing, a dissident says, picked for the job by Deutch's executive director, Nora Slatkin, spoke no Chinese and suffered from a conspicuous skin disease which the Chinese find particularly offensive. The loss of language speakers was not limited to the agency; the National Security Agency, a dissident claims, has only one Pashto speaker—a problem solved by sending transcripts of intercepted communications to Pakistan for translation by the ISI, an organization with a long history of involvement with the Taliban and Osama bin Laden. Some intelligence officials even believe that it was the ISI who warned bin Laden to get out of Khost before American cruise missiles struck in August 1998 in retaliation for the embassy bombings.

The dissidents say that the CIA is still staffed with hard-working people of talent and dedication and that it can still do competent work. They know how vast the agency's resources are and are familiar with the technical marvels which collect intelligence. Above all, they recognize that the apparent success of the military effort in Afghanistan seems to have reassured the public that things are now going well. But all the same the dissidents insist that things have gone badly wrong at the agency. Years of public criticism, attempts to clean house, the writing and rewriting of rules, and efforts to rein in the Directorate of Operations have all conspired to make the agency insular, risk-averse, and gun-shy. So have catch-up hiring of women and minorities, public hostility that makes it hard to recruit at leading colleges, complacency following victory in the cold war, the humiliation of the Ames case, even the long economic boom which put CIA salaries farther and farther behind routine offers to recent graduates by business and industry. The dissidents don't say that all of these problems are somehow the doing of George Tenet, but they do say they have undermined the CIA's ability to follow terrorists through the streets of the Arab world. A few months ago theirs was only the opinion of a group of disaffected officials; since September 11 it ought to be considered seriously.

3.

It is hard to find anyone in the intelligence community who dislikes George Tenet. He is an open-faced, hefty man, a reformed cigar smoker, friendly in manner, a slapper of backs and a clutcher of arms, earnest, interested, quick to take a point, and open to new ideas. "The outgoingness is a genuine gift," said Helms, who has watched many directors of central intelligence come and go. "Who else could lecture Arafat on the Middle East—up close with his hand on Arafat's lapel—and get away with it?" Tenet's confirmation in July 1997 also brought a welcome end to the revolving door on the seventh floor of CIA headquarters, where Tenet replaced Deutch, who had replaced James Woolsey, who had replaced Robert Gates, with a number of failed nominations in between. Tenet has set a recent record for peaceful tenure of the DCI's long, wood-paneled office overlooking the imposing main entrance to the building which Tenet renamed (before the last presidential election) the Bush Intelligence Center. The

Bush in question is the President's father, who was director for ten days short of a year in 1976–1977 and is still remembered as the ideal intelligence consumer when he was in the White House.

The bureaucratic clout of DCIs can be measured by how often they meet with the president. With some it's practically never; with most it starts often and fades off. In the case of Tenet and the current President Bush it is reported to be every day, with the arrival of the DCI at the White House carrying the President's Daily Brief, a printed document reporting much as a newspaper might the classified intelligence take and hot issues of the moment. Trust and personal liking of this sort is rare and CIA officials, happy to have the attention of the Oval Office, don't want to mess with it.

Tenet got the job by an unusual route through a succession of staff jobs dealing with intelligence issues for congressional committees. After several years as an aide to Senator John Heinz, Tenet joined the forty-member staff of the Senate Intelligence Committee in 1985. Four years later he was appointed staff director and then in 1993 he moved to the White House, where he handled intelligence matters for the National Security Council and met John Deutch, who brought him out to Langley in 1995 as deputy director of central intelligence. Even Tenet's admirers concede he got the top job mainly because Clinton did not want to risk another confirmation failure after Lake bowed out, and Tenet had already been confirmed once by the Senate. "George is a service kind of guy," said an officer who worked with him at the agency. "He knew what congressmen wanted and needed and he dealt with the White House the same way." What is remarkable about Tenet's career is that he had no intelligence background or experience of the usual kind; his expertise was all learned in the corridors of power where the deciding question is what will fly. His largely trouble-free years at the CIA prove that he knows how to navigate the maze of a political town.

Three years ago Tenet invented a new position—"counselor" to the DCI—and hired the sixty-four-year-old lawyer and businessman A. B. Krongard to fill it. A Princeton graduate and martial arts enthusiast, Krongard had recently retired after selling his share in a Baltimore stock brokerage firm to Bankers Trust for $70 million. Last March Tenet moved Krongard up into the job of executive director, where he is in charge of managing the agency, including its secret operations, while the director deals with broader issues of policy and strategy. The dissidents say that Krongard may know how to run a financial firm and make a pot of money, and George Tenet may know how to keep out of bureaucratic fights he can't win; but neither one of them, the dissidents say, really knows in any depth what effective intelligence requires, and on-the-job training isn't enough. It is impossible for any outsider to fairly judge what the dissidents are saying—and certainly not anyone as far outside as a journalist like myself. That is a matter for some official body.

When things go awry in the intelligence business it is customary to do a damage report. The Ames damage report—a four-hundred-page document written by then CIA Inspector General Frederick Hitz—in effect cost James Woolsey his job. In 1961, by the time the agency's inspector general, Lyman Kirkpatrick, got around to writing his assessment of the embarrassing failure of a CIA-trained and -financed rebel army at the Bay of Pigs, the DCI at the time, Allen Dulles, was already gone. That disaster was big enough to get a second report from a blue-ribbon panel headed by General Maxwell Taylor. The problem wasn't simply that the rebel army got shot to pieces as soon as it crossed the beach; it was that the agency had deceived itself about the real support throughout Cuba for Fidel Castro. The agency's plan couldn't work, and Taylor's job was to make sure that never happened again.

When I began to work on this article, the first person I called was the CIA officer I have known longest, a man who started his career during World War II, joined the CIA at its birth, and worked closely with just about every chief of covert operations until he retired after the first round of CIA scandals and subsequent reengineerings in the early 1970s. This man remains extremely active in retirement. He is a member of numerous study groups, panels, and commissions, and he rarely misses a conference on intelligence. He hates to criticize the agency he served all his life, but the failure of September 11 is not something he is ready to pass over in silence. "I don't think even Pearl Harbor matches this one," he said. "How often do you lose half a division in a day? Nothing has ever happened on this scale before. This was totally beyond anybody's beliefs or dreams. Nobody wanted to think the unthinkable."

Was anybody talking about an investigation—a post-mortem to figure out what went wrong?

"I don't understand it," said my friend. "There was a little talk but then it suddenly quieted down. Not even [Senator Richard] Shelby [former chairman of the Senate Intelligence Committee]—he knows he can't raise his head. Nobody is pushing for an investigation."

Is it possible to handle the problem—whatever the problem—without an investigation?

"No."

What would an investigation require?

"You need presidential and congressional authority. You can't just do it in-house."

Could it be done while Tenet was still running the CIA?

"If he's still there everybody will know he's watching. People won't tell you the truth. Everybody will be covering his ass, protecting his boss. They try to get rid of rivals. They hide paper and destroy evidence. I've seen it. You can overcome it by being a sonofabitch but only if the top guy is gone."

There is nothing this man hates more than the way politics has torn apart the CIA over the years. I would say he about half agrees with the dissidents—not 100 percent on half what they say, but 50 percent on all of it. But he has little sympathy for people who talk out of school, and he knows how hard it is for investigators to keep political meddlers at bay, get to the bottom of what went wrong, and fix what isn't working. He was the first one to tell me, like someone describing a jewel, that Tenet had the President's ear, which meant the agency could do its job. To give that away, take your chances with someone new, open up a whole can of worms by asking how this could have happened... Talking about it he sounds like a man facing open-heart surgery.

But?

"It ought to be done. He ought to go."

—*December 19, 2001*

APPENDIX

The British Summary

The following document summarizing both the public and newly declassified material linking Osama bin Laden and al-Qaeda to the attacks of September 11 was published by the British Prime Minister's office on November 14, 2001, and updates a similar document published on October 4. It is reproduced here from the 10 Downing Street Web site, www.number-10.gov.uk.

This document does not purport to provide a prosecutable case against Usama Bin Laden in a court of law. Intelligence often cannot be used evidentially, due both to the strict rules of admissibility and to the need to protect the safety of sources. But on the basis of all the information available HMG [Her Majesty's Government] is confident of its conclusions as expressed in this document.

RESPONSIBILITY FOR THE TERRORIST ATROCITIES IN
THE UNITED STATES, 11 SEPTEMBER 2001
AN UPDATED ACCOUNT

INTRODUCTION

1. The clear conclusions reached by the government are:
   - Usama Bin Laden and Al Qaida, the terrorist network which he heads, planned and carried out the atrocities on 11 September 2001;
   - Usama Bin Laden and Al Qaida retain the will and resources to carry out further atrocities;
   - the United Kingdom, and United Kingdom nationals are potential targets; and

- Usama Bin Laden and Al Qaida were able to commit these atrocities because of their close alliance with the Taleban régime, which allowed them to operate with impunity in pursuing their terrorist activity.

2. The material in respect of 1998 and the USS *Cole* comes from indictments and intelligence sources. The material in respect of 11 September comes from intelligence and the criminal investigation to date. The details of some aspects cannot be given, but the facts are clear from the intelligence.

3. The document does not contain the totality of the material known to HMG, given the continuing and absolute need to protect intelligence sources.

SUMMARY

4. The relevant facts show:

BACKGROUND

- Al Qaida is a terrorist organisation with ties to a global network, which has been in existence for over 10 years. It was founded, and has been led at all times, by Usama Bin Laden.
- Usama Bin Laden and Al Qaida have been engaged in a jihad against the United States, and its allies. One of their stated aims is the murder of US citizens, and attacks on America's allies.
- Usama Bin Laden and Al Qaida have been based in Afghanistan since 1996, but have a network of operations throughout the world. The network includes training camps, warehouses, communication facilities and commercial operations able to raise significant sums

of money to support its activity. That activity includes substantial exploitation of the illegal drugs trade from Afghanistan.

- Usama Bin Laden's Al Qaida and the Taleban régime have a close and mutually dependent alliance. Usama Bin Laden and Al Qaida provide the Taleban régime with material, financial and military support. They jointly exploit the drugs trade. The Taleban régime allows Bin Laden to operate his terrorist training camps and activities from Afghanistan, protects him from attacks from outside, and protects the drugs stockpiles. Usama Bin Laden could not operate his terrorist activities without the alliance and support of the Taleban régime. The Taleban's strength would be seriously weakened without Usama Bin Laden's military and financial support.
- Usama Bin Laden and Al Qaida have the capability to execute major terrorist attacks.
- Usama Bin Laden has claimed credit for the attack on US soldiers in Somalia in October 1993, which killed 18; for the attack on the US Embassies in Kenya and Tanzania in August 1998 which killed 224 and injured nearly 5000; and was linked to the attack on the USS *Cole* on 12 October 2000, in which 17 crew members were killed and 40 others injured.
- They have sought to acquire nuclear and chemical materials for use as terrorist weapons.

IN RELATION TO THE TERRORIST ATTACKS ON II SEPTEMBER

5. After 11 September we learned that, not long before, Bin Laden had indicated he was about to launch a major attack on America. The detailed planning for the terrorist attacks of 11 September was carried out by one of UBL's close associates. Of the 19 hijackers involved in 11 September 2001, it has been established that the majority had links with Al Qaida. A senior Bin Laden associate claimed to have trained some of the hijackers in Afghanistan. The

attacks on 11 September 2001 were similar in both their ambition and intended impact to previous attacks undertaken by Usama Bin laden and Al Qaida, and also had features in common. In particular:
- Suicide attackers
- Co-ordinated attacks on the same day
- The aim to cause maximum American casualties
- Total disregard for other casualties, including Muslim
- Meticulous long-term planning
- Absence of warning.

6. Al Qaida retains the capability and the will to make further attacks on the US and its allies, including the United Kingdom.

7. Al Qaida gives no warning of terrorist attack.

THE FACTS

USAMA BIN LADEN AND AL QAIDA

8. In 1989 Usama Bin Laden, and others, founded an international terrorist group known as "Al Qaida" (the Base). At all times he has been the leader of Al Qaida.

9. From 1989 until 1991 Usama Bin Laden was based in Afghanistan and Peshawar, Pakistan. In 1991 he moved to Sudan, where he stayed until 1996. In that year he returned to Afghanistan, where he remains.

THE TALEBAN RÉGIME

10. The Taleban emerged from the Afghan refugee camps in Pakistan in the early 1990s. By 1996 they had captured Kabul. They are

still engaged in a bloody civil war to control the whole of Afghanistan. They are led by Mullah Omar.

11. In 1996 Usama Bin Laden moved back to Afghanistan. He established a close relationship with Mullah Omar, and threw his support behind the Taleban. Usama Bin Laden and the Taleban régime have a close alliance on which both depend for their continued existence. They also share the same religious values and vision.

12. Usama Bin Laden has provided the Taleban régime with troops, arms and money to fight the Northern Alliance. He is closely involved with Taleban military training, planning and operations. He has representatives in the Taleban military command structure. He has also given infrastruture assistance and humanitarian aid. Forces under the control of Usama Bin Laden have fought alongside the Taleban in the civil war in Afghanistan.

13. Omar has provided Bin Laden with a safe haven in which to operate, and has allowed him to establish terrorist training camps in Afghanistan. They jointly exploit the Afghan drugs trade. In return for active Al Qaida support, the Taleban allow Al Qaida to operate freely, including planning, training and preparing for terrorist activity. In addition the Taleban provide security for the stockpiles of drugs.

14. Since 1996, when the Taleban captured Kabul, the United States government has consistently raised with them a whole range of issues, including humanitarian aid and terrorism. Well before 11 September 2001 they had provided evidence to the Taleban of the responsibility of Al Qaida for the terrorist attacks in East Africa. This evidence had been provided to senior leaders of the Taleban at their request.

15. The United States government had made it clear to the Taleban

régime that Al Qaida had murdered US citizens, and planned to murder more. The US offered to work with the Taleban to expel the terrorists from Afghanistan. These talks, which have been continuing since 1996, have failed to produce any results.

16. In June 2001, in the face of mounting evidence of the Al Qaida threat, the United States warned the Taleban that it had the right to defend itself and that it would hold the régime responsible for attacks against US citizens by terrorists sheltered in Afghanistan.

17. In this, the United States had the support of the United Nations. The Security Council, in Resolution 1267, condemned Usama Bin Laden for sponsoring international terrorism and operating a network of terrorist camps, and demanded that the Taleban surrender Usama Bin Laden without further delay so that he could be brought to justice.

18. Despite the evidence provided by the US of the responsibility of Usama Bin Laden and Al Qaida for the 1998 East Africa bombings, despite the accurately perceived threats of further atrocities, and despite the demands of the United Nations, the Taleban régime responded by saying no evidence existed against Usama Bin Laden, and that neither he nor his network would be expelled.

19. A former Government official in Afghanistan has described the Taleban and Usama Bin Laden as "two sides of the same coin: Usama cannot exist in Afghanistan without the Taleban and the Taleban cannot exist without Usama."

AL QAIDA

20. Al Qaida is dedicated to opposing "un-Islamic" governments in Muslim countries with force and violence.

21. Al Qaida virulently opposes the United States. Usama Bin Laden has urged and incited his followers to kill American citizens, in the most unequivocal terms.

22. On 12 October 1996 he issued a declaration of jihad as follows:

"The people of Islam have suffered from aggression, iniquity and injustice imposed by the Zionist-Crusader alliance and their collaborators...

"It is the duty now on every tribe in the Arabian peninsula to fight jihad and cleanse the land from these Crusader occupiers. Their wealth is booty to those who kill them.

"My Muslim brothers: your brothers in Palestine and in the land of the two Holy Places [Saudi Arabia] *are calling upon your help and asking you to take part in fighting against the enemy—the Americans and the Israelis. They are asking you to do whatever you can to expel the enemies out of the sanctities of Islam."*

Later in the same year he said that

"terrorising the American occupiers [of Islamic Holy Places] *is a religious and logical obligation."*

In February 1998 he issued and signed a "fatwa" which included a decree to all Muslims:

"...the killing of Americans and their civilian and military allies is a religious duty for each and every Muslim to be carried out in whichever country they are until Al Aqsa mosque has been liberated from their grasp and until their armies have left Muslim lands."

In the same "fatwa" he called on Muslim scholars and their leaders and their youths to

"launch an attack on the American soldiers of Satan"

and concluded:

> *"We—with God's help—call on every Muslim who believes in God and wishes to be rewarded to comply with God's order to kill Americans and plunder their money whenever and wherever they find it. We also call on Muslims...to launch the raid on Satan's US troops and the devil's supporters allying with them, and to displace those who are behind them."*

When asked, in 1998, about obtaining chemical or nuclear weapons he said *"acquiring such weapons for the defence of Muslims* [is] *a religious duty,"* and made the following claim in an interview printed in the Pakistan newspaper *Dawn* in November 2001:

> *"I wish to declare that if America used chemical or nuclear weapons against us, then we may retort with chemical and nuclear weapons. We have the weapons as deterrent."*

In an interview aired on Al Jazira (Doha, Qatar) television he stated:

> *"Our enemy is every American male, whether he is directly fighting us or paying taxes."*

In two interviews broadcast on US television in 1997 and 1998 he referred to the terrorists who carried out the earlier attack on the World Trade Center in 1993 as *"role models."* He went on to exhort his followers *"to take the fighting to America."*

23. From the early 1990s Usama Bin Laden has sought to obtain nuclear and chemical materials for use as weapons of terror.

24. Although US targets are Al Qaida's priority, it also explicitly threatens the United States' allies. References to *"Zionist-Crusader alliance and their collaborators,"* and to *"Satan's US troops and the devil's supporters allying with them"* are references which unquestionably include the United Kingdom. This is confirmed by more specific references in a broadcast of 13 October, during which Bin Laden's spokesman said:

> *"Al Qaida declares that Bush Sr, Bush Jr, Clinton, Blair and Sharon are the arch-criminals from among the Zionists and Crusaders... Al Qaida stresses that the blood of those killed will not go to waste, God willing, until we punish these criminals... We also say and advise the Muslims in the United States and Britain... not to travel by plane. We also advise them not to live in high-rise buildings and towers."*

25. There is a continuing threat. Based on our experience of the way the network has operated in the past, other cells, like those that carried out the terrorist attacks on 11 September, must be assumed to exist.

26. Al Qaida functions both on its own and through a network of other terrorist organisations. These include Egyptian Islamic Jihad and other north African Islamic extremist terrorist groups, and a number of other jihadi groups in other countries including the Sudan, Yemen, Somalia, Pakistan and India. Al Qaida also maintains cells and personnel in a number of other countries to facilitate its activities.

27. Usama Bin Laden heads the Al Qaida network. Below him is a body known as the Shura, which includes representatives of other

terrorist groups, such as Egyptian Islamic Jihad leader Ayman Zawa-hiri and prominent lieutenants of Bin Laden such as Mohamed Atef (also known as Abu Hafs Al-Masri). Egyptian Islamic Jihad has, in effect, merged with Al Qaida.

28. In addition to the Shura, Al Qaida has several groups dealing with military, media, financial and Islamic issues.

29. Mohamed Atef is a member of the group that deals with military and terrorist operations. His duties include principal responsibility for training Al Qaida members.

30. Members of Al Qaida must make a pledge of allegiance to follow the orders of Usama Bin Laden.

31. A great deal of evidence about Usama Bin Laden and Al Qaida has been made available in the US indictment for earlier crimes.

32. Since 1989, Usama Bin Laden has conducted substantial financial and business transactions on behalf of Al Qaida and in pursuit of its goals. These include purchasing land for training camps, purchasing warehouses for the storage of items, including explosives, purchasing communications and electronics equipment, and transporting currency and weapons to members of Al Qaida and associated terrorist groups in countries throughout the world.

33. Since 1989 Usama Bin Laden has provided training camps and guest houses in Afghanistan, Pakistan, the Sudan, Somalia and Kenya for the use of Al Qaida and associated terrorist groups. We know from intelligence that there are currently at least a dozen camps across Afghanistan, of which at least four are used for training terrorists.

34. Since 1989, Usama Bin Laden has established a series of businesses to provide income for Al Qaida, and to provide cover for the procurement of explosives, weapons and chemicals, and for the travel of Al Qaida operatives. The businesses have included a holding company known as "Wadi Al Aqiq," a construction business known as "Al Hijra," an agricultural business known as 'Al Themar Al Mubaraka," and investment companies known as "Ladin International" and "Taba Investments."

USAMA BIN LADEN AND PREVIOUS ATTACKS

35. In 1992 and 1993 Mohamed Atef travelled to Somalia on several occasions for the purpose of organising violence against United States and United Nations troops then stationed in Somalia. On each occasion he reported back to Usama Bin Laden, at his base in the Riyadh district of Khartoum.

36. In the spring of 1993 Atef, Saif al Adel, another senior member of Al Qaida, and other members began to provide military training to Somali tribes for the purpose of fighting the United Nations forces.

37. On 3 and 4 October 1993 operatives of Al Qaida participated in the attack on US military personnel serving in Somalia as part of the operation "Restore Hope." Eighteen US military personnel were killed in the attack.

38. From 1993 members of Al Qaida began to live in Nairobi and set up businesses there, including Asma Ltd, and Tanzanite King. They were regularly visited there by senior members of Al Qaida, in particular by Atef and Abu Ubadiah al Banshiri.

39. Beginning in the latter part of 1993, members of Al Qaida in

Kenya began to discuss the possibility of attacking the US Embassy in Nairobi in retaliation for US participation in Operation Restore Hope in Somalia. Ali Mohamed, a US citizen and admitted member of Al Qaida, surveyed the US Embassy as a possible target for a terrorist attack. He took photographs and made sketches, which he presented to Usama Bin Laden while Bin Laden was in Sudan. He also admitted that he had trained terrorists for Al Qaida in Afghanistan in the early 1990s, and that those whom he trained included many involved in the East African bombings in August 1998.

40. In June or July 1998, two Al Qaida operatives, Fahid Mohammed Ali Msalam and Sheik Ahmed Salim Swedan, purchased a Toyota truck and made various alterations to the back of the truck.

41. In early August 1998, operatives of Al Qaida gathered in 43, New Runda Estates, Nairobi to execute the bombing of the US Embassy in Nairobi.

42. On 7 August 1998, Assam, a Saudi national and Al Qaida operative, drove the Toyota truck to the US Embassy. There was a large bomb in the back of the truck.

43. Also in the truck was Mohamed Rashed Daoud Al 'Owali, another Saudi. He, by his own confession, was an Al Qaida operative, who from about 1996 had been trained in Al Qaida camps in Afghanistan in explosives, hijacking, kidnapping, assassination and intelligence techniques. With Usama Bin Laden's express permission, he fought alongside the Taleban in Afghanistan. He had met Usama Bin Laden personally in 1996 and asked for another "mission." Usama Bin Laden sent him to East Africa after extensive specialised training at camps in Afghanistan.

44. As the truck approached the Embassy, Al 'Owali got out and threw a stun grenade at a security guard. Assam drove the truck up to the rear of the Embassy. He got out and then detonated the bomb, which demolished a multi-storey secretarial college and severely damaged the US Embassy, and the Co-operative bank building. The bomb killed 213 people and injured 4500. Assam was killed in the explosion.

45. Al 'Owali expected the mission to end in his death. He had been willing to die for Al Qaida. But at the last minute he ran away from the bomb truck and survived. He had no money, passport or plan to escape after the mission, because he had expected to die.

46. After a few days, he called a telephone number in Yemen to have money transferred to him in Kenya. The number he rang in Yemen was contacted by Usama Bin Laden's phone on the same day as Al 'Owali was arranging to get the money.

47. Another person arrested in connection with the Nairobi bombing was Mohamed Sadeek Odeh. He admitted to his involvement. He identified the principal participants in the bombing. He named three other persons, all of whom were Al Qaida or Egyptian Islamic Jihad members.

48. In Dar es Salaam the same day, at about the same time, operatives of Al Qaida detonated a bomb at the US Embassy, killing 11 people. The Al Qaida operatives involved included Mustafa Mohamed Fadhil and Khaflan Khamis Mohamed. The bomb was carried in a Nissan Atlas truck, which Ahmed Khfaklan Ghailani and Sheikh Ahmed Salim Swedan, two Al Qaida operatives, had purchased in July 1998, in Dar es Salaam.

49. Khaflan Khamis Mohamed was arrested for the bombing. He

admitted membership of Al Qaida, and implicated other members of Al Qaida in the bombing.

50. On 7 and 8 August 1998, two other members of Al Qaida disseminated claims of responsibility for the two bombings by sending faxes to media organisations in Paris, Doha in Qatar, and Dubai in the United Arab Emirates.

51. Additional evidence of the involvement of Al Qaida in the East African bombings came from a search conducted in London of several residences and businesses belonging to Al Qaida and Egyptian Islamic Jihad members. In those searches a number of documents were found including claims of responsibility for the East African bombings in the name of a fictitious group, "the Islamic Army for the liberation of the Holy Places."

52. Al 'Owali, the would-be suicide bomber, admitted he was told to make a videotape of himself using the name of the same fictitious group.

53. The faxed claims of responsibility were traced to a telephone number, which had been in contact with Usama Bin Laden's cell phone. The claims disseminated to the press were clearly written by someone familiar with the conspiracy. They stated that the bombings had been carried out by two Saudis in Kenya, and one Egyptian in Dar es Salaam. They were probably sent before the bombings had even taken place. They referred to two Saudis dying in the Nairobi attack. In fact, because Al 'Owali fled at the last minute, only one Saudi died.

54. On 22 December 1998 Usama Bin Laden was asked by *Time* magazine whether he was responsible for the August 1998 attacks. He replied:

"The International Islamic Jihad Front for the jihad against the US and Israel has, by the grace of God, issued a crystal clear fatwa calling on the Islamic nation to carry on Jihad aimed at liberating the holy sites. The nation of Mohammed has responded to this appeal. If instigation for jihad against the Jews and the Americans ... is considered to be a crime, then let history be a witness that I am a criminal. Our job is to instigate and, by the grace of God, we did that, and certain people responded to this instigation."

He was asked if he knew the attackers:

"... those who risked their lives to earn the pleasure of God are real men. They managed to rid the Islamic nation of disgrace. We hold them in the highest esteem."

And what the US could expect of him:

"... any thief or criminal who enters another country to steal should expect to be exposed to murder at any time ... The US knows that I have attacked it, by the grace of God, for more than ten years now ... God knows that we have been pleased by the killing of American soldiers [in Somalia in 1993]. This was achieved by the grace of God and the efforts of the mujahideen ... Hostility towards America is a religious duty and we hope to be rewarded for it by God. I am confident that Muslims will be able to end the legend of the so-called superpower that is America."

55. In December 1999 a terrorist cell linked to Al Qaida was discovered trying to carry out attacks inside the United States. An Algerian, Ahmed Ressam, was stopped at the US-Canadian border, and over 100 lbs of bomb-making material was found in his car. Ressam admitted he was planning to set off a large bomb at Los Angeles International

airport on New Year's Day. He said that he had received terrorist training at Al Qaida camps in Afghanistan and then been instructed to go abroad and kill US civilians and military personnel.

56. On 3 January 2000, a group of Al Qaida members, and other terrorists who had trained in Al Qaida camps in Afghanistan, attempted to attack a US destroyer with a small boat loaded with explosives. Their boat sank, aborting the attack.

57. On 12 October 2000, however, the USS *Cole* was struck by an explosive-laden boat while refuelling in Aden harbour. Seventeen crew were killed, and 40 injured.

58. Several of the perpetrators of the *Cole* attack (mostly Yemenis and Saudis) were trained at Usama Bin Laden's camps in Afghanistan. Al 'Owali has identified the two commanders of the attack on the USS *Cole* as having participated in the planning and preparation for the East African Embassy bombings.

59. In the months before the September 11 attacks, propaganda videos were distributed throughout the Middle East and Muslim world by Al Qaida, in which Usama Bin Laden and others were shown encouraging Muslims to attack American and Jewish targets.

60. Similar videos, extolling violence against the United States and other targets, were distributed before the East African Embassy attacks in August 1998.

USAMA BIN LADEN AND THE 11 SEPTEMBER ATTACKS

61. Nineteen men have been identified as the hijackers from the passenger lists of the four planes hijacked on 11 September 2001. Many

of them had previous links with Al Qaida or have so far been positively identified as associates of Al Qaida. An associate of some of the hijackers has been identified as playing key roles in both the East African Embassy attacks and the USS *Cole* attack. Investigations continue into the backgrounds of all the hijackers.

62. From intelligence sources, the following facts have been established subsequent to 11 September; for intelligence reasons, the names of associates, though known, are not given.

- In the run-up to 11 September, Bin Laden was mounting a concerted propaganda campaign amongst like-minded groups of people—including videos and documentation—justifying attacks on Jewish and American targets; and claiming that those who died in the course of them were carrying out God's work.
- We have learned, subsequent to 11 September, that Bin Laden himself asserted shortly before 11 September that he was preparing a major attack on America.
- In August and early September close associates of Bin Laden were warned to return to Afghanistan from other parts of the world by 10 September.
- Immediately prior to 11 September some known associates of Bin Laden were naming the date for action as on or around 11 September.
- A senior associate claimed to have trained some of the hijackers in Afghanistan.
- Since 11 September we have learned that one of Bin Laden's closest and most senior associates was responsible for the detailed planning of the attacks.
- There is evidence of a very specific nature relating to the guilt of Bin Laden and his associates that is too sensitive to release.

63. In addition, Usama Bin Laden has issued a number of public

statements since the US strikes on Afghanistan began. The language used in these, while not an open admission of guilt, is self-incriminating.

64. For example, on 7 October he said:

> *"Here is America struck by God Almighty in one of its vital organs, so that its greatest buildings are destroyed. Grace and gratitude to God... I swear to God that America will not live in peace before peace reigns in Palestine, and before all the army of infidels depart the land of Mohammed, peace be upon him."*

65. On 9 October his spokesman praised the *"good deed"* of the hijackers, who *"transferred the battle into the US heartland."* He warned that the *"storm of plane attacks will not abate."*

66. On 20 October Bin Laden gave an inflammatory interview which has been circulating, in the form of a video, among supporters in the Al Qaida network. In the transcript, when referring to the US buildings that were attacked, he says:

> *"It is what we instigated for a while, in self-defence. And it was in revenge for our people killed in Palestine and Iraq. So if avenging the killing of our people is terrorism, let history be a witness that we are terrorists."*

Later in the interview he said:

> *"Bush and Blair... don't understand any language but the language of force. Every time they kill us, we will kill them, so the balance of terror can be achieved."*

He went on:

> *"The battle has been moved inside America, and we shall continue until we win this battle, or die in the cause and meet our maker."*

He also said:

> *"The bad terror is what America and Israel are practising against our people, and what we are practising is the good terror that will stop them doing what they are doing."*

67. Usama Bin Laden remains in charge, and the mastermind, of Al Qaida. In Al Qaida, an operation on the scale of the 11 September attacks would have been approved by Usama Bin Laden himself.

68. The modus operandi of 11 September was entirely consistent with previous attacks. Al Qaida's record of atrocities is characterised by meticulous long-term planning, a desire to inflict mass casualties, suicide bombers, and multiple simultaneous attacks.

69. The attacks of 11 September 2001 are entirely consistent with the scale and sophistication of the planning which went into the attacks on the East African Embassies and the USS *Cole*. No warnings were given for these three attacks, just as there was none on 11 September.

70. Al Qaida operatives, in evidence given in the East African Embassy bomb trials, have described how the group spends years preparing for an attack. They conduct repeated surveillance, patiently gather materials, and identify and vet operatives, who have the skills to participate in the attack and the willingness to die for their cause.

71. The operatives involved in the 11 September atrocities attended flight schools, used flight simulators to study the controls of larger aircraft and placed potential airports and routes under surveillance.

72. Al Qaida's attacks are characterised by total disregard for innocent lives, including Muslims. In an interview after the East African bombings, Usama Bin Laden insisted that the need to attack the United States excused the killing of other innocent civilians, Muslim and non-Muslim alike.

73. No other organisation has both the motivation and the capability to carry out attacks like those of the 11 September—only the Al Qaida network under Usama Bin Laden.

CONCLUSION

74. The attacks of the 11 September 2001 were planned and carried out by Al Qaida, an organisation whose head is Usama Bin Laden. That organisation has the will, and the resources, to execute further attacks of similar scale. Both the United States and its close allies are targets for such attacks. The attack could not have occurred without the alliance between the Taleban and Usama Bin Laden, which allowed Bin Laden to operate freely in Afghanistan, promoting, planning and executing terrorist activity.

Notes on the Contributors

DANIEL BENJAMIN is a Senior Fellow at the Center for Strategic and International Studies in Washington. STEVEN SIMON is Assistant Director of the International Institute for Strategic Studies in London. Both served on the National Security Council Staff between 1994 and 1999.

CHRISTOPHER DE BELLAIGUE has worked in India for *India Today* and in Turkey for *The Economist*. He currently represents *The Economist* in Iran and is writing a book about Iran since the 1979 revolution.

ISAIAH BERLIN (1909–1997) was Professor of Social and Political Theory and a Fellow of All Souls College, Oxford. He served as the first President of Wolfson College, Oxford, and as President of the British Academy. HENRY HARDY, a Fellow of Wolfson College, Oxford, is Berlin's editor and one of his Literary Trustees. For more information visit http://berlin.wolf.ox.ac.uk/.

TIMOTHY GARTON ASH's books on the recent history and politics of Europe include *The Magic Lantern*, *The File*, and *History of the Present*. A regular contributor to *The New York Review*, he is Director of the European Studies Centre at St. Antony's College, Oxford, and a Senior Fellow at the Hoover Institution, Stanford.

RICHARD L. GARWIN is Reed Senior Fellow for Science and Technology at the Council on Foreign Relations and Adjunct Professor of Physics at Columbia University. His most recent book, *Megawatts and Megatons: A Turning Point in the Nuclear Age?*, appeared in October 2001.

STANLEY HOFFMANN is Paul and Catherine Buttenwieser University Professor at Harvard University. He is working on a book on the politics and ethics of global society.

TIM JUDAH is a journalist and writer based in London. He is the author of *Kosovo: War and Revenge* and *The Serbs: History, Myth and the Destruction of Yugoslavia*.

TONY JUDT directs the Remarque Institute at New York University. He is writing a history of Europe since the Second World War.

KANAN MAKIYA was born in Baghdad and teaches at Brandeis University. His books include *Republic of Fear: The Politics of Modern Iraq, Cruelty and Silence: War, Tyranny, Uprising, and the Arab World*, and, most recently, *The Rock: A Tale of Seventh-Century Jerusalem*. HASSAN MNEIMNEH is a director of the Iraq Research and Documentation Project based at Harvard University and a regular contributor to the London-based Arabic newspaper *al-Hayat*.

MATTHEW MESELSON is Thomas Dudley Cabot Professor of Natural Sciences at Harvard University. He is engaged in research on molecular genetics and evolution.

PANKAJ MISHRA lives in New Dehli and Simla. He is the author of *Butter Chicken in Ludhiana: Travels in Small Town India* and *The Romantics: A Novel*, and is currently writing a book about the Buddha.

ORHAN PAMUK is the author of six novels, most recently *My Name Is Red*. He is the recipient of major Turkish and international literary awards, and his work has been translated into more than twenty languages. He lives in Istanbul.

THOMAS POWERS is the author of *The Man Who Kept the Secrets, Heisenberg's War*, and *The Confirmation*, a novel.

PHILIP C. WILCOX JR. is a retired Foreign Service Officer who served from 1994 to 1997 as Ambassador at Large and Coordinator for Counter-Terrorism in the US Department of State. He is now President of the Foundation for Middle East Peace.